# PRAISE FOR THE POPULAR CULT~~URE PSYCHOLOGY~~ SERIES

TRAVIS LANGLEY, PHD, SERIES EDITOR

## *Captain America vs. Iron Man: Freedom, Security, Psychology*

"A thought-provoking collection."

— Comics Grinder

"An excellent example of how psychology can be applied beyond mere case studies and real-life events . . . sure to be of interest to both psychology readers and comic-book fans alike."

— The Psychologist (British Psychological Society)

"If you're looking to delve deeper into the mythos, crack this open immediately."

— Geek Chic Elite

## *Doctor Who Psychology: A Madman with a Box*

"A cracking read. They know their Who inside out and the science is impeccable . . . This is an exceptional example of what must now be regarded as a legitimate genre."

— The Psychologist (British Psychological Society)

"This book is a must-read for every Whovian!"

— Night Owl Reviews

## *Game of Thrones Psychology: The Mind Is Dark and Full of Terrors*

"It's super interesting and inspired me."

— PBS BrainCraft

"Literate, well written, and informative."

— *Pittsburgh Post-Gazette*

"An entertaining collection . . . It is the perfect companion for the philosophical fan who wants to gain a better of understanding of what it means to be a hero or for the casual fan who just left the theater wanting to slip into their hero's shoes."

— Amazing Stories

### Supernatural Psychology: Roads Less Traveled

"An entertaining textbook. . . . the editors of this book, as well as those who contributed the essays, are to be applauded for laying everything out in such a clear and informative fashion."

—Clearing Out the Clutter

### Star Trek Psychology: The Mental Frontier

"Five stars."

—Dawn Reviews Books

### Star Wars Psychology: Dark Side of the Mind

"Thought-provoking."

—Kirkus Reviews

"There's something for everyone in this fun and fascinating volume, a good addition to any Star Wars fan's bookshelf."

—The BiblioSanctum

"The book is awesome."

—Sci-Fi & Fantasy Buzz

### The Walking Dead Psychology: Psych of the Living Dead

"The perfect blend of insightful scholarship, pop-culture savvy and bloody good fun. Highly recommended!"

—Jonathan Maberry, best-selling author

"One of the most fascinating books I read this year . . . Required reading for zombies with brains."

—Brian Keene, best-selling author

"Those interested in #TWD and/or psychology, check it out."

—actor Andrew J. West (Gareth on The Walking Dead)

### Wonder Woman Psychology: Lassoing the Truth

"Absolutely fantastic!"

—Retroist

"The best Wonder Woman book ever!"

—Christie Marston, Wonder Woman Family Network

# BLACK PANTHER

## PSYCHOLOGY

### HIDDEN
### KINGDOMS

EDITED BY

TRAVIS LANGLEY AND ALEX SIMMONS

FOREWORD BY DON MCGREGOR

STERLING
New York

STERLING
New York

An Imprint of Sterling Publishing, Co., Inc.
1166 Avenue of the Americas
New York, NY 10016

ISBN 978-1-4549-3400-4

Distributed in Canada by Sterling Publishing Co., Inc.
c/o Canadian Manda Group, 664 Annette Street
Toronto, Ontario M6S 2C8, Canada
Distributed in the United Kingdom by GMC Distribution Services
Castle Place, 166 High Street, Lewes, East Sussex BN7 1XU, England
Distributed in Australia by NewSouth Books
University of New South Wales, Sydney, NSW 2052, Australia

For information about custom editions, special sales, and premium and corporate
purchases, please contact Sterling Special Sales at 800-805-5489
specialsales@sterlingpublishing.com.

Manufactured in Canada

2 4 6 8 10 9 7 5 3 1

sterlingpublishing.com

Cover design by David Ter-Avanesyan and Igor Satanovsky
Interior design by Nancy Singer

Cover images: Shutterstock.com: 3000ad (city), James Cohen (lightning),
Eky Studio (metal pattern), ksanask.art (emblem), PictuLandra (inside pattern)

Interior images: Depositphotos.com: © Aguirre_mar: 81; © Doom.ko: 97;
© jenyako86.gmail.com: 68; © roxanabalint: 8; © YokoDesign: 154 Getty
Images: DigitalVision Vectors: bgblue: 224; bubaone: 21; ROBOTOK: 52;
yogysic: 132, 214; LizaLutik/iStock/Getty Images Plus: vi, x, 10, 70, 120, 156,
202 Shutterstock.com: Sovenko Artem: 157; Anar Babayev: 172; bignoze: 121;
Serhii Borodin: 191; draco77vector: 109, throughout (claws); Egor Shilov: 71;
tcheres: 11; Vector Art Factory: 240; Vilingor: 36; Zlava74: 118, 181; zzilazz: 144

to Marc Nadel

—*Travis*

to Emmett "Babe" Wallace

—*Alex*

and in memory of
T'Challa's creator Jack Kirby
and co-creator Stan Lee

# CONTENTS

ACKNOWLEDGMENTS

# OUR CREW

## I.

## TRAVIS LANGLEY, PHD

### EDITOR

Once upon a time, illustrator Marc Nadel and I were discussing book publishing as we wove our way through New York Comic Con when we crossed paths with Connie Santisteban, my former editor on *Batman and Psychology: A Dark and Stormy Knight*.[1] There in the hallway, we had the conversation that led to the launch of this Popular Culture Psychology anthology series. During a more recent New York Comic Con, I told Marc about the then-upcoming book *Black Panther Psychology: Hidden Kingdoms*. Soon, he introduced me to Alex Simmons, the comic book writer who would become my co-editor this time. Having someone onboard such as Alex, who is both a great guy and a writer who worked on *Black Panther* features, is a huge help. Thank you, friend Marc, for all of that and more. Alex is a treasure—not only a valuable co-editor but also a fine, fun human being. I thank our mutual friend Michael Uslan, doctor of comic books and *Batman/The Dark Knight*[2] executive producer, through whom I first met Marc.

While we were working on *Black Panther Psychology: Hidden Kingdoms*, Stan Lee left this world to embark on his next adventure out in the multiverse. While Black Panther appears to have been artist/collaborator Jack Kirby's creation more than Stan's, and it was clearly Jack whose style first made the Black Panther so majestic, Stan wrote the text for those *Fantastic Four* stories in which T'Challa originally appeared.[3] Together, they gave us this character that we love today. On a more personal level (or at least a different kind of personal level), we lost a valued member of our own crew when we lost Stan. He'd contributed forewords to both *Captain America vs. Iron Man: Freedom, Security, Psychology* and *Daredevil Psychology: The Devil You Know.*[4] This is our first Marvel topic without him. We thank the man born Stanley Martin Lieber again for joining our journey, and I miss him. We owe him and Jack for giving us the character we're exploring in this particular stretch in the trek.

# A PERSONAL NOTE ON STAN

I was lucky enough to work with Stan Lee for a time, and luckier still that he agreed to do two interviews that led to the forewords for *Captain American vs. Iron Man: Freedom, Security, Psychology* and *Daredevil Psychology: The Devil You Know.* Every moment that we spent in interviews, between tapings of our YouTube show *Cocktails with Stan,* or behind the scenes at convention panels, Stan was gloriously cheerful and exceedingly lovely. He never failed to put his fans first and had a kind word for everyone. No one has ever worked harder, yet there was never a moment when he didn't have a smile on his face. I feel blessed to have known him and his work will live on forever.

—Jenna Busch, writer and editorial assistant

Many writers, artists, editors, actors, filmmakers, and other creative individuals have guided the Black Panther for more than fifty years. Reginald Hudlin and Ta-Nehisi Coates deserve shout-outs for how often we cite their work. We thank them all, with a special recognition to director Ryan Coogler and actor Chadwick Boseman, who showed the world how great Black Panther can be. We must heap extra appreciation upon those who directly helped us on this book. Back when our foreword author Don McGregor wrote the "Panther's Rage" storyline in *Jungle Action*, he was the first writer to present T'Challa as the lead character, not as a guest star, supporting character, or member of a crowded American super team. In that story, Don created Killmonger, expanded our knowledge of Wakanda, and laid the foundation for many other creators' stories yet to come. Actor Keith David Williams (a.k.a. Keith David), who was the first actor to play T'Challa in any form; writer Christopher Priest; Academy Award-winning costume designer Ruth E. Carter; Marine veteran Tara Bachman; and artists Arvell Jones and Ken Lashley were all so gracious for speaking with us and letting us include their interviews in this book.

Because I met several of them through fan conventions, I thank the organizers of ComiConway (Jimmy Dyer, Kara Rimmer Dyer) and Wizard World shows (Ryan Ball, Peter Katz, Jerry Milani) for featuring me as a special guest. And because I met many of our writers through other cons, I thank the organizers of San Diego Comic-Con International (Eddie Ibrahim, Gary Sassaman, Cathy Dalton, Sue Lord, Adam Neese, Amy Ramirez, Chris Sturhann), New York Comic Con, and the Comics Arts Conference (Peter Coogan, Randy Duncan, Kate McClancy).

I am fortunate to teach at a university where so many helpful people assist and support my unusual writing endeavors. Henderson State University administrators (President Glendell Jones, Provost Steve Adkison, Dean Angela Boswell) encourage creative ways of teaching. Library director Lea Ann Alexander and staff maintain an impressive graphic novel reading room and stock their shelves with fantastic resources as I make one strange request after another. David Bateman, Lecia Franklin, Carolyn Hatley, Ermatine Johnson, and Salina Smith help me and my students go where we need to go. Latrena Beasley and Sandra D. Johnson handle a whole lot of mail for me. Our faculty writers' group (Anji Boswell, Matthew Bowman, Jennifer Dawes, Maryjane Dunn, Brian George, Nydia Jeffers, Vernon Miles, David Sesser, Michael Taylor, Al Valbuena, Constanze Weise) reviewed portions of this manuscript.

The fine folks at Sterling Publishing help me and my writers bring you these Popular Culture Psychology anthologies—including Ardi Alspach, Toula Ballas, Michael Cea, Sari Lampert, Blanca Oliviery, and Lauren Tambini. Editor Kate Zimmermann stays on top of it all, is wonderful to work with, and makes a great Captain Marvel when she cosplays. My original editor, Connie Santisteban, continues to help as consultant and friend. Thanks also to David Ter-Avanesyan, who designed the cover. My literary agent, Evan Gregory of the Ethan Ellenberg Literary Agency, takes care of more details than you probably want to know.

For putting up with us when we get lost in Wakanda and helping us make our way through, our writers thank David, Mike, Charlie, Madison, Kally, and Christina Adams; Adam Griffis; Jeffrey Henderson; Katrina Hill; Consuelo, Aurelio, and Rizalina Ingresso; Isabel, Asher Jr., Sage, and Sophia Johnson; Linda, Marissa, and Teagan Jordan; Rose Kyungyun Kong; Rose Elijah Mastin; Dustin McGinnis; Shannon Merritt of 901 Comics in Memphis; Phil Rosier; Farouk "Roo" Shaaban; Bethany and Fermina San Juan; Christian, Lennon, Ezra, and Gavin Vozar; Amanda Wesselmann; Keenan Wimbley; and Apryl's siblings at BLM 5280. We thank FirstGlance Films' Bill Ostroff and others who shot our author photos. Eric Bailey helped me access older comic book issues. He and Nicholas Langley have been my favorite traveling companions for so many events. Danny Fingeroth, Christopher Jansen, Wanda Jones, Sean Kleefeld, Lynda Langley and Travis Sr., Hayley Lewis, Jonathan Maberry, J. B. Manas, Cordell Moss, William Patrick Murray, Ed O'Neal, Dennis O'Neil, Matt Smith, Len Wein, and a little guy named Spencer deserve mention for reasons diverse and sometimes hard to explain. And words are not strong enough to express my affection, adoration, appreciation, and other words that start with the letter *a* for Rebecca Manning Langley.

# II.
# ALEX SIMMONS
## VOLUME CO-EDITOR

Acknowledgment is a tricky thing.

I mean, who do you thank for where you are in life at any one particular moment? You can thank parents, friends, a favorite teacher, your mentor, or any number of other folks. You could even thank the writers who made you fall in love with storytelling so much that you wanted to be a part of that world.

Well, over the years I've thanked my family and friends for supporting my dreams and goals, and for putting up with me while I pursued them. I'll always be grateful and will probably say so a million times more. But I think this time I'll thank someone who is long gone, but never forgotten by me.

This book is dedicated to Emmett "Babe" Wallace. He was a Black* singer, hoofer (dancer), and film actor who performed alongside the likes of Bill "Bojangles" Robinson and Lena Horne in the 1940s.

---

* "Racial and ethnic groups are designated by proper nouns and are capitalized. Therefore, use *Black* and *White* instead of *black* and *white*. . . ."—American Psychological Association (2010/2013), p. 75.

In the '70s I had the honor of being in a play with him when I was only 18. I was new to all of it and especially insecure about my dramatic acting skills. And wouldn't you know it—a situation came up in the production where I had to face that fear, and was not ready. Mr. Wallace, in a kind and sage voice, gave me one piece of advice. But he said it with such quiet and solid conviction that it got through. I portrayed the scene successfully and learned something that has stayed with me all these years.

So thank you, Emmett. Here's to an elder who passed on wisdom to a young one. That wisdom has served him well throughout his life, and I have certainly tried to pass it along.

## NOTES

1. Langley (2012).
2. *Batman* (1989 motion picture); *The Dark Knight* (2008 motion picture); and more.
3. *Fantastic Four* #52–53 (1966).
4. Langley (2016; 2018).

# LIVING INSIDE THE HEAD OF THE KING OF THE WAKANDANS

## Don McGregor

I lived inside the head of T'Challa, the King of the Wakandans, for six years. I listened for his voice every day inside my head. Who could know the Black Panther, in those initial years of his life, better? I am sure that in many places over the years you have heard or seen people write or say, "They have to get the voices *out* of their heads." The storyteller has to "hear" the voices in his or her head, day in and day out, not just of T'Challa, but also of his adversaries like Killmonger, and every other character, friend or foe, around him.

If you can't hear them, you can't know them!

When Stan Lee and Jack Kirby created the Panther and Wakanda, it was a new and exciting concept for comics in the pages of the *Fantastic Four*.[1] But the concept could not be explored and defined in just a couple of comic book issues. There were villains to fight, and the new dynamic personality in T'Challa to introduce.

It wasn't until years later, in 1973, when I was told there would be series that would be the Panther's own in a comic titled *Jungle Action*, and that it would be set in Wakanda, that it then became my daily duty to not only hear the voices, but discover and come to know this magical place hidden in the African continent.

Before a story was written, I had to map out Wakanda, know its different locales that would give it visual distinction but also reality so that when T'Challa showed up in those places in the months to come the reader would already know they exist.

In fact there were a number of decisions that had to be made before I felt I could write anything on the Black Panther. *Jungle Action* was a bi-monthly published comic title, and in the beginning I would only have 13 pages to tell whatever story would become a major part of the Black Panther's history. Now what this means is that if you don't write a character into an issue, you the reader don't get to see or know or care about that character for four months.

And if a character doesn't appear for two issues in a row that's the span of time of half a year that they are missing! That is a long time for a storyteller to hope that you will even remember the character by the time he or she reappears.

This also was something I felt I had to seriously consider as I spent those first months researching the Panther: If T'Challa came back to Wakanda (Marvel comics had brought him to New York City for guest stories he would appear in), what would the Wakandans think if as soon as he came back, every two months, for 13 pages, a new villain would show up and threaten them and the Panther would have to save everybody from destruction and death?

To me, it wouldn't be long before his people would be saying, "You should go back to America; we had it pretty calm before you came back!"

Realizing this, I decided in that time while developing Wakanda that whatever story I told would only make sense if it all were connected, and thus I decided it had to be a novel, in comics form, because then whatever the threat was it wasn't some new, easily defeated villain of the month. This led me to a further thought, as I came up with the umbrella title, "Panther's Rage," for this fledgling, sprawling epic.[2] It would showcase as many jungle genre set pieces and iconic images that its followers loved, but the first time it would be a Black character in the title role and not some jungle White God or Goddess saving the natives, the mainstay go-to plot for many "Jungle Action" tales.

"Panther's Rage" would also become a Hero's Journey, a way of passage where, hopefully, you all would come to know what made T'Challa tick, and what he had to overcome, and how many of the doubts and beliefs he had were a reflection of what we feel as individuals.

His leaving Wakanda to pal around with the Avengers left the country open to revolution.

And thus was born Erik Killmonger. Every hero needs a villain in this kind of genre, and as I developed Killmonger, I believed he would become memorable in who he was and how he challenged our King. Killmonger was so fierce and righteous that when he first appeared on the cover of *Jungle Action* #6,[3] Editorial told me he could not appear on the covers anymore. People have asked me why they made that demand, and I have often answered, "You would have to ask the editors," because I was never told, but I'm pretty sure it was because the comics had never had such a ferocious Black character with such power and intense anger that it made them reluctant to have him so much in the forefront.

When the movie[4] would come out decades later, Killmonger would finally be embraced.

One of the things the movie people have a luxury of when doing a film like *Black Panther* is they have access to a number of specialists, so they can hire people who can research costuming, they can find set designers who can offer ideas of what the places in Wakanda can look like. They have people who are knowledgeable in all different areas of expertise.

When creating a comic in 1973, you had you and the artist. And as the writer, I not only had to hear T'Challa's voice in my head, know and analyze who he was and how events would change him, but I also had to research as best I could in that limited time-frame of a bi-monthly comic everything from costuming to the look and feel of Wakanda.

And I got lucky, because I had met artist Rich Buckler, and in our becoming friends, he insisted with Marvel Editorial, who wanted him to be on high-profile books like *Fantastic Four* and *The Avengers*, that he and I were going to work together on the *Black Panther*.

Those books could not have been what they were if I had not had an artist as dynamic as Rich to draw them.[5] Editorial did not read my scripts; they looked at the art, and as long as it was visual and had fights, that's all they really knew until the book came out. They had too many other, more important, for them, books to oversee than the *Black Panther*.

For me, nothing was more important than T'Challa and Wakanda and the people around him.

Over 40 years ago, I had Rich draw Killmonger throwing T'Challa over Warrior Falls!

For *Jungle Action* #7, I asked him to turn pages 2 and 3 on their side so we could emphasize visually the sheer steep drop of the waterfall and include the title of that "Panther's Rage" chapter.[6] Rich pulled it off.

As the Panther plunged down that deadly descent, I would explore how such violent onslaught affects our hero, what thoughts stab through him, what scars it leaves physically and well as psychologically.

If I could not have Killmonger on the covers, I suspected I would never be allowed to do "Panther's Rage" if I asked. In comics at that time, if you were told "No" and you try to do it anyhow, that is open defiance, and there will be consequences, and odds are you won't be able to do what you hoped anyhow, no matter how valid the reasons you believe.

So, what I did was have Rich draw a title *Panther's Rage* logo. Then I went to Stu Schwartzberg, who ran the huge Stat machine room and asked him to shoot that logo into various sizes. One of the upsides to working on staff at Marvel back then was that you were there to protect your book, but also to see it safely off to the printers. And what I would do, while hearing T'Challa's voice, is slap a *Panther's Rage Continues* logo onto the title page of every new chapter as it went out.

I don't think anybody in the Hallowed Halls noticed until Billy Graham became the artist.[7] Many people believe I chose Billy to be artist to take over the art when Rich finally could put Marvel Editorial off no more, but that is not true. In the 1970s, I did not yet have any power to choose artists. Yes, Billy and I were friends from years back when we both worked at Warren Magazines, but the reason I got lucky and Billy was assigned to the *Panther* is that it was what Marvel Editorial did in those days. Black artists, who were just finding entrance into the field, were often put on Black titles. Thus, I had another friend and partner who believed enough in me to give me the kind of powerful visual dynamics I needed, but who could also see past the physical pain and into the wounds of the spirit that would plague T'Challa and the people around him.

As the series progressed, readers began to write to us, and the enthusiasm for Wakanda, as a unique and individualistic place within the Marvel Universe, intensified. It was rewarding and stimulating and little frightening. Like T'Challa, there would be self-doubt that we could take this to the finish line. Because if the readers wrote with strong opinions about what the stories and T'Challa meant to them, Editorial was pretty much in an opposite frame of mind.

I don't believe it had occurred to them in the beginning that if the stories were set in Wakanda, it meant the comic would have a virtually all Wakandan cast, which meant an all-Black cast. They wanted to know where the White people were. I kept telling them it was their mythology, not mine. They established that Wakanda was this mystical, hidden, technologically advanced nation, so where the hell were these White people supposed to come from?

Some editorial people wanted the Avengers to appear in the book. It had become important to me as I got further into writing the books that the events in Wakanda and *Panther's Rage* stay isolated. The Black hero did not need some White guys coming in to save his hash. The more I went to comic conventions (back when comic conventions really were all about comics!), I would hear how much it meant to people who followed the series that it stay apart and true to its spirit.

I came to believe that what we were doing was too important.

When doing a huge project like *Panther's Rage*, I look back at it and liken it to an endurance race, the winning line long and distant. For me, I found I had to keep blinders on, the way they do on a racehorse galloping the track. You can't let yourself be distracted by what is going on outside the fence, any of the shouting negative voices there that can corrode your belief. You need to keep what you envisioned clear, what you hoped you would achieve if you finished the story, because it is *always* about the story! If you let derision or challenge derail you, you will never know if you would or would not achieve what you set out to do, what you thought was important. That gets lost. If that gets lost, you lose. If you lose, the readers do, too! And the reasons and passions and insight that drove you on to do this insane, crazy thing, to live inside the head of the King of the Wakandans, might never become reality! If a writer doesn't believe in what he or she is writing, why should anyone else believe it?

When the *Black Panther* movie was released, the filmmakers

received this mammoth display of praise and love for what they had achieved, which was a staggering global response way beyond what I experienced decades ago with "Panther's Rage," this love for the Panther and the ideal of Wakanda.

In probing inside T'Challa's personality, who he was, one of the things I came to believe is that despite the fact that he was a king and in that respect beyond the average person's concerns and ways of life, they related to his humanity. It came to me that many people loved the fact that he was a monarch. T'Challa could do anything he wanted as a leader. Who could say to him, "Nay"?

But what they loved was that he truly worried about the decisions he made. T'Challa truly did want to represent as many of the different factions of his people as he could. His dedication was as much to the technological wizards as to the farmers. His concern for his warriors was as much as for teachers. He was, as far as I was concerned, a leader who truly cared about the fate of all his people, and realistically knew there were times he would fail some of them, but he cared to try to make that loss minimal. And really, I'll bet when you think about it, isn't that what most of us desire: that the political leaders in our life truly want to represent their constituents? And actually care about how what they do affects their daily lives?

Now, if I worry about hearing T'Challa's voice in my head, I am also always concerned about what do I do after I finish that first race. I mean, right from the get go, before I even knew how many books "Panther's Rage" would be I had to know where I could take T'Challa, who would be changed by its conclusion.

I have no inclination to write the same story again and again. It occurred to me when reading all the earlier books on the Panther, no one had ever mentioned his mother. If any of you read "Panther's Rage" you will find I purposefully did not mention her, either, for two and a half years. I was saving her for the next story, "Panther's Quest," which I thought would deal with South Africa, and since this was the 1970s, Apartheid, and that for some reason that I did not yet know, the Panther would become a son searching for his mother in a racist regime that made such a human endeavor almost impossible.

I did not write that story at the end of "Panther's Rage," I did "The Panther vs. The Klan" instead because I was going through an emotionally turbulent time in my personal life and knew I could not do the necessary research for the project properly. Thus, some of you know, "The Panther vs. The Klan" came about, with Billy Graham and Rich Buckler helping me explore how T'Challa would react to racism and extremism in America.[8] We all have to explore how we will deal with this very real threat.

Years later, in the 1980s, I did create his mom Ramonda's character, and I did have to figure out how to go inside her head and learn what had happened to her so that her son never knew her and no one ever talked about her to him.[9] Gene Colan was the artist, and once again I was fortunate to have someone who believed in this emotionally devastating backdrop and depict the human faces caught up in such racist and violent events. You can see the pain in T'Challa's eyes as he holds a burned child in his arms, weeping, in the opening page of "Last Night I Wept for Freedom."[10]

This was among my most challenging efforts to be inside T'Challa's head and try to capture the pain and loss and despair, but also his heroic efforts and determination. The main focus I tried to always have . . . KEEP IT HUMAN! Gene Colan could draw such human dignity, his art seeing right into the eyes and souls of the people I created. It is like Gene lived inside MY head, the way I lived inside T'Challa's!

Later, when I returned T'Challa to Wakanda, I knew everyone had been waiting for years to see where all the Wakandans around T'Challa were, how their lives had changed. Gene

Colan was not available to draw *Panther's Prey* and I made one of the best art choices I ever made in my life, Dwayne Turner, as the artist.[11] The Panther was Dwayne's first big comics story. The Panther was his favorite character. I thought I'd rather have someone starting out who loved the character, who would want to explore and capture T'Challa, the way I did, than have someone to whom the book would be just another comic book gig. Dwayne was magnificent at capturing the grandeur that I wanted for Wakanda, and the gymnastic Olympian feats of the Panther, his agile grace, his poetic power in motion!

I knew I had to expand on the Wakanda mythos, and now see how the country would interact with the global community, and the machinations of outside forces, from the United States' own CIA to other countries' desirous ambitions, and those fearful of Wakanda's incredible accomplishments.

This is the last I will write about living inside the King of the Wakandans' head. I am glad I could be there; it brought out the better human being in me. And, hopefully, you feel there are more positive possibilities because of T'Challa.

Remember, the possibilities of T'Challa lives inside us, too. Be kind to each other. Be kind to yourselves. And hang in there!

—Don McGregor

## NOTES

1. *Fantastic Four* #53–54 (1966).
2. *Jungle Action* #6–18 (1973–1975).
3. *Jungle Action* #6 (1973).
4. *Black Panther* (2018 motion picture).
5. *Jungle Action* #6 (1973) through #8 (1974).
6. *Jungle Action* #7 (1973).
7. *Jungle Action* #10 (1974).
8. Starting with *Jungle Action* #19 (1976).
9. *Marvel Comics Presents* #14 (1989).
10. *Marvel Comics Presents* #27 (1989).
11. Beginning with *Black Panther: Panther's Prey* #1 (1990).

# STARRING . . .
# T'CHALLA THE BLACK PANTHER

**Creators:** Stan Lee & Jack Kirby.

**Debut of Character:** *Fantastic Four* #52 (1966).

**First Ongoing Publication as Lead Character:** *Jungle Action*, starting with issues #5 (reprint of *Avengers* #62) and #6 (original material, Killmonger's debut).

**Debut of Eponymous Series:** *Black Panther* #1 (1977).

**First Television Appearances:**

   Nonspeaking—*X-Men*, episode 4–06, "Sanctuary, Part One" (October 21, 1995).

   Speaking—*Fantastic Four*, episode 2–07, "Prey of the Black Panther" (November 11, 1995). Voiced by Keith David.

**First Television Series:** *Black Panther* motion comic, episode 1–01, "Pilot" (January 23, 2010). Voiced by Djimon Hounsou.

**First Live-Action Theatrical Appearance:** *Captain America: Civil War* (2016 motion picture). Played by Chadwick Boseman.

**First Theatrical Starring Role:** *Black Panther* (2018 motion picture). Played by Chadwick Boseman.

# WHAT YOU WISH FOR

### Alex Simmons

Where do you start talking about someone who represents superhuman bravery and power, as well as the struggle between cultures, religions, and races?

There's no way that I will ever know what truly went on in the mind of Jack Kirby initially when he created the character called the Black Panther, back in the turbulent 1960s. Over the three decades that I've been in the company of many Marvel writers and editors, I've heard one or two stories multiple times. The single repetitive element seems to be that Jack first came up with the concept of a Black superhero who is the king of his own nation. He originally thought of the character as having a cowl mask, much like Batman's, where the jawline and lips and so forth would be exposed. I'm told that concept was rejected and that he was told the face must be completely covered. I wonder who said that. I wonder what their reasoning for it was exactly. But as I said, I'll never know.

The story went on that Jack (possibly alone or probably collaborating with Stan Lee) asked if he could at least expand on the Panther's kingdom in Africa. Jack was given the go-ahead. What was on Jack's mind at that moment, once again, I don't know. Whether or not he sat with Stan and they devised so many of the elements that we've come to know and love, I don't know. So few of those who might have been the proverbial fly on the wall are still with us so many years later. What I was told is that Jack came back days or weeks later with Wakanda. Not a quaint, primitive environment. And not simply thatched huts, woven shields, and simple spears. T'Challa's kingdom was a vibrant, industrious, super-technological nation, in possession of an ore that most of the world would probably kill for—if they knew it existed.

Be careful what you wish for, those on high.

I do know that Stan, being the P. T. Barnum of comics, got the concept published. I know he introduced the character through Marvel's most popular books of the times (the 1960s), that being the *Fantastic Four* and the *Avengers*. And I know it was some time before the Panther received his own storylines, even if it was only half an issue in a series called *Jungle Action*.

It was a while before a certain writer by the name of Don McGregor was brought on to write stories for that series. Of course, Marvel Editorial didn't really know Don McGregor. They had no idea that this short Caucasian man from Rhode Island would come up with the first maxi-series for the Black Panther or that he would title it "Panther's Rage." Don set the entire cast, crew, and storyline in Wakanda, with all its technology, mythology, political intrigue, humanity, and all with characters of color. That storyline eventually became the basis for the movie that so many of us enjoyed in 2018.

It is unfortunate in a way that T'Challa the Black Panther—his lineage, loved ones, even his enemies of the darker hue—cannot be seen strictly as fantastic or entertaining comic book characters. In some ways it's rather frustrating that they must not only represent exciting and exotic adventure, fantasy, and the power struggle between right and wrong. The Panther legacy must also represent—as seen by some—an entire race of people. It represents their individualism, cultural values, history, and their worth in society. No one individual or creation should carry such weight.

But by the same token, it is empowering to see how well they have sustained their existence. They are removed from the stereotypes of street, ghetto, or jungle primitives worshipping all but their own. Their majesty is in the stories, as well as fun and thrills—as a literary and artistic piece as well as a symbol. It is wonderful to see how many people have contributed to creating this iconic canon of material. I won't bother to try and list the roster, but it is long and it is seasoned with the faces and names of people from various cultural and racial backgrounds. In fact, one could say that the Black Panther has existed because of the diversity of strength and talent brought together over 40-plus years. A diverse cadre of talent in Hollywood eventually brought millions of new fans and billions of green dollar bills.

And now we have this book, which goes one step further. It takes a fictitious African (not African-American) comic book character and the world in which he dwells, and places him under the microscope of psychology and human motivation. It probes the stories and symbols to find even greater clarity as to how it represents the human condition. It explores our strengths and flaws, our indomitable will of humankind—perhaps seeking the best of us, no matter what color.

This may or may not change how you see to T'Challa the Black Panther. It may not change how you view society, no matter where you are in the world. But I hope it will offer some interesting insight into the minds and hearts of the creators, the storytellers, the character, and the audience that has embraced him for so very long.

# ROLL CALL

Wakanda, vibranium, and the heart-shaped herb all first appear when T'Challa himself debuts in *Fantastic Four #52* (1966). Other major characters discussed in this book join his growing cast in issues cited below. As points of reference, the list identifies actors who played these characters in the 2018 motion picture *Black Panther* when applicable (in parentheses).

**King T'Chaka**—T'Challa's father (John Kani): *Fantastic Four #53* (1966).

**Ulysses Klaw**, spelled **Klaue** for the movies—T'Chaka's killer (Andy Serkis): *Fantastic Four #53* (1966).

**M'Baku**—a.k.a. Man-Ape (Winston Duke): *Avengers #62* (1969).

**W'Kabi**—head of security (Daniel Kaluuya): *Avengers #62* (1969).

**Monica Lynne**—T'Challa's ex-fiancée: *Avengers #73* (1970).

**Erik Killmonger**—born N'Jadaka (Michael B. Jordan): *Jungle Action #6* (1973).

**Ororo Munroe**—a.k.a. Storm, T'Challa's ex-wife: *Giant-Size X-Men #1* (1975).

**Queen Ramonda**—T'Chaka's widow, Shuri's mother, T'Challa's stepmother whom he addresses as mother (Angela Bassett): *Marvel Comics Presents* #14 (1989).

**Everett K. Ross**—US State Department liaison in comics, CIA operative in movies (Martin Freeman): *Ka-Zar* #17 (1998).

**Nakia**—a.k.a. Malice (Lupita Nyong'o): *Black Panther* #1 (1998).

**Okoye**—Dora Milaje leader (Danai Gurira): *Black Panther* #1 (1998).

**Shuri**—T'Challa's half-sister (Letitia Wright): *Black Panther* #4 (2005); later becomes a Black Panther in *Black Panther* #5 (2009).

**S'Yan**—T'Chaka's brother and T'Challa's predecessor as Black Panther: *Black Panther* #4 (2005).

**Zuri**—special attendant to Wakanda's king (Forest Whitaker): *Black Panther* #1 (1998).

**Ayo**—Dora Milaje member (Florence Kasumba): *Ultimates* #1 (2016).

**N'Yami**  T'Challa's mother, who dies shortly after his birth: *Black Panther* #7 (2016).

# THE PUBLISHER: IT'S ALL MARVEL

Black Panther and related Marvel Universe characters originate in publications from Marvel Comics. The company has undergone several name changes during its history.

**Founder:** Martin Goodman (1908–1992), who sold the company in 1968 and remained as publisher until 1972.

**First Original Comic Book Publication:** *Marvel Comics* #1 (1939).

**Timely Publications:** Founded in 1939, then renamed **Timely Comics** in 1941.

**Atlas Comics:** New company name starting in 1951. (Goodman later reused this name after he left Marvel. Under the parent company of **Seaboard Periodicals**, he published the second **Atlas Comics** in 1974 to compete with Marvel and DC, but this enterprise folded in 1975.)

**Marvel Comics:** Rebranded in summer 1961. Official company name has been **Marvel Publishing**, **Marvel Comics Group**, and **Marvel Worldwide**.

**Parent Company:** Timely Publications (1939); Magazine Management (by 1947); Perfect Film & Chemical Corporation (1968); Cadence Industries (1973); New World Pictures (1986); Andrews Group (1989); Marvel Holdings (1994); Icahn Enterprises (1997). Marvel Enterprises became Marvel Entertainment (part of The Walt Disney Company as of 2009).

**Location:** New York, NY.

Marvel Comics reset the *Black Panther* series' numbering repeatedly in later years, so the comic book series has had #1 issues published in 1977, 1988, 1998, 2005, 2009, 2016, and 2018. Even though fans assign volume numbers, Marvel typically does not. Publication dates therefore indicate story order better than issue numbers do. Because Marvel published most of the comics cited herein, references will identify a comic book's publisher only for the few instances in which an outside company (such as DC Comics) published the work.

I

A
PANTHER
IS
BORN

When T'Challa first appears in comics and films, he is already a man. He is already the Black Panther. Unlike many of the best-known superheroes,[1] his debut appearance does not yet depict his origin.[2] It will be told in flashback,[3] and his life will be revealed in pieces over time. A person's life story follows meandering paths with many choices, and each choice made leaves other possibilities behind. Why does one person take the path of great resistance where others take the least? And when two people follow similar paths so far along the way, why does one become a hero where others might go astray?

Life's beginning is not the only time or only way that a Panther is born.

**NOTES**

1. e.g., Superman—*Action Comics* #1 (1938); Wonder Woman—*All-Star Comics* #8 (1941); Captain America—*Captain America Comics* #1 (1941); Marvel Comics' most prominent Silver Age superheroes beginning with the Fantastic Four—*Fantastic Four* #1 (1961).
2. *Fantastic Four* #52 (1966); *Captain America: Civil War* (2016 motion picture).
3. *Fantastic Four* #53 (1966).

# 1

# THE FIRST PANTHER

## INTERVIEW WITH ACTOR KEITH DAVID

### Alex Simmons & Travis Langley

Actor Keith David Williams, known professionally as Keith David, was the first person to play the role of T'Challa. Although the Black Panther previously made a non-speaking appearance in the original *X-Men* cartoon,[1] his true debut came a few weeks later in the *Fantastic Four* episode, "Prey of the Black Panther,"[2] a 1995 retelling of his 1966 comic book introduction.[3] In addition to his many live-action roles in films such as *The Thing, Barbershop,* and *Platoon,*[4] Keith has narrated numerous films including *The War,*[5] and voiced characters in a variety of video games (e.g., *Mass Effect*[6] series) and cartoons (e.g., *Gargoyles, Rick and Morty, Todd McFarlane's Spawn),*[7] along with many television commercials. You probably know his face, and you certainly know his voice.

Not only was Keith the original voice of T'Challa, but he has also been a vocal supporter for other portrayals of the character. Among other things, he made a YouTube appearance just to say,

"Don't forget to see the *Black Panther*,"[8] encouraging people to see the movie starring Chadwick Boseman.[9] The original T'Challa actor shared his experiences with us, along with his thoughts on the nature and importance of the Black Panther character.

## VOICE OF THE PANTHER

**Alex Simmons:** When did you first encounter T'Challa and the Black Panther?

**Keith David Williams (actor Keith David):** When I was growing up, my best friend owned a comic book store. And the Black Panther was one of the few [Black] characters in comic books. So you know he became somewhat my favorite character. I felt was it was overdue, the whole idea of Wakanda and a Black community and a Black superhero. I was fine with Nick Fury's . . .

**Alex:** If you're talking about *Sgt. Fury and His Howling Commandos*, that series from Marvel, the Black character in that was called Gabe. He was a jazz musician, but he was one of the fighting soldiers in that team.[10]

**Keith:** That's the guy, because I played a guy similar to him in a movie called *The Fifth Commandment*.[11] I was a jazz musician. So that [Gabe] set the bar. That would have been in the Sixties.

**Alex:** Yes. [At that time] Marvel would bundle their books together for the different distributors, and the distributors would receive Spider-Man, Sgt. Fury, and whatever else was in those bundles. And the story is that supposedly when some of those bundles hit the South and the distributors or retailers saw Gabe in that comic, they returned everything. They didn't just return Sgt. Fury, but they returned everything.

**Keith:** Really?

**Alex:** Yes. Not all, but a lot. Enough of them, so I can see where that character would have stood out in your mind.

**Keith:** It never ceases to amaze me the depths to which racism in this country descends. Or the manifestations of it, you know, just like when you listen to their stories: He [the Black man] was nothing, there was no getting along, no Black and White togetherness at all—which is a fallacy. However, you know there are certain places that would have you believe that when things seemed to be doing better, it really wasn't. So then, few people can even fathom in a comic book, a Black man having any class or dignity whatsoever.

**Alex:** Or value even, right!

**Keith:** Yes, or value. I mean that's amazing to me, because that's definitely a taught mentality. It's something you have to learn. It's not only something that you have to learn, it's something that has to be reinforced within your closest environment. That is to say, at home.

**Alex:** Well certainly when you're growing up, you're in your most vulnerable developmental stages.

**Keith:** That's when you learn that lesson. I had a great affinity for my grandfather. I'm named David after my grandfather. If he had harbored any "isms" that he would have deigned to pass onto me—which he did not—I probably would have adopted them and probably would have nurtured them, because they were his and because of me wanting to be like him, to emulate him.

**Alex:** He was your role model.

**Keith:** Right. You know it's like these people who insist upon keeping statues of scumbag war heroes in the South, because you say you're a historian. Well, most of these guys were just racist; they weren't heroes. They just wanted to keep the status quo the way it was, let it all be White, and anybody else, the hell with them.

**Alex:** It's funny that you bring that up. I feel the Black Panther also challenges people's conceptions of heroes. What is a hero? Are they favoring the heroes, like the ones you and I probably encountered when we were growing up, both historical as well as fictional, or the antiheroes? When you were growing up, you were seeing Gabe in the Howling Commandos, you were also seeing T'Challa in some of the Marvel comics. Was the impact on you at that time significant? Or as a kid at that time, were you just thinking, this was cool? How do you remember that?

**Keith:** I would have to say it was probably more "cool" than I would register any grand significance. But you know, that certainly turned into being both cool and significant, you know what I mean. But I can't say I really grew up with any "shame in my game." I never not wanted to be Black. There was a time I can remember when people were talking about it, and there were such negative connotations around being Black that I certainly wish *that* [the negativity] wasn't so. But in my house, my father was a pretty militant guy as far as "Black Power" and owning your blackness in a way that again "no shame in the game."

**Alex:** How did you go from that into pursuing an acting career? Was it something you always wanted to do? Or was it inspired by something in particular?

**Keith:** I wanted to be an actor my whole life. I don't even know why I wanted to be an actor. I wanted to be a preacher, I wanted to be a pediatrician when I saw roles that I liked. And I feel very strongly that acting is a calling, like ministry. And people come to it for different reasons. Like my desire to be a preacher. I just felt that God wanted me to be an actor, and that's what I wanted to do. And like ministry, if I play a character within a story, that makes you want to be like him or that makes you *not* want to be like him, well, again that's ministry.

**Alex:** You're influencing your audience in one way or another, so absolutely, you're speaking to them and you're bringing a message to them. Whether or not they become engaged and pulled into the story, that speaks to the merit of that delivery.

**Keith:** And that brings us back to T'Challa. I mean somebody has nobility and then regard for his people. Someone who has the desire to do the right thing and the next rightest thing and the next, for all people involved. And to learn that it's not just about my people.

**Alex:** Did the Black Panther character stay with you during your growing-up years? Were you still reading comics, or did you move away from that?

**Keith:** I sort of dropped off of my comic book reading after I went to college.

**Alex:** Once you got to college, you gave up on reading comics and you began pursuing your acting career. At what point did you find yourself back with the Black Panther? How did that happen?

**Keith:** There was a brother who was a Black producer on one of the cartoon networks.

**Alex:** Dwayne McDuffie.

**Keith:** Yeah, so he wanted to introduce the Black Panther, and we talked about if we could make him an animated series. He thought the world wasn't ready for that at that time, so it never happened, but how wonderful that it did finally come to fruition. And it couldn't have been better portrayed than by Chadwick Boseman. He's just wonderful.

**Alex:** You enjoyed the movie?

**Keith:** I *loved* it. It was wonderful! And he was phenom-
enal. He really embraces that character quite wonder-
fully and Michael [B. Jordan] playing his nemesis was
also wonderful. He was also quite brilliant.

**Alex:** You did voice the Black Panther in an episode of the
*Fantastic Four* animated series. When you did that, how
did you approach the role? How did you feel about it?

**Keith:** I was honored to be able do it. I mean, here I
am voicing the Black Panther for the first time. Again,
I really wanted to make more of it, but it wasn't the
time. And then a few years later, I got to do Goliath
in *Gargoyles*. He wasn't the Black Panther, but he was a
man of color.

**Alex:** Yes, whether people thought of it that way or not,
absolutely.

**Keith:** The truth of the matter is, inherently, yes, we're
all human beings. We're all one human race, we all
come from different cultures, and we come from a
magnificent mixture of cultures, where climate, environment, and other things cause us to have different
habits and customs. And I think, inherently, like the
first Americans, we are far more welcoming by nature.
Inherent in the White man's history, he's always trying
to conquer somebody. As if his own, wherever that is,
is not enough. You say that, and then there are people
who say, well, Africans sold Africans to other countries. And, yes, there have always been warring factions
within the same culture. But you can't compare the
American slave trade to any other form of slavery in the
world. It was the worst aberration of all.

**Alex:** Let's look at the power of the image of Wakanda and
T'Challa as a superhero. It's not like Superman, where
there's no Krypton any more. Here you have T'Challa,

who's come to the United States, is seen as a superhero alongside the Fantastic Four and the Avengers, and then he goes home, back to his kingdom, the most technologically advanced in existence. He's also wealthy, so much so that he once bought out Tony Stark in a particular deal.[12] So do you feel that this kind of imagery in the real world you're talking about is viewed—as a threat or a titillation? Or do you feel some people just don't know what to do with that imagery?

**Keith:** They don't know what to do with that. How fantastic is that? How wonderful is that? It's like how they tried to undermine the technological advances of the Egyptians and the Black people in Africa or all over Africa, in other forms of historical documentation. Whenever the White man came across a culture that was in any way, shape, or form advanced, especially above the barbaric Anglo-Saxon culture where they were still—

**Alex:** And throwing the sewage out the window.

**Keith:** And others were doing brain surgeries in Egypt. Anytime they came across that, they wanted to undermine that somehow in their written documentation. By nature, any explorer is unique, there's not a whole lot of people doing that, so they [the public] have to take your [the explorer's] word for it. So depending on the prejudice of the explorer, that's the history that you got. You got *his story*. Far too many times, it was far from objective; in fact, there was nothing objective about it.

**Alex:** As I understand the history, it was Jack Kirby who created the Black Panther and a lot of the world of Wakanda. I'm sure Stan Lee collaborated on the project, because that's what Stan often did. And I know they received some pushback from some executives.

But it was most certainly Stan who got the project out to the world, because he was a showman. He was the P. T. Barnum of comics.

And so, we have this, and we look at how it's transpired, and how it's influenced people over the years. That's one of the reasons I wanted to have your take on the character, and your experience with him as well. Earlier, you talked about the movie. Do you think you would have any more involvement in the Black Panther world in some way? Or would you like to?

**Keith:** I hope to God they ask me to do something in the *Black Panther*. I want to have some part in it.

**Alex:** One of the things I liked about the film was developed in the comic books. The Black Panther character showed up in a lot of the *Avengers* and the *Fantastic Four* comics as another character without full stories and issues on his own, initially. When writer Don McGregor had a shot to take over the Black Panther, one of the many things he did was make sure the women in his stories were strong characters. Over the years, between writers Reggie Hudlin and Christopher Priest, we have Shuri, the Panther's sister.[13] She even earned her way into becoming the Black Panther in one storyline.[14] In the movie we have his girlfriend who is a very capable spy, his mother, and the women warriors who protect T'Challa. So what do you think is the impact of seeing so many strong Black women, affecting the world in and outside of Wakanda?

**Keith:** As you say yourself, it has done wonders for the image and stereotype of what Black women are capable of. They were beautiful, and they were *badass*!! And, I think you know, I cannot commend them [various creators] enough for changing that paradigm. They definitely initiated a paradigm shift and we can't go back from that. Nobody wants to go back from that. That was powerful! That was beyond powerful; it was empowering. And oh my God, it's a beautiful, beautiful thing what they did. Whoever initiated it, my hat is off to them, and for the continuance. As for Ryan Coogler, I hope I get my opportunity to work with him again someday because I just think he's just fantastic.

I'd like to see more Black Panther–type characters developed and nurtured, brought to fruition. Because we need them; White people need them. White people need to know that the old history that they learned from their grandfathers, a lot was false, and that if it wasn't for the Black man in America, there would be no America as we know it. Bringing forth the truth— there is nothing more powerful than that. Jesus said, "The truth will set you free!"[15] I mean, that's an edict from God! That's not even man-sourced, that's God-sourced. The truth *will* set you free. That's the real deal.

## NOTES

1. *X-Men*, episode 4–06, "Sanctuary, Part One" (October 21, 1995).
2. *Fantastic Four*, episode 2–07, "Prey of the Black Panther" (November 11, 1995).
3. *Fantastic Four* #52 (1966).
4. As Childs in *The Thing* (1982 motion picture); Lester Simmons in *Barbershop* (2002 motion picture); King in *Platoon* (1986 motion picture).
5. *The War* (2007 documentary).
6. As David Anderson, beginning with *Mass Effect* (2007 video game).
7. As Goliath, beginning with *Gargoyles*, episode 1–01, "Awakening, Part 1" (October 24, 1994); the President, beginning with *Rick and Morty*, episode 2–05, "Get Schwifty (August 23, 2015); Al Simmons/Spawn, beginning with *Todd McFarlane's Spawn*, episode 1–01, "Burning Visions" (May 16, 1997).
8. *Relentless* (2018).
9. *Black Panther* (2018 motion picture).
10. The character Gabriel Jones first appeared in *Sgt. Fury and His Howling Commandos* #1 (1963).

11. He played Max "Coolbreeze" Templeton in *The Fifth Commandment* (2008 motion picture).
12. *Black Panther* #42–43 (2002).
13. Hudlin introduced Shuri in *Black Panther* #4 (2005).
14. *Black Panther* #5 (2009).
15. John 8:32.

# 2

# GROWING UP IN WAKANDA

## UNDERSTANDING THE PSYCHOLOGICAL
## FEATURES OF SOCIAL LIFE

### Justin F. Martin

*"To live in society is to form a diversified understanding of
human character, of its capacities for good and evil."*

—social psychologist Solomon Asch[1]

*"Who, in full sanity, would try to hold a nation under their feet?"*
—Changamire, Wakandan philosopher[2]

If the society in which a person lives offers insight into its
individuals, as social psychologist Solomon Asch seems to
suggest in the quote above, understanding Wakanda may be
critical to understanding T'Challa. Due to its display of diverse
socio-moral judgments and their underlying concepts, understanding Wakanda might also inform our thinking about the
psychological features of its citizens' (and ruler's) social life.[3]

How we form, evaluate, and apply concepts related to our treatment of others, such as friends, family, colleagues, and acquaintances, can underscore our relationships with them during times of cohesion and times of conflict.[4]

In other words, the ways in which we make moral, immoral, or amoral choices, and the ways in which we interact with people in our lives, are shaped by the way we developed our ideas about morals and relationships in the first place. So the differences in how T'Challa and Killmonger make their choices and treat others likely depend on how and even where they learned moral and social ideas as they each grew up.

## THE DEVELOPMENT OF SOCIO-MORAL CONCEPTS

*Social domain theory* suggests that what makes humans unique— our ability to have diverse relationships and use various concepts to understand those relationships—also makes social life complex and at times challenging. Under what circumstances should T'Challa uphold Wakandan tradition and when should he seek to change it? How does Okoye choose the best outcome when being loyal to T'Challa means betraying her husband? In Wakanda and in everyday life, dilemmas involving competing considerations are by-products of our decisions to pursue meaningful relationships with one another.

Social domain theory contends that our relationships tend to involve interactions that fall into one of three distinct domains: *moral* (harm/welfare, justice/fairness, rights, and civil liberties), *social-conventional* (e.g., authority, group norms, group functioning, laws, policies, and customs), and *personal/psychological* (e.g., autonomy, personal jurisdiction, and mental/emotional characteristics). Black Panther stories explore similar themes, including (1) moral themes related to harm (e.g., protecting Wakanda from outside influences) and justice (e.g., making sure the throne is occupied in a fair manner), (2) socio-conventional themes related to tradition/custom (e.g., ensuring that the ceremonial battle is carried out properly) and foreign policy (e.g., how to interact with other nations), and (3) personal/psychological themes related to autonomy/personal jurisdiction (e.g., choosing a life for oneself not bound by tradition or cultural/societal expectations).

Although Wakanda is often portrayed through the struggles and perspectives of adults, research on socio-moral development suggests that many of the concepts related to or implicated in these struggles and perspectives—such as harm, fairness, rights, democracy, authority, and personal choice—have their origins in childhood.[5] Examples include T'Challa's struggles to be a moral leader as both king and Black Panther, O'Koyes' difficulties maintaining her loyalty to the throne as a leader of the Dora Milaje, and Nakia's strivings for a life not primarily defined by Wakandan tradition and expectations. One potential interpretation regarding the nature of these struggles and perspectives is that they stem—at least in part—from concepts within the moral, socio-conventional, and personal/psychological domains.

Individuals' ability to understanding the moral,[6] socio-conventional,[7] and personal/psychological[8] domains improve with age. These age-related changes are often reflected in older individuals' increased ability to reason about such concepts in ways that are more abstract, multifaceted, and/or applied to a wider variety of situations. Therefore, just as children's developing understanding of the moral treatment of others[9] may serve as a foundation for the more sophisticated moral understanding that can develop later, T'Challa's childhood understandings of harm and fairness likely prepared him for the morally complex intervention versus isolation debate he contends with throughout the film. Just as children's early understanding of rules and authority[10] may serve as a foundation for more elaborate and complex perspectives on these concepts, Okoye's childhood understandings of these concepts may have prepared her for the nuances and complexities that come with preserving Wakandan tradition as leader of the Dora Milaje. Similarly, it is plausible that the relationship between Nakia's childhood and adult understandings of personal choice may parallel the relationship between early[11] and later understandings of personal matters as suggested by literature. In the film, these understandings may partially explain her noncommittal response to T'Challa's suggestion that she become his wife. The conceptual bases underlying the strivings of fully formed adults have to originate much earlier in life.

## THE APPLICATION OF SOCIO-MORAL CONCEPTS

In many ways, social domain theory suggests that the presence of distinct domains of social judgment and the extent to which they undergo conceptual changes across development are parts of a larger story when it comes to understanding the psychological features of social life. Specifically, how individuals apply these concepts in the context of their varying relationships and interactions is closely associated with three other psychological phenomena believed to be prevalent in social life: *domain-relevant concept interactions, coordinations,* and *social construals.* Given the myriad of socio-moral issues reflected in the struggles and decisions of various Wakandans, their society provides a rich social setting to illustrate these psychological features of social life.

### DOMAIN-RELEVANT CONCEPT INTERACTIONS

Social domain theory identifies three ways[12] in which domain-relevant concepts tend to interact with each other. One way is through *within*-domain combinations, which occur when a situation (or judgment) includes multiple concepts or considerations within the same domain. For instance, two friends may get into an argument because one kid getting teased by a group of other children may be upset that the kid's friend does not stick up for him or her. Despite understanding that the teasing could cause the first kid some psychological harm (moral understanding), the friend has decided not to intervene out of fear that the kids would then tease him or her, too, or even do something worse, such as inflict physical harm. One interpretation of the film's central theme— the intervention-versus-isolation debate—is that it reflects a within-domain combination with regard to the moral domain. Both Killmonger and T'Challa appeal to the use of force when debating Wakanda's relationship with other countries, although Killmonger more directly addresses harm/welfare considerations. Killmonger believes Wakanda should use its vibranium to weaponize oppressed peoples throughout the world so they can improve their way of life (i.e., welfare). Although T'Challa does not explicitly reference welfare considerations, it is worth considering whether his emphasizing that Wakanda does not go to war with other countries is at least partly based on welfare considerations of a different sort (e.g., the possibility that Wakanda's use of force in other countries could ultimately harm more lives than it helps).

A second type of interaction is a *between*-domain combination and occurs when a situation (or judgment) includes concepts or considerations from multiple domains. The ceremonial fight between T'Challa and Killmonger represents a potential between-domain combination when it appears that Killmonger is about to kill T'Challa. Given the concerns the film raises prior to this fight, regarding Killmonger's fitness as king, T'Challa's imminent demise at the hands of Killmonger could potentially alter the situation for some of the observers. For these observers, the situation might be a conflicting one, whereby socio-conventional considerations (e.g., letting the fight play out as tradition/custom demands) are in conflict with moral considerations (e.g., preserving T'Challa's life). Indeed, one could argue that it is this conflict that explains Okoye's visible discomfort with this particular part of the fight and Zuri's decision to intervene at the cost of his own life.

A *second-order* combination can occur when an act in one domain has implications for another domain. Even if observers generally understand the ceremonial fight as straightforward— meaning primarily viewed through the lens of one domain (say, the socio-conventional domain)—the ceremony itself still has implications for the moral domain since the combatants are inflicting harm on each other. Similarly, changes in Wakandan policy regarding humanitarian aid could be considered a second-order combination, whereby socio-conventional acts (e.g., modifying laws and policies) can have moral implications (e.g., improving people's physical and psychological welfare).

The dilemma that Wakandan philosopher Changamire faces at the height of the escalation of a major political conflict depicted in the comics[13] may also be viewed in terms of a second-order combination. After realizing that his teachings calling for Wakanda to be ruled by the people are influencing his pupil Tetu to commit acts of violence against Wakandans in the name of political revolution, he agrees to take an active role in helping T'Challa resolve the conflict.[14] Although he believes that doing away with Wakanda's monarchy is the best path forward, his decision to help may be driven by his belief that the costs (moral implications) of altering Wakandan government and policy (socio-conventional acts) in this manner are too great.

## COORDINATION

In light of social domain theory's assertions about our relationships with others, one might expect domain combinations to be commonplace in social life. Consistent with this idea, the theory highlights the importance of coordination,[15] a process whereby individuals acknowledge various competing considerations in a given situation and attempt to balance or weigh them in order to arrive at a resolution. Across many phenomena—some examples include discrimination,[16] rights and civil liberties,[17] and harm[18]—the increasing ability to understand issues related to the treatment of others is considered a key feature of socio-moral development. In general, research in this area suggests that by the time we are introduced to Wakanda and those fighting to preserve its livelihood, its adults have developed the capacity to consistently balance multiple and sometimes competing considerations when dealing with complex issues facing the nation.

Despite often having to infer film characters' mental processes through their actions, instead of relying on their reasoning (the latter of which is often used to assess coordination ability), the actions of some of the characters in *Black Panther* are generally consistent with the characteristics of coordination. For instance, initially a proponent of isolationism with regard to Wakanda's knowledge and resources, T'Challa struggles with whether or not this policy is in the best interests of Wakanda and the world as the film progresses. His struggles are understandable, given the complex nature of the issue and the implications an isolationist or interventionist policy could have for the welfare of Wakandans and the world at large.

The complex or ambiguous features of the issue are also reflected in the fact that although, at the film's end, he resolves the ambiguity to an extent by informing the United Nations that Wakanda will indeed start sharing its knowledge and resources with the outside world, he makes no mention of Wakanda getting involved in other nations' military or political affairs. Nor does he decide to use vibranium to arm oppressed people throughout the world, thus remaining opposed to the position held by Killmonger.

In a way, T'Challa's struggles with this complex issue are akin to findings on children's and adolescents' ability to resolve a complicated situation involving indirect harm.[19] Research participants were presented with a hypothetical scenario where $10 falls out of one person's pocket, and the main actor in the scenario (who needs money for a particular activity but is short $10) is considering whether or not to take the money. Whereas 8-year-olds tended to understand the situation as straightforward (e.g., primarily as a matter of stealing, which is wrong), 10- and 14-year-olds appeared to view the situation as more ambiguous in that they were more likely to struggle with whether or not keeping the money was wrong. The 16- and 17-year-olds, however, appeared to resolve the potential ambiguities by prioritizing the wrongness of stealing over these other considerations. Similarly, as the film progresses T'Challa becomes better able to resolve the intervention-versus-isolation debate in a way that prioritizes certain moral considerations (e.g., improving the welfare of others) over certain socio-conventional ones (e.g., maintaining full adherence to Wakanda's isolationist tradition).

Other examples from the film that are consistent with this "struggle/ambiguity" characteristic of coordination include the actions of Okoye during the ceremonial battle between Killmonger and T'Challa, when she believes T'Challa dies. Although visibly uncomfortable watching Killmonger apparently defeat T'Challa and then kill Zuri, Okoye does not intervene and remains silent when a fellow Dora Milaje asks her, "Is there nothing that can be done?" Immediately following the battle, Nakia visits Okoye to convince her to leave and join her, Ramonda, and Shuri as they find a way to overthrow Killmonger. Okoye refuses, leading to an argument about whether loyalty toward or rebellion against the throne is in Wakanda's best interest. Okoye's apparent prioritizing of socio-conventional considerations (e.g., maintaining tradition and social stability) over moral ones (e.g., preserving the welfare of Zuri) is consistent with findings from investigations of children's, adolescents', and adults' understandings of hypothetical dilemmas that include socio-conventional (e.g., group norms and functioning, rules, authority) and moral (e.g., harm, fairness, rights, and civil liberties) considerations.[20] Collectively, these findings reveal that, across many situations children, adolescents, and adults are aware of, care about, and attempt to balance socio-conventional and moral considerations in situations where both kinds of considerations are present and may be in conflict.

Once it is discovered that T'Challa is not dead (and thus the challenge is still "live" because T'Challa never submits), Okoye and W'Kabi's differing responses to this revelation are in line with research in the area of social construals,[21] which in many ways relates to the process of coordination. The general idea behind this line of inquiry is that both the nature of people's social experiences and the domain-relevant considerations they believe are most salient in those experiences influence how they make sense of them. Thus, one implication is that in multifaceted or ambiguous situations, where multiple domains are apparently or potentially relevant (e.g., politically charged issues, such as immigration, gun rights, abortion, and universal health care), it is possible for multiple people to experience the same situation yet construe the situation differently.

Seeing T'Challa alive, Okoye takes a neutral position with the expectation that the ceremonial battle will commence as per Wakandan tradition. Once it is clear that Killmonger will not honor tradition, Okoye turns on him, believing that his heart is too hardened to be king. Okoye's husband W'Kabi is also present when T'Challa declares that he is alive, yet W'Kabi's reaction is different. Although his own story arc suggests that he is also struggling with competing considerations, he still follows Killmonger's orders to attack T'Challa and anyone else in Killmonger's way. It is not until W'Kabi realizes that his wife is now one of the people standing in Killmonger's way that he resolves this struggle and surrenders to her.

What makes Okoye and W'Kabi respond in different ways to the same revelation? Specifically, why is Okoye prepared to fight her spouse but not T'Challa, yet the opposite is true for W'Kabi? This variability in responses to a multifaceted or ambiguous situation illustrates the relationship between social construals and coordination. Namely, if the ways in which people's construals of multifaceted or ambiguous situations can vary, so can the ways in which people coordinate the considerations they bring to bear on those situations. Therefore, as suggested by research on the development of coordination ability,[22] predicting one's ability to coordinate multiple considerations in a given complex situation does not necessarily mean that one can predict exactly how that coordination will play out.

## COHESION AND CONFLICT: THE COMPLEXITIES OF SOCIAL LIFE

What do these psychological features suggest about the complexities of social life? If one assumes that (1) social interactions and relationships between individuals vary in terms of relevant considerations, (2) considerations can interact in various ways, and (3) people can differ in how they make sense of social interactions and relationships, then it might be best to characterize social life (e.g., within families, societies, etc.) as normatively entailing both agreement (cohesion) and disagreement (conflict) among individuals.[23] It is with regard to these complexities of social life that Wakanda asserts itself as the main "character" in the Black Panther mythology. Examples of issues that Wakandans seem to generally agree on in the film include (1) having a monarchy-based government, (2) the importance of the ceremonial battle and the criteria to determine legitimate participants and combat, and (3) initially maintaining a "closed borders" policy regarding foreign trade, aid, and intervention. Some examples of disagreements or differing perspectives include (1) the shifting opinions on foreign policy (intervention versus isolation), (2) T'Challa disagreeing with his father and ancestors on whether the ends (e.g., protecting Wakanda) always justify the means (e.g., leaving a young Erik in Oakland instead of bringing him back to Wakanda), and (3) Okoye (who remains silent) reacting differently from Zuri (who intervenes) when it appears that Killmonger is about to kill T'Challa, although both are visibly troubled by the situation.

In addition to using social domain theory as a lens to examine the ways the interactions between Wakandans are consistent with research regarding the psychological features of social life, it can also serve as a bridge for identifying certain parallels between the diversity of perspectives portrayed among Wakandans and the diversity of perspectives that currently exist among Americans. Regarding the latter, a Pew Research study[24] suggests that potential similarities and differences exist between generations across many socio-political issues. Insofar as these similarities and differences can be partially explained by the psychological features discussed above, the results of this study are in line with research that has found support for the influence of these features on people's understandings of their experiences in real-life situations.[25]

Perhaps T'Challa's dual responsibilities—and the myriad of perspectives he has to take into account to maintain the well-being of the nation—contribute to his popularity and may partly explain why he was recently chosen to serve as leader/chairperson for the Avengers.[26] Unlike his American

# From Boy to King: A Rite of Passage

Sarah Rizkallah

All people across various cultures and races around the world undergo public rituals that signify the redefinition of their social status—*rites of passage.*[27] These changes typically occur in adolescence or young adulthood and can mark an individual's transition from child to adult, also known as that person's *coming of age.*[28] These shifts fall in numerous categories and may include events with which you are familiar, such as obtaining a learner's permit to drive (legal), graduation from school (economic), being of voting age (political), or marriage (interpersonal).[29] Physical symbols of change often accompany these changes, acting as a public declaration that an individual has successfully made the transition from one status to another[30] (such as a driver's license, a graduation cap and gown, or a wedding gown). Within non-Western cultures, other symbols of status might include the possession of tribal tattoos, piercings, or scarification.[31]

As with any new Black Panther, T'Challa undergoes an elaborate rite of passage.[32]

- *Separation phase:* Attendees to the formal ceremony are decorated with body paint and tribal attire to signify the impending change. Here, T'Challa is separated from his existing status and power.

- *Liminal phase:* In a period of ambiguity regarding his future status, wooden masks and chants mark the beginning of a ceremonial fight against any challenger who also wants to become the Black Panther.

- *Reincorporation phase:* He drinks of the heart-shaped herb, enters into the spirt world, and reemerges with a new status and identity as both Black Panther and king of Wakanda.

# Religious Freedom versus Threat: M'Baku across the Universes

Travis Langley

Jabari tribe leader M'Baku challenges T'Challa for the Wakandan throne and loses, but accepts his loss in the *Black Panther* film.[33] He even leads the Jabari in coming to T'Challa's assistance in the climactic battle against Killmonger's forces, playing out the classic cavalry trope to turn the odds in T'Challa's favor.[34] In the comics, however, M'Baku is T'Challa's enemy. Even though the film version of M'Baku might seem like a different character from the print version, these depictions might instead show how the same individual could change under different circumstances.

Before becoming the villain Man-Ape, M'Baku is a great warrior trusted to govern Wakanda in T'Challa's absence.[35] After he joins the outlawed White Gorilla Cult, though, he tries to usurp the throne and to replace the official state religion, to get every Wakandan to worship the White Gorilla instead of the panther god Bast. This is unlike the film version, in which he and his tribe freely worship a gorilla god and no one else seems to mind. Movie-M'Baku does not have to rebel in order to worship as he pleases because he already has religious freedom. So these different versions could show how the same person might follow different paths under conditions of religious freedom versus religious oppression.

People living under conditions of *authoritarianism*, in which authority figures are strict and punish anything other than unquestioning obedience, might show *authoritarian obedience* or they might rebel. A new convert to a banned religion might immediately feel the inherent threat of consequences even before any repercussions have occurred. People who feel threatened will experience physiological arousal that needs an outlet.[36] In the classic *fight-flight-freeze* response to threat,[37] M'Baku is the kind of person whose baseline response is to fight. In the movie universe, where his religion is not threatened, he does not feel the same need to fight for power.

superhero counterparts (such as Iron Man, Captain America, and Spider-Man) who can operate solely as protectors and sometimes avengers of their city, the country, or the world without also being responsible for addressing the various perspectives of its inhabitants, T'Challa does not have that luxury. Indeed, it appears that Wakandan philosopher Changamire is right to point out the difficulties of being king.

## NOTES

1. Asch (1952), p. 6.
2. *Black Panther* #10 (2016).
3. Martin (2018).
4. Turiel (1983, 2002).
5. Elenbaas & Killen (2016, 2017); Helwig (1997, 1998); Helwig et al. (1995); Killen & Smetana (1999); McNeil & Helwig (2015); Mulvey & Killen (2016); Nucci (1981); Prencipe & Helwig (2002); Rizzo et al. (2016); Smetana (1981); Smetana & Bitz (1996).
6. Arsenio & Willems (2017); Helwig (1997, 1998); Nucci & Turiel (2009); Rizzo et al. (2016).
7. McNeil & Helwig (2015); Midgette et al. (2016); Prencipe & Helwig (2002); Turiel (1983).
8. Helwig (1995, 1997); Komolova et al. (2017); Recchia et al. (2015).
9. Smetana (1981); Smetana et al. (2012).
10. Helwig (1998); Smetana & Bitz (1996).
11. Killen & Smetana (1999).
12. Turiel (1983).
13. *Black Panther* #9 (2016).
14. *Black Panther* #12 (2016).
15. Nucci & Turiel (2009).
16. Killen et al. (2010).
17. Helwig et al. (2013).
18. Jambon & Smetana (2014); Nucci & Turiel (2009).
19. Nucci & Turiel (2009).
20. Cooley & Killen (2015); Helwig (1997); Mulvey & Killen (2016); Prencipe & Helwig (2002); Shaw & Wainryb (1999); Turiel (2008).
21. Turiel et al. (1991); Wainryb (1991); Wainryb & Brehl (2006); Wainryb et al. (2005).
22. Jambon & Smetana (2014); Nucci & Turiel (2009).
23. Turiel (2002).
24. Pew Research Center (2018).
25. Komolova et al. (2017); Recchia et al. (2012); Recchia et al. (2015); Turiel (2008); Wainryb et al. (2005).

26. *Avengers* #8 (2018).
27. Van Gennep (1960/2013).
28. Arnett & Tanner (2006).
29. Steinberg (2005); Holmbeck et al. (2006), Thompson (2013).
30. Charon & Cahill (2004); Warner (1949).
31. Garve et al. (2017); Ludvico & Kurland (1995); Rush (2005).
32. *Black Panther* #2 (2005); *Black Panther* (2018 motion picture).
33. *Black Panther* (2018 motion picture).
34. Perfecting Your Craft (2018); TV Tropes (n.d.).
35. *Avengers* #62 (1969).
36. Endler & Shedletsky (1973).
37. Bracha et al. (2004); Webster et al. (2016).

# 3

# STAGES OF MINORITY IDENTITY DEVELOPMENT

## A JUXTAPOSITION OF T'CHALLA AND ERIK KILLMONGER

Vanessa Hicks

*"In times of crisis, the wise build bridges, while the foolish build barriers. We must find a way to look after one another as if we were one single tribe."*
—T'Challa[1]

> *"Our glorious diversity—our diversities of faiths and colors and creeds—that is not a threat to who we are; it makes us who we are."*
>
> —former U.S.A. First Lady Michelle Obama[2]

T'Challa has been locked in combat with his archnemesis Erik Killmonger in the comic books since the 1970s.[3] Their long-standing feud, from its first telling in comics through

the blockbuster on-screen adaptation, remains all too proverbial to many people of color in America. The United States is a
country in which government officials not only decreed racism
as one of its most divisive forces, but also concluded that historical racial vestiges have continued to marginalize minority
groups, causing racial inequities to be so deeply woven into
the very fabric of American society that they are nearly invisible.[4] The tension between American citizens—fueled by the
aforementioned chronically tense nature of race relations in
this country—not only makes Black Panther's quarrel with
Killmonger an inspirational hero's story, but also provides the
backdrop for this so-called villain's ideals to be openly debated
and widely accepted. The idea that T'Challa and Killmonger
are "cut from the same cloth," so to speak, lends itself to
countless discussions concerning the impacts of oppression on
minorities around the world, as well as morally "appropriate"
methods for coping with cultural discrimination.

## THE MINORITY IDENTITY DEVELOPMENT MODEL

Just as individuals develop physically and cognitively over time,
one's sense of cultural identity is something that is considered to
have the capacity for change and maturation. There have been
several models for cultural development introduced, each of
which outlines different stages, or segments, of identity development, specifically as they relate to matters of race and ethnicity. *Minority identity development models* apply to "ethnoracial
minorities or individuals who consider themselves members
of a marginalized group," with "precipitators for the development of a sense of minority development [being] described
as oppression and discrimination."[5] These models differ from
those concerning members of the majority culture, as they
integrate potential impacts of marginalization on individual
development. Oppression is largely understood to occur when

# THE AFROFUTURIST PARADISE: WAKANDA'S AESTHETICS

Upon seeing Wakanda for the first time, a comic book character named Queen Divine Justice weeps while taking in the allure, not only of the nation's technological advancements but also of its inhabitants. For Queen, an African-American woman raised in a nation perpetually wrought with tense racial relations, "seeing these beautiful faces—it, it changes everything."[6] I experienced an emotional state like Queen the first time I watched the *Black Panther* film. While not an *in vivo*, real-life experience, given that Wakanda is a fictional place, the images of individuals of African descent thriving in a nation seemingly untouched by widespread discrimination and hardships seemed *perfect*. As an African-American woman who has spent much of my life in densely populated urban areas, Queen's description resonated with me in a way that I believe it could resonate with a majority of African Americans as well.

Black people in America are more accustomed to seeing our likeness on the big screen reflecting the adverse experiences throughout African-American history, including slavery, mass incarceration, and widespread disenfranchisement. The *Black Panther* film, while not the first of its kind, uniquely introduces Black Americans—myself included—to a visually appealing, Afrofuturist paradise devoid of the marginalization and minority status we are so accustomed to donning. This "reworking" of Black characters in mainstream film not only deepened the personal relevance and impact of the movie, but likely also contributed to the movie's overwhelming box office success, both domestically and abroad.

acts of prejudice, discrimination, or violence interfere with one's ability to evolve as a complete individual.[7] One minority identity development model describes "five stages of development that oppressed people may experience as they struggle to understand themselves in terms of their own minority culture and the oppressive relationship between the minority and majority cultures."[8] While these stages are supposedly separate, the model is more accurately understood as a continuous cycle of growth with blurred boundaries between each of the different phases.

## STAGE ONE: CONFORMITY

Individuals in this initial stage of minority development most often interpret their minority status as "less than"—both consciously and unconsciously. They tend to hold unfavorable views about themselves and other minorities, and often prefer norms and values promoted by the dominant cultural group. Individuals in this first stage *conform* to the conventions of the dominant group, often holding opinions of themselves that mirror the assumptions of the majority culture.[9] Both Prince N'Jobu and Zuri ("James") have essentially disavowed Wakandan traditions and have adopted mainstream American customs. This is evident not only in their style of dress when they live in California but also in their whispered planning of some sort of crime.[10] Both Wakandan and American traditional values likely discourage this sort of criminal activity. However, in the conformity stage, both Zuri and N'Jobu seem to willingly embody one of the negative stereotypical views of people of color in America (i.e., that minorities tend to commit crimes at a higher rate than the majority group).

## STAGE TWO: DISSONANCE

Transitioning to this second stage of identity development is often the result of some race-related event. For instance, if a young college student is denied membership into a student organization solely based on her race and/or ethnicity, this would be considered a "race-related event." Following this exclusion, the student is likely to experience some conflict, or *dissonance*, between the negative attitudes she held toward herself and other minorities in the previous stage, and the positive opinions that are now beginning to form. This second stage is transitional and fraught with discordant feelings toward self and others.[11] The *Black Panther* film introduces W'Kabi as one of T'Challa's trusted advisors and as the leader of the Border Tribe. W'Kabi openly expresses his distrust of others, indicating that allowing others to find refuge in Wakanda will only create further problems.[12] However, following T'Challa's failure to apprehend Klaue, as he had promised he would, W'Kabi begins to express some dissonance concerning his previously held beliefs about allowing outsiders into Wakanda. Ultimately, this discord leads W'Kabi to back Erik Killmonger in his quest to overthrow T'Challa as king of Wakanda.

## STAGE THREE: RESISTANCE AND IMMERSION

The middle stage of the minority identity development model represents a complete 180-degree shift from the initial stage. Individuals in this stage of development often wholly reject, or *resist*, ideas and values promoted by the dominant culture. This is largely attributed to further understanding of societal forces (i.e., racism, oppression, and discrimination), as well as to the awareness that the individual has been personally victimized by these forces.[13] Individuals in this third stage of development most often hold sweeping negative views concerning members

of the majority group, which are fueled by desires to eradicate oppressive forces. Because of these general negativeatti-
tudes, resistance against the majority culture is followed by full
*immersion* into one's minority culture, including adherence to
certain values and customs. Perhaps the most glaring example
of a character thrust into the trenches of this third stage is
Erik Killmonger. In his many altercations with T'Challa,
Killmonger continues to assert that all his actions are in direct
response to oppressive forces, which subjugate individuals of
African descent around the globe. Killmonger appears to find
some semblance of nobility in this quest, and often attempts to
point out the similarities between himself and T'Challa. Not
only does Killmonger find similarity in the fact that both he
and T'Challa have lost their fathers, but he also claims that
neither he nor T'Challa can be "men of peace," as both have
seemingly dedicated their lives to ensuring that their father's
deaths have meaning, even if this requires them to "settle conflicts with violence."[14]

## STAGE FOUR: INTROSPECTION

Individuals transition into the fourth stage of identity development while questioning the rigidly held beliefs they adopted
in the previous stages. Through a process of self-reflection,
or *introspection*, individuals often move toward more flexible
views of themselves and others, adhering to the notion that
all cultures have both positive and negative elements. Okoye,
Wakanda's highest-ranking general and leader of the Dora
Milaje, appears to alter her thoughts concerning the majority
culture (i.e., Americans) when she, T'Challa, and Nakia are
unexpectedly forced to work with Agent Ross while trying
to apprehend Klaue. Upon first meeting Agent Ross, Okoye
threatens to "impale him" on a desk and refuses to speak in
English, which she acknowledges is purposeful.[15] As the mission

continues to unfold and Okoye is presented with Killmonger's threats to Wakanda, she must work with Ross in her quest to return T'Challa to the throne. At the end, we see Okoye standing proudly at T'Challa's side as he announces his plans to share Wakandan technological advancements with the rest of the world, which illustrates Okoye's ideological evolution concerning previously held negative views of other cultures.

## STAGE FIVE: SYNERGY

Minority individuals in this final stage of development experience a sense of security regarding their cultural identity. These individuals often view their racial identity as a singular aspect of who they are, and not one that is wholly defining.[16] People experiencing cultural synergy are likely to regard other cultural groups with selective respect and gratitude. T'Challa represents this pinnacle of minority identity development, as he continually attempts to bridge divides between Wakanda and the rest of the world. For T'Challa, "Now, more than ever, the illusions of division threaten our very existence. We all know the truth: More connects us than divides us."[17] T'Challa's individual trek toward cultural identity development is chronicled further in the vignette below.

## T'CHALLA'S JOURNEY TO CULTURAL SYNERGY

In T'Challa's journey toward cultural enlightenment, he is (1) a citizen of Wakanda, and thus, not *necessarily* subjected to the by-products of racial tensions faced by African Americans, (2) a member of the royal family and thus held in the highest regard in Wakandan society, and (3) often forced to confront—albeit, indirectly—racial tensions throughout the rest of the world, given his dealings with foreign nations, as well as his affiliation with the Avengers.[18] When audiences are first introduced to T'Challa as the Black Panther—whether it be in print or on-screen—he is, arguably, well beyond the first two stages of minority identity development. T'Challa is a shining beacon of optimism for most Black people, given that he is a fictional representation that serves as a "grand vision of Afrofuturist blackness, where black folk are no longer over-determined by racism and colonialism."[19] T'Challa does not initially encounter resistant and rigidly held views of other cultures, as he is not directly confronted with oppressive forces. For most African Americans, who have never lived in a world in which racial disparities are nonexistent, the Black Panther, and the entirety of Wakanda, serve as representations of what *could have been*, "outside of American enslavement, European colonialism, inner-city stereotypes, and hip-hop hypermasculinity."[20]

T'Challa's on-screen adaptation provides more evidence of his movement between different stages. When he first appears in the movies, T'Challa, as a diplomat, is attending a world leaders' summit with his father, King T'Chaka.[21] At this point, he seems to be teetering in between the third and fourth stages of minority identity development, given that both he and his father seem content with shielding Wakanda and all its technological glory from the rest of the world. There is some allusion to T'Challa's questioning of his father's rigidly held views concerning Wakanda's relationship with the rest of the world; however, T'Challa is unable to explore his dissonance further, given his father's untimely death. This great tragedy seems to propel T'Challa into a previous stage in his cultural development, as he begins to question the need for *any* interaction between Wakanda and other nations.

T'Challa demonstrates dissonance in his understandings of how Wakanda should fit into the global cultural landscape. The imposition of Erik Killmonger presents even more uncertainty for T'Challa concerning Wakanda's *responsibility* to African descendants around the globe. Through his various confrontations with Killmonger, T'Challa moves through the introspective stage, as is evident in a conversation with the elders on the ancestral plane, ahead of his decisive battle with Killmonger, now king of Wakanda. In this conversation, T'Challa expresses contempt for the decisions of his elders, referring to Killmonger as a "monster of our own making," while vowing not to allow "fear of discovery" to stop him from "right[ing] this wrong."[22]

T'Challa has now distanced himself from the inflexible beliefs of his ancestors, and he has outwardly disavowed the idea that Wakanda has no duty to share its advancements with others around the globe. In making this assertion, T'Challa moves into a place of cultural synergy, as he acknowledges that Wakandans, along with others around the world, have all made mistakes, but there is much to be gained from mutual respect and collaboration. King T'Challa recognizes the wisdom of "building bridges," and ultimately finding "a way to look after one another as if we were one single tribe.[23] Hence, T'Challa has achieved a sense of enlightenment regarding his opinions of his own culture. As someone who has reached a level of cultural synergy, T'Challa exudes a well-balanced appreciation for other cultures, while also working actively to fight against the oppression and discrimination that remain a painful part of the lives of people of color around the world.[24]

## KILLMONGER'S STUNTED CULTURAL DEVELOPMENT

Erik Killmonger, whose birth name is N'Jadaka, is the son of N'Jobu. Like T'Challa, the death of N'Jadaka's father thrusts N'Jadaka into an adverse mindset in terms of his cultural development. According to this minority identity development model, "the movement into the dissonance stage is most often a gradual process, but . . . a monumental event . . . may propel the Black person into the next stage."[25] Not only is the death of N'Jadaka's father a "monumental event," but it also occurs when N'Jadaka is at a young, developmental stage, in which his individual cultural identity is just beginning to take shape. Thus, though N'Jadaka may have previously held somewhat optimistic views of other people in the world, the fatherless child, abandoned in the United States, becomes the man known as Killmonger, who is obsessed with avenging the unjust, oppressive forces responsible for his cruel upbringing.[26]

Unlike T'Challa, Killmonger does not demonstrate the same movement through different stages of cultural identity development. Killmonger cements himself in the Resistance and Immersion stage following his father's death; rather than moving back and forth between various stages, his adverse views of others intensify over time. Killmonger experiences a kind of rebirth following his father's death, in that he is left with nothing meaningful in his life, other than the hatred he holds toward those he deems responsible for his difficult circumstances. Because of this, the only things Killmonger has to motivate himself to move forward are anger at the world and the promise that he will one day be responsible for inflicting pain and suffering on his enemies. The depth of his resistance to embrace others is ever-present in his numerous altercations with T'Challa; he often urges T'Challa to "liberate" and allow free expression of his hate for those who have wronged him. Killmonger notes, at times, that his life seems devoid of anything meaningful, other than the disdain he feels toward his enemies.[27]

The dynamic between T'Challa and Killmonger is more complex than their apparent idealistic differences suggest. In the on-screen adaptation of this feud, Killmonger's father is the brother of King T'Chaka; and, Prince N'Jobu has died at his brother's hand. As a result, Killmonger views T'Challa as one who receives privileges that Killmonger could only dream of, given that he grew up fatherless in the heart of Oakland's inner city. Killmonger's outward disdain toward T'Challa's

# RACIAL SOCIALIZATION AND THE PROACTIVE PANTHER

Amber A. Hewitt

A few days after the *Black Panther*[28] movie release, a friend (who is a Black woman and the mother of two Black children) shared on social media how she rearranged her son's schedule to see the film, stating, "I needed him to see himself." Her statement speaks to the impact *Black Panther* may have on Black youth who see such powerful images on-screen. Importantly, her statement depicts *proactive racial socialization,* the process of Black parents transmitting messages (both verbal and nonverbal) about what it means to be Black and of African descent.

*Cultural pride,* a sense of positive attachment to a person's culture of origin, involves knowledge about racial/ethnic/cultural heritage, history, customs, and traditions. As a core component of racial-ethnic socialization, cultural pride is protective against a host of adverse mental health outcomes.

*Racial-ethnic socialization* consists of (1) preparing for bias, (2) promoting mistrust of other racial/ethnic groups, (3) egalitarianism, and (4) instilling cultural pride.[29] Its goal is to provide children with a healthy sense of themselves while giving them tools to actively cope with varying forms of oppression. Black youth who know of society's negative stereotypes, but also experience positive racial-ethnic socialization, show greater resilience in the face of adversity.[30]

Regarding mental health outcomes, research shows that racial socialization is positively related to prosocial behavior,[31] positive mental health,[32] psychological well-being,[33] and reduction of susceptibility to stereotype threat[34] for US ethnic minority youth and adults. In one study, Black parents who provided their children with messages about cultural pride also reported less psychological distress for their children.[35] Interventions designed to promote racial socialization in youth have been found to decrease relational aggression and problem behaviors and increase positive racial identity.[36]

*Black Panther*, in part, is a story about identity and cultural socialization: a young man's discovery of who he is in connection with his ancestry. Throughout his story, he receives many messages from his parents, loved ones, and friends, which help to instill in him a positive sense of self. That quest for self-definition is evident when T'Challa's mother tells him, "Show him who you are!" Or when T'Challa's close friend and love interest, Nakia, tells him, "You get to decide what kind of king you are going to be." I think Nakia's message is exactly what my friend wanted to relay to her children: You are more than someone else's perception or stereotype.

privilege is strengthened by his belief that Wakanda, while entirely capable, has failed to protect the "two billion people all over the world that look like us, but [have] lives [that] are a lot harder."[37]

From Killmonger's perspective, his hatred encompasses all he deems responsible for the plight of African descendants on a global scale, which includes not only the oppressors themselves, but also the individuals with the knowledge and weapons strong enough to end the suffering. Killmonger remains steadfast in his far-reaching negative views of others up to the end, electing to die by T'Challa's hand, rather than

live out his days in captivity. In Killmonger's view, all his
experienced hardships—both on the individual and societal
levels—are direct products of oppression. Because of this, no
progress would be lasting until those oppressors were elim-
inated. Ultimately, the tragedy and adversities Killmonger
experienced at an early age—the death of his father, racial
prejudice, and economic hardships—were too deep-rooted to
overcome, forever consigning him to an individual cultural
identity plagued by pessimism and resistance.

## THE SIGNIFICANCE OF INTERSECTIONALITY

The juxtaposition of T'Challa's and Killmonger's paths to individual cultural identity development illustrates the importance
of examining aspects of culture holistically, rather than individ-
ually. The term *intersectionality* is used to describe how certain
cultural systems (i.e., gender, race, class, and nation) mutually
construct one another.[38] In this instance, while both native sons
of Wakanda—and, generally, similar in terms of race and ethnicity—T'Challa and Killmonger demonstrate two radically
different journeys to individual cultural identity. T'Challa is
born into royalty and remains a royal throughout the entirety
of his life. Along with the privilege of wealth and prestige,
T'Challa is raised in Wakanda, and afforded the best that life
has to offer—technologically, spiritually, and financially. By
contrast, Killmonger is plucked from his utopian home and
brought to the United States. While a land of opportunity
all its own, America pales in comparison to Wakanda, and,
because of his racial and economic circumstances, Killmonger
is not privy to the same kinds of privilege and opportunity
as T'Challa. This disparity, while no fault of his own, breeds
levels of resentment and hate in Killmonger, which, ultimately
become too much for him to overcome.

Herein lies the moral ambiguity concerning the acceptance of Killmonger's ideals. On the one hand, Killmonger's plans to eradicate all members of the majority, oppressive group seem extreme. At what point, though, does blame shift from the individual to the larger, societal systems and circumstances that fostered—and, arguably, created—Killmonger's radical views? For T'Challa, it seems as if Killmonger's plight has enough of an influence on him to encourage the king to share his nation's advancements with the rest of the world. Whether it be through Black Panther's fictional dealings with the Avengers or via the real-world implications that mainstream, Black super-heroes have on minorities around the world, the landscape of minority identity development has undoubtedly changed with the current resurgence of the Black Panther. In addition, the long-standing conflict between Wakanda's patriarch and the antihero, Erik Killmonger, serves a dual purpose, in providing African Americans with a creative outlet with which to discuss oppressive, societal forces, while also utilizing these charac-ters as anchors with which to evaluate their own individual minority development.

## NOTES

1. *Black Panther* (2018 motion picture).
2. Reilly (2017).
3. *Jungle Action* #6 (1972).
4. Advisory Board to the President's Initiative on Race (1998).
5. Fouad & Arredondo (2007), p. 24.
6. *Black Panther* #20 (2000).
7. Schwarzbaum & Thomas (2008).
8. Atkinson (2004), p. 40.
9. Schwarzbaum & Thomas (2008).
10. *Black Panther* (2018 motion picture).
11. Schwarzbaum & Thomas (2008).
12. *Black Panther* (2018 motion picture).
13. Atkinson (2004), p. 42.
14. *Black Panther* #20 (2000).

# THE PSYCHOLOGY OF DIFFERENCE

One of the five general principles of the American Psychological Association's Code of Ethics emphasizes that psychologists should be "aware of and respect cultural, individual, and role differences."[39] In essence, *cultural competence* is something that is expected of all practicing psychologists. Culturally competent psychologists are not only fully aware of their individual identity within multiple contexts and layers, but also how the development of this identity influences attitudes for both the self and others.[40]

Cultural competence becomes even more important within the therapeutic relationship when there are ostensible cultural differences between the client and the therapist. Specifically, individuals who have experienced oppression often feel similarly marginalized and powerless when their therapist appears to be a member of a different cultural group. For instance, Killmonger would likely make little (no) progress with a therapist who was culturally different than himself. By contrast, T'Challa, with his sense of fulfillment regarding cultural identity, would likely not experience the same difficulties connecting with a therapist who presented as culturally dissimilar.[41]

When faced with clients who may be distrusting within the therapeutic relationship, humility is perhaps the most effective tool psychologists have for decreasing tensions stemming from cultural differences. Psychologists who are humble are often the most effective helpers, as they understand that others' viewpoints may be just as valid as their own.[42] Essentially, humility allows psychologists and therapists to "better understand themselves as racial and cultural human beings, which will reduce the likelihood of causing harm to clients whose cultural identity differs from their own."[43]

15. *Black Panther* (2018 motion picture).
16. Schwarzbaum & Thomas (2008), p. 62.
17. *Black Panther* (2018 motion picture).
18. *The Avengers* #52 (1968).
19. Nama (2009), p. 138.
20. Nama (2011), p. 66.
21. *Captain America: Civil War* (2016 motion picture).
22. *Black Panther* (2018 motion picture).
23. *Black Panther* (2018 motion picture).
24. Atkinson (2004), p. 46.
25. Atkinson (2004), p. 41.
26. *Black Panther* #19 (2000).
27. *Black Panther* #20 (2000).
28. *Black Panther* (2018 motion picture).
29. Hughes et al. (2006).
30. American Psychological Association (2008), p.3.
31. Caughy et al. (2003).
32. Shaw & Fischer (1999).
33. Yoon (2004).
34. Davis & Salinas (2006).
35. Bannon et al. (2009).
36. Whaley & McQueen (2004).
37. *Black Panther* (2018 motion picture).
38. Collins (2012), p. 246.
39. American Psychological Association (2017), p. 4.
40. Schwarzbaum & Thomas (2008).
41. Atkinson (2004).
42. Hays (2008).
43. Trahan & Lemberger (2014), p. 120.

# 4

# DEATH, DESCENT, AND DELIVERANCE

## THERAPEUTIC VISITS TO THE ANCESTRAL PLANE

### Travis Langley

*"Sometimes you have to kind of die inside in order to rise from your own ashes and believe in yourself and love yourself to become a new person."*
—singer Gerard Way[1]

*"The Black Panther is dead."*
—M'Baku's messenger[2]

**H**uman beings appear to be unique in our awareness of our mortality, our understanding that death follows every life, including our own.[3] Human *symbolic ability*, our extensive capacity for letting one thing represent something else,[4] allows us to perceive connections between diverse stimuli, whether any logical connection exists between them or not, and we are particularly likely to symbolize our existential states of life and death.[5] So not only are we conscious of our mortality, we find reminders of it all around us. Because we try to look beyond death for signs that we might continue to exist in some form anyway,[6] death itself can be a symbol as well when it represents change, the end of our old status and the beginning of something new.[7] Cultures and religions everywhere develop customs regarding the literal components of mortality—birth, maturation, procreation, death—with the concepts of life and death intertwined. The concept of rebirth is a cornerstone of many faiths. While some conceptions refer to literal rebirth through reincarnation over multiple lifetimes, others refer to a figurative or spiritual rebirth through symbolic death of one's old self and previous way of living as requisite to getting a fresh start within the same physical lifetime.[8]

The process by which a character becomes Black Panther is not unlike real-world traditions. After defeating challengers in ritual combat, each prospective Black Panther enters a death-like state, buried alive in the motion picture version. The candidate enters a spirit world or ancestral plane to commune with ancestors and, in the comics, to be judged by the goddess Bast for purity of intent.[9] Such esoteric themes, even those of spiritual confrontation and divine judgment, sometimes help people grow and heal.[10] People also report achieving peace, epiphany, or reinvigoration as a result of unplanned encounters with death. When an attack by Doctor Doom leaves T'Challa critically injured and comatose,[11] the entity Death conjures illusions of figures, including T'Challa's father, in an attempt to lure him out of his limbo state and to get him to accept his demise. Near Death, T'Challa has a *near-death experience* (NDE). The event occurs literally for T'Challa, not figuratively. In our own world, many people believe that such experiences involve supernatural encounters and prove that consciousness exists beyond death,[12] whereas skeptics argue that NDEs are simply a natural state our brains undergo and that *near-death* means exactly that, being nearly dead physically but not truly dead.[13] Regardless of why, numerous individuals find the experience to be life-changing and profound.[14]

Figuratively dying and emerging reborn could be therapeutic. Ritual simulations of death are not restricted to religious and cultural practices. A number of different kinds of therapy also make individuals face death in order to feel more alive.

## FACING DEATH

> *"It can lead to more appreciation of life, a fuller life,*
> *and hopefully a life that you'll have a better*
> *impact on people around you."*
>
> —terror management theorist Jeff Greenberg[15]

Even though others see T'Challa as fearless,[16] he has fears, especially for his nation and his loved ones.[17] He simply manages fear very well most of the time. *Terror management theory*[18] has grown increasingly popular as a psychological model for examining human life. A growing body of empirical evidence supports aspects[19] of its basic contention that awareness of our own mortality drives much of people's behavior. This basic idea is not new. *Existential psychologists* beat terrorist management theorists to the punch. Building on existential philosophy, existential psychologists examine how we ask and attempt to answer key questions about our mortal existence.[20] Both theoretical perspectives have led some clinicians to develop therapeutic techniques in which clients vividly contemplate their own deaths in order to rethink life.[21]

The characters in superhero stories are regularly shown to be correct in their beliefs that ghosts, reincarnation, and other forms of afterlife existence are real—for example, when T'Challa visits the ancestral plane or his sister Shuri trains with a griot spirit during her time as a ghost in the years between her death and resurrection.[22] Even if they were wrong, though, they could nonetheless be normal and mentally healthy to hold these beliefs. The majority of the world's people believe in some form of continued personal existence beyond death. If it's normal within a culture, then it's not sufficient reason to deem that culture's people mentally ill. The relationship between such beliefs and mental health is complicated, though.[23] For example, afterlife beliefs may help bereaved individuals cope with personal losses,[24] but, then again, they may compound grief among those who believe the departed now suffer eternal consequences or they may increase suicide risk among those who believe self-termination might reunite them with those they've lost.[25]

## DEATH EXERCISES

Characters undergoing the ritual to become a Black Panther enter a death-like state during which they encounter supernatural entities such as ghosts and a goddess. In the comics, T'Challa and Shuri have each gotten killed at different times and later returned from the dead, as have antagonists such as Killmonger, M'Baku, Morlun, and Klaw.[26] They differ in what they take from these experiences—for example, Killmonger does not gain the same kind of insight gained by others who visit the ancestral plane. Even though people in our world might not undergo literal resurrections, a great many have brushes with death, such as life-threatening traumas, comas, and near-death experiences, and they vary widely in their reports. Plenty of them describe these experiences as enlightening, inspiring, or life-affirming, but not all, because some instead suffer feelings or torture, torment, or depression with a range of responses along the spectrum between these extremes.[27]

# VARIETIES OF NEAR-DEATH EXPERIENCES

Alex Langley

After nearly dying, some who are resuscitated report *near-death experiences* (NDEs), dream-like out-of-body experiences that provide feelings of peace and contentment generally involving heavy reflection on a person's life events or encounters with deceased relatives and religious figures.[28] T'Challa's and Killmonger's visions after consuming the heart-shaped herb[29] are consistent with real people's NDE descriptions. Both relive key moments in their lives and meet with deceased relatives. Killmonger's vision and T'Challa's second vision are far from the peaceful experiences most describe, but some people do report unpleasant NDEs.[30]

Research on NDEs finds that people's experiences are generally consistent with their spiritual belief systems. In one well-known incident, a child reported meeting his great-grandfather and Jesus Christ during his NDE, in accordance with his family's Christian ideology.[31] T'Challa meeting his father on the ancestral plane is in line with his family's Wakandan ideology. Killmonger, seemingly lacking in any such religious upbringing, has a mundane vision of his childhood home, lacking any of the religious hallmarks. His vision reflects the NDEs of nonreligious individuals, such as Stephanie Savage, an avowed atheist who spent six weeks in a coma and had an NDE devoid of religious figures.[32]

Given that the visions in *Black Panther* take place in a universe where magic and super-science exist, one would not be remiss to assume that T'Challa and Killmonger were having true out-of-body experiences. Their experiences nevertheless remain true to the descriptions of NDEs reported by real-world survivors whose visions are a source of continuing contention between the spiritual community, who often point to NDEs as proof positive of an afterlife, and the scientific community, who often refer to the more rational explanation that trauma is a matter of shutting the brain down and the NDE constitutes the brain placing itself in a dream-like state as a defense.[33]

In different places in our world, the therapeutic techniques built around symbolizing or facing death sometimes include rehearsing one's own demise. Therapies that focus on death and rebirth vary in their objectives and goals. Therapists differ in theoretical outlooks and clients differ in their needs, just as each Black Panther finds his or her own personal meaning in the near-death visit to the ancestral plane. The therapeutic goals include changing how stressful death seems, finding closure by imagining interactions with people who are now departed, achieving a sense of rebirth with a fresh start in this world, or developing a sense of transcendence above it all.

## PRACTICE DEATH

A key difference among various *practice death* therapies—techniques aimed at getting clients to contemplate their deaths by physically rehearsing either the process of death or post-death activities, such as resting in a coffin—lies in their purpose: How do they make clients feel about death itself? Some focus on reducing *death anxiety* by making it seem not so bad—which seems to happen the first time we see T'Challa visit the ancestral plane, where he embraces his departed father and beholds the spirits of previous Black Panthers.[34] Other techniques, however, make unpleasant aspects salient in order to discourage suicide.

In South Korea, China, and Taiwan, a few psychotherapists have guided thousands of people through practice deaths in which clients write down their final words or last will and testament, then lie down in a closed coffin for five minutes before it opens.[35] Clients seek out this "death experience" in the belief that it will help them leave old troubles behind and experience a sense of rebirth. A scroll on the wall in one Shanghai facility translates as "If you don't know death, how will you know life?"[36] Lying in a closed coffin even briefly carries some inherent risk. What if a client's fear sets off a panic attack or seizure while no one else can see what's occurring in the coffin? What if the client happens to doze off when an attendant at the clinic gets distracted and fails to check before the client in the closed coffin can suffocate? Ukrainian psychologist Andrey Zhelvetro has taken the process further with the riskier practice of burying clients in coffins and leaving them in shallow graves (each with a metal air pipe) for two hours at a time.[37]

When potential Black Panthers lie down in sand while others bury them alive, there is risk. After T'Challa and Killmonger experience their visits to the ancestral plane, each jerks upward from the sand, gasping for air.[38] Would every candidate rise in time to avoid asphyxiation? Attendants during the ritual might have stepped in to help candidates in previous centuries, but rituals change over time. Perhaps the scientifically advanced Wakandans have carefully studied the process over the centuries and kept careful records, or perhaps information that is passed down through oral tradition risks getting distorted or lost because memory is a terribly unreliable thing. For that matter, not all therapists rely on evidence-based methods when developing their techniques, and the evidence they offer for their success may be subjective, anecdotal, short on record keeping, and devoid of long-term follow-up interviews.[39] Despite the large number of clients reportedly having undergone practice deaths, there is a dearth of solid evidence regarding the effects.

The Wakandan rituals follow well-established procedures passed down through the generations, with established practices not only regarding how to perform each ritual but also regarding who should oversee it. These coffin therapies are unregulated, without restrictions on who can implement them or how. For example, a Ukrainian coffin maker with no training in psychology has offered "coffin therapy" sessions in which people lie in coffins for 15 minutes, allegedly to help them relax by putting their minds at ease about the idea of being dead somehow in order to feel more alive.[40]

## PSYCHEDELIC DISSOCIATION

Each Black Panther visits the ancestral plane and becomes superhuman through consumption of the otherwise-unnamed heart-shaped herb that is unique to Wakanda and rare even there. Our world's scientists would tend to assume that the supernatural experiences do not occur literally but are instead hallucinogenic experiences induced by the herb. Even in the fictional world where the Black Panther interacts with ancestors' spirits, some of the associated experiences might result from the herb's psychoactive properties. Regardless of the degree to which the experience is "real" within the fiction, it includes similarities to a variety of near-death experiences and substance-induced transcendental experiences reported in the real world.

Before changes in the former Soviet Union allowed its scientists to communicate more freely with those elsewhere in the world, rumors had long circulated about *psychedelic research* that some had been working on, including investigations into a variety of practical applications for consciousness-altering substances. One that came to be referred to as *death-rebirth* induces unpleasant death associations through the use of ketamine.[41] Anesthesiologists had reported that ketamine often produces an *emergence reaction* side effect that induces confusion, feelings of dying, and unpleasant hallucinations.[42] Clinical researchers attempted to use that experience to treat alcoholism through *aversive conditioning* by associating alcohol with such feelings of death and dying. It didn't work. Instead, many participants reported *depersonalization* episodes in which they felt they were floating, as if disconnected from their bodies. For some, these experiences felt mystical and profound, and this gave them fresh perspectives on relationships and the meaning of life. So the researchers developed this into death-rebirth therapy in order to help clients recognize their alcoholism by expanding their perspective and feeling reborn or renewed. Several trends appeared through objective measures and statistical analyses. Among them, commitment to maintaining sobriety increased while anxiety and depression decreased, and patients shifted to more spiritual and wider-reaching worldviews. Other researchers later found ketamine to offer promising results for reduction of death anxiety,[43] but investigators need to proceed with caution due to the risks associated with the drug.[44]

The depersonalization state of feeling unreal reported by some of the ketamine recipients is a form of *dissociation* (i.e., dis-association), a state in which different parts of the mind function simultaneously but are disconnected from one another.[45] One simple example of dissociation is *highway hypnosis*, when one part of the mind is daydreaming while another drives the car.[46] The individual can suddenly realize he or she has no memory of the last five miles. One explanation for hypnosis in general may be that it is a dissociative process. Dissociative experiences can be induced psychologically as a *defense mechanism* (a trick the mind plays on itself to protect against stress)[47] or biologically through means such as drugs, fatigue, or near-death experiences,[48] and so can hallucinations.[49] Even though comic book stories make it clear that ghosts exist in Black Panther's reality, the motion picture depictions leave room for T'Challa's and Killmonger's experiences on the ancestral plane to be no more than what their unconscious minds desired or expected.

## MONOMYTHIC REFLECTIONS

The *Hero's Journey* refers to a pattern, the *monomyth* ("one myth") underlying all heroes' tales. Found in heroic stories throughout all cultures, the pattern includes a cyclical series of encounters and trials that heroic characters undergo in the course of their adventures. In recent years, authors such as *Star*

*Wars* creator George Lucas[50] have intentionally followed this universal pattern as described by author Joseph Campbell.[51] Prior to that, these stories evolved more naturally, whether because storytellers unconsciously followed archetypes identified by psychiatrist Carl Jung[52] or because life circumstances tended to influence the kinds of stories people would tell and the kinds of heroes people wanted in their lives. A number of books in this Popular Culture Psychology series have examined how different heroes' stories lined up with aspects of the Hero's Journey.[53] Regardless of whether Jung and Campbell were right about the unconscious origins underlying this general pattern, it is a popular model for storytelling and for character analysis because something about it resonates with people.[54]

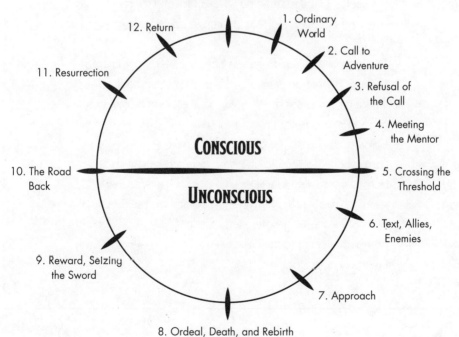

# THE HERO'S JOURNEY

12. Return

1. Ordinary World

11. Resurrection

2. Call to Adventure

3. Refusal of the Call

4. Meeting the Mentor

**CONSCIOUS**

10. The Road Back

**UNCONSCIOUS**

5. Crossing the Threshold

6. Text, Allies, Enemies

9. Reward, Seizing the Sword

7. Approach

8. Ordeal, Death, and Rebirth

# THE WAKANDAN EPIC

Superhero origin stories tend to follow the structure of the entire monomyth figuratively, as the hero-to-be receives the call to adventure, descends into the depths of the unknown, and reenters the world with gifts that can aid others.[55] Black Panther follows the formula more overtly than many others do because the ritual that produces his descent and confrontation with the unconscious either simulates or briefly induces death, he enters a realm of the dead, and then he returns from the underworld transformed. African epics and folktales often emphasize heroes' supernatural encounters and otherworldly powers.[56] "The essential mark of the heroic personality in many African folk epics is in its reliance on supernatural resources."[57] African studies expert Mariam Konate Deme seems to be describing Wakanda and its line of Black Panthers in her analysis of African heroic epics:

> The hero of the African epic is not only the embodiment of perfection in literary terms, but he is also the embodiment of the ideals of the society in which he lives. And for him to set a good example for others, he has to win over their admiration and respect. As a symbol of power that the society as a whole looks up to, the hero accomplishes miraculous actions the society identifies with. . . . In the African worldview, the relationship between the natural and supernatural aims at establishing harmony in society. The cyclical birth and death is a perpetual one in African belief systems, and continuity is thus assured.[58]

A number of modern Jungian therapists use the Hero's Journey as a model for counseling in several ways.[59] Pursuant to the idea that we can all be the heroes of our own stories, these therapists may view a client's life history, the therapeutic process, or a therapist's own personal or professional life in terms of how any of those things fit this epic pattern.[60] The monomyth may offer an analogy to help the client think about his or her own struggles with points of comparison to help that person see that individuals whom they admire, whether fictional or real, also face struggles along the way. "With its ability to reach beyond the typical limitations of socially constructed, Western psychological models, The Hero's Journey represents a strengths-based approach that may provide meaning to a client's struggles while placing them in a universal context and lessening feelings of isolation," a pair of clinicians advocating for this as a therapeutic model suggested. "Counselors can use The Hero's Journey as a template for establishing deep, complex, professional relationships with clients, and in turn, they can help clients do the same with those in their own lives—acts that can facilitate new perspectives and personal development."[61] Key to therapeutic progress is the parts of the process that would correspond with the hero's encounter with death and subsequent return or rebirth.

Two common steps in the monomythic cycle, the *call to adventure* and the *aid of a helper*, prepare the hero to pass through the supernatural world (in this case, therapy) that lies between the old life and a new one. T'Challa's call to adventure, the crisis that pushes him to move past one threshold into a new part of the cycle, is his father's death.[62] He receives aid from mentoring figure Zuri,[63] whom film director Ryan Coogler described as "Black Panther's version of Obi-Wan Kenobi" because he is a spiritual figure to whom T'Challa looks for guidance.[64] In the epic tradition, however, the hero must lose that mentor—such as when Zuri dies—in a representation of how individuals must grow beyond their parents and teachers

in order to stand as adults on their own. In a clinical situation, the call to adventure may occur when circumstances push
the individual to enter therapy, the therapist may perform the
helper or mentor role,[65] and the client should eventually reach
a point when no such helper is needed anymore.

When the hero or therapeutic client crosses from the known
world into the unknown, "the hero begins to engage in self-
reflection with the purpose of rebirth."[66] Many traditional
forms of therapy, especially "talk therapies," which rely on
dialogue rather than activities such as behavior modification
exercises, require self-reflection for clients to make progress
toward greater mental health. Taking a hard look at oneself
can be difficult, so difficult that this model equates it with
experiencing death of the old self in order to resurrect or be
born as someone new. As a basis for narrative therapy, looking
at one's own life in terms of the Hero's Journey might help that
individual feel more hopeful about seeing light at the end of the
long, dark tunnel. Psychologist Lawrence Rubin outlined how
counselors can help clients identify where they see themselves
on that journey, brace themselves to face difficult thresholds
that lie ahead, use examples from movies or literature as anal-
ogies to process their struggles, identify those who might be
helpful along the way, and look for practical answers and solu-
tions.[67] Clients who have difficulty talking about their own
problems may readily share thoughts about fictional characters'
struggles. The more fantastic the fiction, the more easily some
clients will talk about the characters' human qualities without
being hindered by biases and predispositions. Talking about
how characters such as T'Challa, Shuri, and even their enemy
Killmonger persist in pursuing their goals and how well or
poorly these characters face their visits to the underworld may
help clients find meaning in their own struggles, ready themselves for their figurative descents, and look forward to their
rebirth into greater mental health.

## FACING LIFE

*"I have to go back."*
—T'Challa, rejecting the peace of death[68]

Whether a person wants a whole new beginning unburdened by his or her past or perhaps would just like a "soft reboot" that keeps the best of the old life while tidying things up in order to move onto something new, most of us understand the appeal of getting a fresh start. T'Challa can die both figuratively and literally many times in an ongoing cycle of renewal. A number of religious faiths and certain psychotherapies offer symbolic death of the old self and rebirth as something new. Whether spiritual rebirth achieves its goals may be unprovable in this lifetime, but psychological science requires testability.[69] Much of the evidence for the efficacy of death-focused treatments is anecdotal and short on empirical data regarding short-term results or long-time follow-up. Lack of evidence is not evidence, though, either for or against. Many therapists and clients have reported value from these approaches. Whether they are correct or merely fooling themselves with placebo effects, we need better evidence to be sure. Even though what happens beyond literal death remains the Great Unknown, what happens as a result of therapy should be empirically knowable, and so we keep trying and hoping to find a way to start anew.

*"We are in the Kingdom of the Dead."*
—T'Challa[70]

*"In the end, it all begins."*
—author Saji Ijiyemi[71]

## NOTES

1. Jinxxy Winxxy (2012).
2. *Black Panther* #4 (2009).
3. Hayes & Schimel (2018); Hirschberger et al. (2002); Pyszczynski et al. (1996) Wisman & Goldenberg (2005).
4. DeLoache (1995); Piaget (1953); Sharon (2005).
5. Christenfeld et al. (1999); Collier (2003).
6. Florian & Mikulincer (1998); Hui & Coleman (2012); Lambert (2003); Ukpokolo (2012); Wisman & Heflick (2016).
7. Drolet (1990).
8. II Corinthians 5:17; Qu'ran 39:53; Tao Te Ching (4th century BCE). Also Analayo (2018).
9. *Black Panther* #60 (2003); #2 (2005).
10. Becker (1972); Lambert (2003); Tate (1989); Wein (2012).
11. *Black Panther* #1, #3–6 (2009).
12. Carter (2010); Hagan (2017); Piper & Murphey (2004); van Lommel (2010).
13. Savage (2015).
14. Sleutjes et al. (2014).
15. *Terror Management Theory: What It Tells Us about Human Behavior* (2007 DVD program).
16. *Black Panther: The Man without Fear* #513; Wardlow (2018).
17. *Black Panther Annual* #1 (2018).
18. Solomon et al. (1991).
19. e.g., Dunne et al. (2015); Taubman-Ben-Ari et al. (2011); Volini (2017).
20. e.g., Frankl (1946).
21. Major et al. (2016); Lewis (2014); Vos et al. (2015).
22. *Black Panther* #3–7 (2016).
23. Heflick et al. (2015); Hui & Coleman (2013); Riekki et al. (2013); Wolson (2005).
24. Benore & Park (2004); Lee (2016).
25. Krysinska & Lester (2006); Takahashi & Berger (1996).
26. Examples of deaths from which they later returned: T'Challa—*Black Panther* #48–39; Shuri—*New Avengers* #24 (2014); Killmonger—*Jungle Action* #17 (1975); M'Baku—*Black Panther* #4 (2009); Morlun—*Amazing Spider-Man* #35 (2001); Klaw—arguably *Dazzler* #9 (1981).
27. Sleutjes et al. (2014).
28. Moody (1975).
29. *Black Panther* (2018 motion picture).
30. e.g., Wiese (2006).
31. Burpo & Vincent (2010).
32. Savage (2015).
33. Price, S., in *Penn & Teller's Bullshit!* episode 1–12, "Ouija Boards/Near Death Experiences" (April 11, 2003).
34. *Black Panther* (2018 motion picture).

35. Daily Mail Reporter (2012); Shuangjie (2014); Yoon (2016).
36. Shuangjie (2014).
37. Seaburn (2018). See also Palmer (2008).
38. *Black Panther* (2018 motion picture).
39. Tavris (2015).
40. Duchardt (2012); Urquhart (2012).
41. Kungurtsev (1991).
42. Grof (1980).
43. Kolp et al. (2007).
44. Chang et al. (2016).
45. Putnam (1989); Janet (1889, 1894, 1898).
46. Furuya et al. (2009); Williams (1963).
47. Freud (1936).
48. Furuya et al. (1963); Greyson (2000).
49. Furuya et al. (1963); Moskowitz & Corstens (2007); Sheaves et al. (2016);
    Vedat et al. (2007).
50. *The Mythology of Star Wars* (1999 documentary).
51. Campbell (1949).
52. Jung (1942/1961, 1948/1969).
53. e.g., Kuniak & Blink (2015); Langley (2015); Mastin & Garski (2017).
54. e.g., Bulkeley (1998); Predmore (1977); Lu (2005).
55. Coogan (2006).
56. Deme (2009); Okpewho (1979).
57. Okpewho (1979), p. 119.
58. Deme (2009), p. 417–418.
59. Hartmann & Zimberoff (2009); Lawson (2005); Rubin (2009).
60. Duffy (2010); Halstead (2000); Pieraci (1990); Robertson & Lawrence (2015).
61. Robertson & Lawrence (2015), pp. 266–267.
62. *Captain America: Civil War* (2016 motion picture).
63. *Black Panther* (2018 motion picture).
64. Jayson (2017).
65. Halstead (2000).
66. Robertson & Lawrence (2015), p. 268.
67. Rubin (2009).
68. *Black Panther* #4 (2009).
69. LeBel et al. (2017).
70. *Black Panther* #21 (2000).
71. Ijiyemi (2012), p. 103.

# II

# A SENSE OF SELF

T'Challa first appears as a mystery, a man whose purpose and importance are, to other heroes, largely unknown.[1] By the time they meet him, he knows who he is. He always has more to discover even about himself because he has great curiosity. He will weigh alternatives and reevaluate his actions because he is a master strategist whose analytical mind plans for everything and thinks through alternatives for every plan.[2] A strong sense of self, it can be healthy, adaptive, and even heroic when it helps the person stand strong in new situations, stay true to values, and look out for others related to those values and to the individual's own identity.[3] Wisdom includes the ability to know who you are, and sense of self can walk together with sense of others.[4]

### NOTES

1. *Fantastic Four* #52 (1966); *Captain America: Civil War* (2016 motion picture).
2. According to Queen Ramonda in *Black Panther* #168 (2017).
3. De las Cuevas (2014); Palombo (2017).
4. Berggrat et al. (2014); Ickes et al. (2012); Sinigaglia & Rizzolatti (2011).

# 5

# THE RAISING OF A KING

## FATHER-SON ATTACHMENT BETWEEN T'CHALLA AND T'CHAKA

### Apryl A. Alexander & Tracy Vozar

*"I see a great and new Wakanda—the nation of my sons
and their sons after them."*
—T'Chaka[1]

*"Anyone can make a baby, but it takes a man to be a father."*
—author, journalist, Black Panther writer Ta-Nehisi Coates[2]

How does one raise a king? T'Chaka is a well-respected leader of Wakanda prior to his death, and citizens of Wakanda often remark on his leadership style. The father-son relationship between T'Chaka and T'Challa is central to both character and plot development in the Black

Panther stories. Following T'Chaka's assassination,[3] their bond is seen as crucial in T'Challa's development as the leader of Wakanda. The attachment between father and son at an early age sets the stage for their adult relationship and the eventual rupture and repair of their bond. Wakandan cultural norms are important aspects in the father-son relationship, which promote T'Challa's strength as a leader. As T'Challa explores his own leadership style, he vacillates between whether to emulate his father's style or develop his own based on the current needs of Wakanda. T'Chaka's influence extends beyond death, as T'Challa continues to consult with his father and other elders in Djalia when faced with difficult decisions. Overall, the relationship serves as a model for secure attachment bonds and a counternarrative to typical media depictions of father-son relationships, including Black father-son bonds.

## ATTACHMENT

The relationship between T'Challa and T'Chaka provides insight into the development and strength of their father-son bond, as well as the security of each character's relationships with important others. Attachment theory is a manner of describing the foundation for the infant and young child's social-emotional development. But it is also relevant to adult relationship health, as the security of childhood relationships lays the foundation for how the individual behaves in and thinks about his or her future relationships.[4] *Attachment* refers to the infant and young child's tendency to seek closeness, comfort, protection, and support from a few primary caregivers.[5] Findings from the adult attachment literature suggest that there is generally stability in attachment security over time, suggesting that observations of T'Challa and T'Chaka's relationship as adults are pertinent to understanding their prior relationship development.[6]

## EARLY RELATIONSHIP DEVELOPMENT

Attachment theory originates from the work of Bowlby, Ainsworth, and others who discovered that separations from or intense difficulties with a primary caregiver can have lasting impacts on the caregiver-child relationship.[7] Notably, T'Chaka likely served as a primary caregiver for T'Challa because T'Challa suffered two losses of primary maternal caregivers during his early childhood. His mother, N'Yami, dies in childbirth with T'Challa and his stepmother, Ramonda, disappears when he is three (and three decades later is discovered to have been kidnapped). These losses further solidify the father-son relationship as one of primary importance to both.

Based on observations of primary caregivers and young children interacting, four attachment styles exist: secure, insecure-avoidant, insecure-ambivalent, and disorganized.[8] In an insecure-avoidant attachment style, we observe the child showing little distress in response to a separation from the adult and little displayed need for closeness/comfort upon reunion. In an insecure-ambivalent attachment style, we observe the child experiencing a high degree of distress in response to separation from his or her caregiver and difficulty in receiving comfort from the adult upon reunion. Attachment researchers later added the disorganized attachment style in response to observations of children who demonstrate a heterogeneous, disorganized pattern of relating to primary caregivers.[9] Their behaviors include mixed strategies of approaching and avoiding the caregiver as well as aberrant behaviors (e.g., aggression, self-harm, swearing). Notably, disorganized attachment style is most predictive of current and longer-term psychopathology as well as a warning sign of potential child maltreatment and/or neglect.[10] A secure attachment style is one in which we observe the child expressing distress upon separation, seeking comfort from caregivers upon reunion, and being comforted

easily.[11] Children developing in the context of a secure attachment believe they can trust the caregiver to both support them
in exploring the world and provide them with comfort when
care and closeness are needed. We do not have observations of
T'Chaka and T'Challa during his childhood; however, based
on their observed interactions with each other as adults, we
may speculate that their attachment style started as generally
secure and has continued to be a primarily secure, trusting
relationship.

Considering the father-son relationship within an intergenerational attachment frame provides more evidence for
a secure attachment style. *Intergenerational attachment* refers to
the manner in which attachment styles tend to replicate from
generation to generation of parents and children within families, as the ways in which we were parented tend to influence the ways in which we parent.[12] T'Chaka and T'Challa
hail from a long line of warrior chiefs who have safeguarded
Wakanda for generations. The father-son relationship is a
model for how each king cares for his people during his reign.
Both T'Chaka and T'Challa rule with fairness, trust, kindness,
and strength, all qualities consistent with a secure attachment
base. Additionally, T'Challa is known for caring for children,
both in his role as king of Wakanda (e.g., threatening war with
Atlantis and Lemuria to protect the child of Ghaur) and under
the name Luke Charles in the United States (e.g., teaching high
school children and promoting a charity for children).[13] Further
love and reverence for his father are demonstrated by an alter-
nate-universe version of T'Challa when he and wife Storm
name their son T'Chaka II.[14]

T'Challa and T'Chaka have an attachment relationship
where the use of a subcategory is informative in understanding
the nuances of their interactions. Subcategories are commonly
used in attachment-style coding to designate that, although
predominantly rated as one category of attachment style,

some indicators of additional patterns of interaction exist. For T'Challa and T'Chaka, though their relationship is primarily secure, the trauma experienced by each in connection with the losses of maternal figures may have negatively impacted the security of the father-son attachment relationship from the start. T'Chaka has a reputation for being an extreme isolationist, separating Wakanda from the outside world. From a personal perspective, given his prior intimate losses and specifically his belief that Ramonda, a non-Wakandan outsider, abandoned him and their family, it is not surprising that T'Chaka would mistrust those outside of Wakanda. From a political perspective, this mistrust also makes sense; T'Chaka was an isolationist in his determination to protect the technological secrets of Wakanda from misuse by the outside world. Sure enough, his misgivings were validated by his assassination by an outsider, Ulysses Klaw, over an attempted theft of Wakandan vibranium. This mistrust of the outside world may translate into an insecure-avoidant attachment style, making T'Chaka leery of T'Challa's exploration of and trust in the outside world. This mistrust extends to his rule over other Wakandans, who are also encouraged to remain within the protection and safety of Wakandan walls.

The psychological concept of rupture and repair comes into play in T'Chaka and T'Challa's attachment relationship, both in the film and in the comics. In the film, T'Challa learns that T'Chaka withheld from him important information about his uncle and his cousin Erik Killmonger, and, as a result, left Erik abandoned in the United States. At first, T'Challa has difficulty believing that his father withheld this information and abandoned Erik, likely due to his trusting internal working model of his father and their relationship. An internal working model is a useful construct for considering the degree of disappointment and betrayal that T'Challa feels upon realizing that T'Chaka failed to tell him the truth about his cousin for so many years. Internal working models are relationship-specific, established during infancy, and guide attachment behaviors with caregivers and significant others. Internal working models include expectations of how others will behave, selective attention to certain social information and cues, emotional responses to interacting with others, and relevant memories about the attachment person and relationship.[15] T'Challa's internal working model of his father is one of a trustworthy, honest, strong, caring father and king. T'Challa's internal working model of his relationship with his father is one of trust, openness, and honesty. Therefore, upon learning of the cover-up, T'Challa initially doubts that his father is capable of withholding this information from him, and then experiences a rupture in his relationship with T'Chaka. Given the longtime security of their attachment, however, T'Challa feels confident enough in their relationship to confront T'Chaka about the rupture and T'Chaka's truthful and remorseful response promotes the relationship's repair.

Attachment theory is a useful approach for considering relationship dynamics and the manner in which relationships develop and change over time. Despite decades of research documenting the utility of attachment theory, there are notable weaknesses to the theory, some of which may be especially salient in considering T'Challa and T'Chaka's relationship. Critics of attachment theory point out that, in non-Westernized societies, a category within which Wakanda perhaps arguably belongs, approaches to child-rearing tend to differ from Western views in important ways.[16] For example, caregiving for young children may be accomplished in more communal manners than in the nuclear family, predominantly maternal caregiving context that attachment theory derived from. In non-Westernized societies, multiple caregiving arrangements are more commonplace. In more extensive family networks, mothers benefit from alloparental support from grandmothers, siblings, and other relatives, who share the financial and energy costs of child-rearing. As a result, each adult remains able to contribute to domestic activities in addition to child care.[17] In such a communal child-care arrangement, children may develop many primary attachments and the nature of the relationships may differ from those seen in Westernized nuclear families. Therefore, to truly understand T'Challa and T'Chaka's attachment relationship within the context of Wakandan society, what would be needed are research programs that observe, conceptualize, and empirically study the Wakandan culture of child-rearing. The authors of this chapter are prepared to engage in this line of study, contingent upon funding.

## LEGACY AND SPIRITUALITY

Legacy is important to many families, especially individuals with children. For men, the nature of paternal legacy is often framed based on men's childhood experiences.[18] The last two stages of psychosocial development appear to most closely relate to the concept of legacy: generativity versus stagnation, then ego integrity versus despair. *Generativity versus stagnation* is the seventh of eight stages and takes place during middle adulthood (ages 40 to 65). Many feel the need to "leave their mark" in the world through career achievements or through rearing children. When individuals feel they are unproductive, they become stagnant or disconnected from others, which leaves them unfulfilled. The last stage of psychosocial development is the *ego integrity versus despair* stage in late adulthood (age 65 to death). Supposedly, this is when individuals contemplate their accomplishments and hope to see themselves having lived a successful life. Wisdom is prominent during this stage, as the elder adult looks back at his or her life with a sense of closure and completeness, while accepting death without fear. Adults without this sense of life satisfaction may experience depression, hopelessness, and despair.

Social development appears to end, logically enough, at death. However, cultural norms surrounding death and the afterlife have a great influence on one's legacy. In many indigenous and African cultures, ancestors have a great presence in the lives of their descendants. Ethnic rites of passage and racial/ethnic socialization both promote resiliency.[19] In studies examining Black manhood, themes centering on responsibility, independence, and being a provider and spiritual leader in one's family often derive from Black fathers.[20] Although religion and spirituality are not clearly mentioned, the notion of an afterlife and the ability to interact with Wakandan ancestors is present. Djalia, the ancient ancestral plane of Wakanda memory, connects T'Challa with his predecessors and further bonds T'Chaka and T'Challa in the afterlife. T'Challa often travels there when Wakanda is under duress or when he is in need of advice. He connects with his father and other previous Black Panthers in this place. His sister Shuri also ventures to the Djalia and is provided guidance and clarity from the ancestors during a time of need.[21] When the entity Death imitates his father on one occasion, T'Challa realizes that this is not really his father's ghost because he advises him to give up on himself and Wakanda in order to achieve personal peace, which his father would never suggest.[22]

T'Chaka is a well-respected Wakandan leader during his time as the Black Panther. His legacy inadvertently places enormous pressure on T'Challa when he takes the reins. T'Challa may also fear "repeating the cycle" of negative familial traits.[23] T'Challa is often conflicted as to whether or not his father's own leadership style was effective or should be modeled, as he's developing his own identity as the leader of Wakanda. He struggles with respecting his father's legacy while identifying areas where his father was flawed in his approaches to leadership.

During this time, Ramonda offers him comfort, saying, "I watched your father and uncle struggle under the same weight. But, T'Challa, I think you are stronger than you know, perhaps stronger than all the kings who have come before you."[24] T'Challa calls on a council of former Black Panthers in order to seek their wisdom and advice on how to better align the people and the gods, fulfilling the final psychosocial development stage in the afterlife.[25]

## BLACK PANTHER AS COUNTERNARRATIVE

Structural and systemic barriers, such as unemployment, poverty, educational access, and incarceration, have resulted in ruptures within the Black family.[26] *Black Panther* provides a counternarrative to these stereotypes in its depiction of T'Challa's relationship with his father. *Counternarratives* are used to tell the stories from the vantage point of individuals who have been historically marginalized. Much of the literature regarding Black fathers focuses on the dissolution of Black families. Early research on Black families ignored, distorted, or minimized the parenting role of the Black father.[27] Scholars have noted that many of these narratives in the literature are marked by dominant stereotypes, including in academic literature.[28] In general, many father-son relationships in the media are depicted with maladaptive attachment styles and devoid of emotional learning. In studies of Black father-son relationships, Black sons overwhelmingly identify their father as their greatest model of manhood.[29] The relationship between T'Chaka and T'Challa represents a positive father-son connection in terms of attachment and communication. The influence T'Chaka had in developing a king both during his lifetime and beyond is admirable, and reflects good racial and gender socialization, along with leadership development.

# NOTES

1. *Black Panther* #30 (2001).
2. Coates (2015), p. 66.
3. *Fantastic Four* #53 (1966); *Captain America: Civil War* (2016 motion picture).
4. Main et al. (1985).
5. Zeanah & Smyke (2009).
6. Van IJzendoorn (1995).
7. Ainsworth et al. (1978); Bowlby & Fry (1953).
8. Ainsworth et al. (1978).
9. Main & Hesse (1990).
10. Zeanah & Symke (2009).
11. Ainsworth et al. (1978).
12. Main & Hesse (1990).
13. *Avengers* #77 (1970); *Black Panther* #3 (2001).
14. *Exiles* #2 (2009).
15. Bowlby (1953).
16. Keller (2013).
17. Keller (2013).
18. Perry & Lewis (2016).
19. Bowman (2013).
20. Allen (2016).
21. *Black Panther* #3 (2016).
22. *Black Panther* #4 (2008).
23. Perry & Lewis (2016).
24. *Black Panther* #3 (2016).
25. *Black Panther* #14 (2016).
26. Allen (2016).
27. Cochran (1997).
28. Cochran (1997).
29. Allen (2016).

# 6

# WHO IS THE BLACK PANTHER?

## THE SELF AS EMBODIED OTHERS

### J. Scott Jordan & Daniel Jun Kim

*"How many could we have helped, how many could we have saved, if we chose not to be hidden, not to be set apart? Many times because we did nothing, men, women and children died, and we did this because it was best for our people and Wakanda. That is a king's morality."*
—T'Chaka[1]

*"Moral development could be thought of as progressively broadening one's concept of a person."*
—social psychologist Stefano Passini[2]

Who are you?"[3] asks the wide-eyed youth, clearly awe-struck by the sudden appearance of what looks to be a spaceship in his inner-city neighborhood. The king of Wakanda smiles as if to say, "The answer, young friend, is the story of my life, and of all lives ever lived."

From the birthplace of the species to the backstreets of New York to incursion points in the multiverse, the tale of the Black Panther exemplifies the perpetual struggle to live as if we were all one single tribe, in a world dominated by stories that seem to tell us we are not. But why is it so hard to be one tribe? Why do we cling to cultural narratives of division and exclusion? The answer lies in the borders between *self* and *other* we develop during our lives, and the ways in which cultures influence our decisions about whom we let in, and whom we keep out.[4]

## GROUPS, BORDERS, AND WORLDVIEWS

*"We recount as the blowing branches recount the wind.*
*We recount as the stones recount the sea*
*that batters them to sand."*
—Shuri[5]

To Western ears, these words sound like poetry. To Shuri, they reveal the Wakandan worldview that each of us is a living embodiment of the larger world in which we live. Our heart, lungs, muscles, and bones, for example, are embodiments of the constraints we have to address when we move through Earth's gravitational field.[6] As we strain, exert force, and work to maintain balance, the beating of our hearts, the billowing of our lungs, and the contractions of our muscles reflect (i.e., "recount") the larger context in which we strain, exert, and work. Thus, just like the *blowing* branch and the *battered* stone, we, ourselves, are *recountings* of our world. We are *embodiments of context.*[7]

Psychologists refer to cultures that are organized around this worldview as *holistic.* Within such societies, people believe that "the universe is a vast integrated unit rather than discrete mechanistic parts,"[8] and they experience themselves, "as parts of various holistic entities, who adopt identities from the wholes they are part of, and strive to act in unison with other parts in the wholes."⁹ Black Panther is an embodiment of Wakanda's holistic culture. While visiting the souls of previous Black Panthers in Necropolis, the City of the Dead, he says, "I seek your counsel, honored fathers, warriors and priests. Black Panthers all." One of the souls responds, "You can speak plainly, T'Challa, there is no need for such formality, or subtlety. After all, are we not now all one?"¹⁰

## HOLISTIC VERSUS INDIVIDUALISTIC SELVES

*"You must take us all!"*
—T'Challa¹¹

While he himself is a holist, Black Panther has seen enough of the world to know that *individualistic*¹² cultures also exist, in which each of the people experience themselves as living as an internal, subjective *self* that is separate from and independent of external, objective reality, including other people.¹³ His awareness of this difference is expressed beautifully when he offers his soul to the demon Mephisto if he agrees to never bother another Wakandan. Mephisto accepts the offer and is surprised to find himself suddenly located in a jungle-like spiritual realm, surrounded by the souls of many prowling black jungle cats. T'Challa informs him they are in this realm because "my spirit has been forever joined to that of the panther god!" Mephisto mocks the idea of a panther god, calling it "tribal superstitious claptrap," and further claims, "There is no 'panther god.' I'd have known it."¹⁴

This exchange represents the different forms of thought that characterize holistic and individualistic cultures. Mephisto, as a single, individualistic spirit, reflects the Western tendency to observe and think about reality *analytically* in terms of individual objects, the properties they "possess," and the categories they belong to. These individual objects are thought of as being connected in terms of logic and universal laws that guide their behavior.[15] As a result, members of individualistic cultures tend to experience people as independent agents who are connected to each other through their own subjective powers of choice and free will, and "reason" is thought of as "an internally driven, cognitive process . . . in which meaning is *made*."[16] This analytic type of thought is reflected in Mephisto's belief that his argument with T'Challa is between two individuals and their separate, subjective desires. His statement, "I'd have known it," reveals his commitment to the idea that "reason" is a subjective, individual, cognitive process of making observations and combining them into theories about external reality.

Black Panther's way of perceiving the world, on the other hand, is more *holistic*, "attending to the entire field and assigning causality to it."[17] Members of holistic cultures do not experience "objects" as being independent, and connected through logic and universal laws. Rather, objects are embedded in a larger cosmic order; they are subsets or "wholes" within the larger, cosmic whole; and they derive their "properties," including their causal powers, from their existence in this larger, cosmic order. As an example, in ancient Greek culture, scholars relied more on analytic forms of thought, and explained a stone's falling through the air as if the stone had the property of "gravity" *within itself*. In holistic Chinese culture, on the other hand, "gravity" was considered a property that emerged out of the stone's inescapable *relation* to the larger context in which it was embedded.[18]

In holistic thinking, persons are experienced in terms of their connectivity and interrelatedness with both each other and the larger, cosmic order. In addition, "reason" is not so much a subjective, cognitive process, as it is an individual's ability to "turn the soul in the proper direction to see the external order of the cosmos."[19] Within this way of thinking, meaning is *found* as one becomes increasingly aware of one's connection to the cosmic order.[20]

T'Challa's holistic thinking is evident when he transports Mephisto and himself to the cosmic realm of the panther god. When Mephisto denies the panther god's existence, simply because he didn't know about it, T'Challa says, "You did know it. You just dismissed it."[21] Black Panther's holistic outlook, as well as his experiences with individualistic cultures, allows him to "see" the *analytic* thought structures at the root of Mephisto's argument. By conceptualizing Black Panther as an independent "thing" that is connected to the world through his subjective desires and free will, Mephisto has missed the fact that Black Panther is connected to reality *holistically.* Aware of the differences in their thought processes, Black Panther declares, "My ancestors are the most noble souls that ever walked the earth, and my soul is forever entwined with theirs. My soul is yours now, which means, you must take us all!" Still not understanding Black Panther's holistic message, Mephisto begins to consume the souls of the Panther spirits, squealing in delight over his apparent victory. Gorged, Mephisto stops to rest. T'Challa then reveals, "You're satiated. They are not," and the remaining Black Panther spirits consume the single, individualistic demon.[22]

This delightfully wicked parable serves as a cautionary tale regarding the allure of individual freedom and the lack of constraint supposedly offered by individualistic cultures. Mephisto believes the defining features of an "individual" are independence and free will. This analytic perspective renders him unaware that the purity and nobility he "tastes" while consuming the souls of the Black Panthers derives from their *holism*—from their connectedness to each other and the larger, cosmic order of the panther god. In short, the individual soul tastes "better" because it lives with the awareness that it is connected to, and part of, *everyone* and *everything.*[23]

# HOLISM, RELIGION, CONTEMPT, AND COMPASSION

When T'Challa brings New York blues singer Monica Lynn to Wakanda and she saves a young boy from a charging rhino, the boy's mother, Karota, refuses to thank her. As Monica and Black Panther walk away, Karota says to her husband, "It's that outworlder. That Moan-A-Ca! Look at them! Shameless, that's what it is."[24] While one might claim that Wakanda's holistic religion is responsible for Karota's contempt for an out-group member—even one who saves her son—research indicates that those who attend religious rituals and use religion for nonreligious reasons, such as business networking or because a spouse attends, express more hostility toward out-group members than those who are devoted to, and practice, actual religious principles (e.g., "love thy neighbor").[25] T'Challa is aware of this distinction. When Monica interrupts an important ritual because she believes he is being harmed, and she accuses the attendees of working with Killmonger, W'Kabi says to her, "That's the final indignity, outlander! Your very presence profanes this ceremony!" As Monica and Black Panther walk away, he says to her, "Too many people warp the word *heritage*, Monica. They use it to mean *superiority* when it is only meant to give one *identity!*"[26] Because of his genuine devotion to the Panther religion, T'Challa is more likely to feel compassion for the suffering of out-group members.

## RELATION-BASED VERSUS CATEGORY-BASED GROUPS

*"Whose heroes?"*
—The Thing[27]

While it might seem as if holistic cultures are more group-oriented than individualistic cultures, it turns out that both types foster high levels of *collectivism*, in which, "people are integrated into strong, cohesive in-groups."[28] What differs is how the collectivism is expressed. Members of individualistic cultures engage in *group-based* collectivism, which stresses, "obligations to a group as a whole, valuing obedience to group norms and authority, and subordinating individual interests to those of the collective."[29] Members of holistic cultures maintain *relational* collectivism, which "emphasizes relationships, mutual cooperation, dependence, and concern for each other in a closely interconnected social network."[30] Because of these differences, members of individualistic cultures are more sensitive to distinctions between in-groups and out-groups based on *categorical* group membership, while members of holistic cultures are more focused on personal relationships within the group, and working to create a more relationally based collective.[31]

The differences between these forms of collectivism are clearly expressed as Black Panther stands on a rooftop in New York City, attempting to calm a crowd that has gathered to get a glimpse of the king of Wakanda.

> **T'Challa:** "What do you want? Why have you come?"
> **Crowd member:** "To see if it was true. To see if you were really here."
> **T'Challa:** "I don't understand, I have always been among you."[32]

Black Panther's seeming confusion reveals his *relational collectivism*, in that he experiences the members of the predominantly African–American crowd relationally, as if they were *part of him*. In addition, his surprise that they don't experience him the same way reveals his expectation that he and they should be working toward a more relational form of collectivism.

In response to Black Panther's plea, a different member of the crowd explains the group's concerns: "You were with them, the Avengers, the Fantastic Four. They don't care nothin' about us." This person is experiencing Black Panther in terms of *group-based collectivism*; that is, in terms of a categorical, in-group/out-group distinction. As a result, seeing him "with" the Avengers is experienced as a violation of an in-group expectation. He is a member of *their* group, not the Avengers' group. The crowd member puts a finer point on this idea when he says that the Avengers are "not our heroes" but are instead "their heroes."[33] The point is driven home even harder when the next frame depicts the Fantastic Four's Ben Grimm (a.k.a. the Thing) watching the verbal exchange on television and failing to understand, as he wonders, "Whose heroes?"

What is brilliant about using the Thing in this scene is that he actually embodies the tension between *group-based* and *relationally based* collectivism. When interacting with the Fantastic Four, he is able to experience himself as part of a relationally based collective; that is, he is an essential component of the group, and he is their friend. Outside of the Fantastic Four, however, he often finds it difficult to identify with any category-based collectives because his physical attributes are so totally unique. During the Fantastic Four's first visit to Wakanda, the Thing falls for a trap set by Black Panther and is briefly incapacitated. When he comes to, he says, "He said I'd be weak for five minutes, but it's only been a couple'a minutes, and I feel like my ol' beautiful self again!"[34] Referring to himself in terms of a dimension based on physical appearance (i.e., beauty) reveals how much his identity is based on in-group/out-group categories. And by doing so ironically, by claiming to be beautiful while he believes others think he is not, he reveals the level of loneliness his group-based form of collectivism brings to his life.

Given this distinction between group-based and relationally based collectivism, it seems that when T'Challa asks us to "look after one another, as if we were one single tribe,"[35] he is actually pleading for us to work together toward creating a more relationally based collectivism, to experience ourselves as being part of each other and sharing a common fate. But how do we do this? How do we create a culture in which we experience each other in terms of *relations*, versus *in-group/out-group categories*? The answer seems to lie in the nature of *rhythm*—in the pulses that permeate the movements of our bodies, the meter of our songs, and the arcs of our stories.

## MANAGING GROUP BORDERS

*"Start at the beginning of the story, child.*
  *For in the end, only the story matters."*
—the griot spirit[36]

The griot spirit, caretaker of all Wakandan histories, says these words to Shuri as they walk through the Djalia—the plane of ancient memory, in one of many examples of Black Panther characters visiting otherworldly realms. As the griot informs Shuri of the power of stories, she is expressing the holistic view that as embodiments of context, each of our lives is a story that is a part of the larger tale of the cosmic order, including the otherworldly realms. The ebbs and flows of happiness and sorrow, strength and weakness, victory and defeat—all of these are lived embodiments of the patterns entailed in reality as a whole.[37] Thus, the rhythms of these lived patterns are the rhythms of life. Given this notion of reality as nested rhythms, Wakandans use the rhythms of collective ritual to keep their individual stories connected to both each other and the larger cosmic order.

## BECOMING ONE BY MOVING TOGETHER

*"I, Zuri, son of Badu, give to you, Prince T'Challa,*
  *the Black Panther."*
—Zuri[38]

T'Challa extends his arms outward and to the side, spear and shield held in opposing hands. He crosses his arms over his head, then brings them down rapidly, to his sides, while simultaneously bowing on one knee to the throng of gathered Wakandans. In synchrony, the community answers T'Challa's gesture with the Wakandan salute, fists crossed over the chest, followed by a swift, graceful extension downward, and to the side. This group gesture is just one of the many moments of synchrony Wakandans deliberately generate during T'Challa's coronation ritual.

Research on synchrony clearly reveals its ability to create a sense of group cohesion. In one study, persons who engaged in synchronous behaviors, such as marching, singing, and drumming, were more likely to contribute to the good of their group than members of groups that did not behave synchronously.[39] In addition, when group members share the goal of synchronizing with each other, they experience their relationship to the group much more *holistically*; that is, with an increased sense that they are a true *part* of the group, which is referred to as *interdependent self-construal*.[40]

## BECOMING ONE BY THINKING TOGETHER

*"Let us begin, Shuri, in the ancient Wakandan duchy of Adowa."*
—the griot spirit[41]

As Shuri and the griot spirit practice fighting with long staffs, the griot tells the tale of how Wakanda first became united as a nation. This image of bodies and minds, moving together, reflects the Wakandan understanding of the rhythm and power of stories. Data indicate that behavioral synchrony leads to more prosocial behavior if it is accompanied by a mythological narrative, as opposed to a secular narrative.[42] In addition, those who read more narrative fiction over the course of their lives are better able to understand that other people might have ideas, thoughts, and goals that are different from their own,[43] and also score higher on measures of empathy.[44] Finally, children whose parents reminisce with them in emotionally elaborative ways about past events, particularly negative ones, develop stronger self-concepts and have greater insight into their own feelings, as well as those of others.[45]

Clearly, stories matter. As members of a group share knowledge, their conversations render some memories stronger, and others, weaker. This process of socially constructing collective memories, over time, is known as *mnemonic convergence*,[46] and as groups engage in it, they eventually give rise to what are known as "We" narratives. The "We" narrative "provides the typical format for the attribution of joint agency; it contributes to the formation of group identity, and it generates group stability.[47] As Shuri and the griot complete their training exercise, the griot ends her tale by exclaiming, "Either you are a nation, or you are nothing."[48] Bringing the arc of the story and the rhythm of the training exercise to a conclusion, simultaneously, expresses the Wakandan understanding that the rhythms of both serve as a medium for the transference of memory and, ultimately, a stronger sense of who *We* are.

# THE *WILD* NATURE OF GROUP NARRATIVES

Because group narratives emerge out of our lived lives, they are *wild*.[49] Usually we live in them unconsciously, and experience surprise when we find that the world is different from what we have lived. Such surprise is expressed beautifully when Everett K. Ross, a state department liaison, and Queen Divine Justice, a Chicago girl of Wakandan descent, find themselves on a monorail in Wakanda. Ross's life as a Washington, DC bureaucrat has led him to harbor a wild narrative in which he unconsciously experiences groups in terms of potential conflict. Thus, when he sees city dwellers and tribal villagers sitting next to each other, he thinks, "There was this huge diversity of cultures—all peacefully riding the 'A' train. But that peace was fragile." Queen Divine Justice has a quite different reaction. Wiping a tear from her eye, she states, "We're riding a monorail into one of the world's most technologically advanced cities, built and occupied by Black people . . . seeing these beautiful faces, it, it changes everything."[50] Clearly, the wild narratives embodied by these two characters reveal the differences in their lived lives, as well as the overwhelming influence wild narratives have on our moment-to-moment experiences of life, even though we are completely unaware that we harbor them.

## BECOMING A *NEW* ONE

*"But didn't life start right here on this continent?*
*So ain't all people your people?"*
—Erik Killmonger[51]

Erik Killmonger has arrived in Wakanda with a hate-fueled desire to write a new story for its future. He says these words to T'Challa as he chastises the members of the Wakandan royal family for their country's centuries-old policy of secluding themselves from the rest of the world. When Killmonger then challenges T'Challa for the throne and T'Challa accepts the challenge, we see how collective rituals serve a conservative role in transmitting a culture's values, on the one hand, and a progressive role, on the other, by providing a way for the culture's worldview to change. Specifically, by accepting Killmonger's challenge, T'Challa is honoring his commitment to the Wakandan ritual of ascension. By instituting ritualized combat as a means of ascension, however, Wakandan tradition is allowing for the emergence of a new leader with a different worldview, one who might set Wakanda on a different course for the future.

Of course, their different perspectives on Wakanda's future constitute a major source of tension between Killmonger and T'Challa. And, somewhat ironically, despite their differing views, it is the synchrony that emerges during their ritualized combat that provides T'Challa with the strength he needs to change himself. During their battle, T'Challa and Killmonger engage in *mimicry*, which is similar to synchrony in that both involve similar movements. However, in synchrony the behaviors happen at the same time, while in mimicry there is a time lag—merely seconds, usually, but a lag nevertheless.[52] In addition, unlike synchronous behaviors, mimicked actions occur spontaneously and outside conscious awareness.

As T'Challa and Killmonger engage in combat, we see two

highly skilled, well-matched martial artists whose strikes and parries begin to mirror each other, albeit unintentionally, with highly similar moves occurring seconds apart from each other. Research reveals that such mimicry, like synchrony, promotes affiliation, empathy, prosocial behavior, and even a blurring of the self with another.[53] Thus, while the two are intent on defeating each other, the mimicry that spontaneously emerges during their combat provides a medium for T'Challa to unconsciously empathize with Killmonger's plight. And although T'Challa ultimately defeats Killmonger, Wakanda, in fact, does have a new king. When Ramonda feeds T'Challa's unconscious body the heart-shaped herb, he has a vision in which he confronts his father and ancestors and tells them that he must "right these wrongs"[54] and that he cannot join them in the Djalia until he does. It is clear that T'Challa's decision to return to physical reality and reclaim the throne is not made out of a lust for power but out of a sense of moral responsibility. But the responsibility he feels does not end merely with overthrowing Killmonger and reclaiming the throne. He must stop Killmonger because, although he has become newly sympathetic to Killmonger's suffering and plight, he cannot allow the violent uprisings that Killmonger is planning. However, due in no small part to their ritualistic battle, the unconscious mimicry that occurred, and the empathy it elicited, T'Challa goes further and does what no Black Panther before him has ever done: He overturns centuries of Wakanda's stringently observed tradition of isolationism and spearheads an international outreach program.

## THE EVER-GROWING *WE*

*"When I was younger, you told me to always consider my actions, father."*
—T'Challa[55]

T'Challa says these words as he contemplates whether or not to set off a bomb that will destroy an entire alternate earth that is about to crash into and annihilate our own. Because of his holistic culture, its commitment to experiencing itself as part of the larger cosmic order, its maintenance of cultural stability through collective ritual, and its understanding that collective narratives need to reflect our ever-changing world, T'Challa has come to experience himself and all of Wakanda as an embodiment of the struggle to be one single tribe, including unknown inhabitants of the multiverse. And just as his ever-growing "We" narrative gave him the courage to defy his father's spirit, and break Wakanda's centuries-old isolation,[56] it now gives him the strength to defy his father's wishes yet again, as he refuses to destroy the alternate earth.

Who is the Black Panther? He is the leader of those who would work to be an example of how to create a more relationally connected collective. It is important to note that in his speech to the UN, he explicitly states, "We will *work* to be an example,"[57] for such a line reflects the insight that lived life always lies at the intersection of choice and chance. T'Challa is inviting us to join him in the hard, holistic work of being one single tribe. The more we tell each other such a story, and the more we organize our collective lives around living in a more holistic way, the more it will become our collective narrative. In short, we, too, can become one with the Black Panther.

## NOTES

1. *New Avengers* #18 (2014).
2. Passini (2010), p. 439.
3. *Black Panther* (2018 motion picture).
4. Jordan & Wesselmann (2015).
5. *Black Panther* #8 (2016).
6. Jordan (2013).
7 Jordan et al. (2015).
8. Lim et al. (2011), p. 24.
9. Lim et al. (2011), p. 24.
10. *New Avengers* #18 (2014).
11. *Black Panther* #5 (1998).

12. Lim et al. (2011).
13. Christopher & Hickinbottom (2008).
14. *Black Panther* #5 (1998).
15. Nisbett et al. (2001).
16. Christopher & Hickinbottom (2008), p. 579.
17. Nisbett et al. (2001), p. 291.
18. Nisbett et al. (2001).
19. Christopher & Hickinbottom (2008), p. 579.
20. Christopher & Hickinbottom (2008).
21. *Black Panther* #5 (1998).
22. *Black Panther* #5 (1998).
23. Jordan et al. (2017).
24. *Jungle Action* #9 (1974).
25. Lynch et al. (2017); Matthew 22:38.
26. *Jungle Action* #8 (1974).
27. *Black Panther* #6 (1999).
28. Lim et al. (2011), p. 22.
29. Lim et al. (2011), p. 24.
30. Lim et al. (2011), p. 24.
31. Brewer & Chen (2007).
32. *Black Panther* #6 (1999). Compare Matthew 18:20, 28:20.
33. *Black Panther* #6 (1999).
34. *Fantastic Four* #52 (1966).
35. *Black Panther* (2018 motion picture).
36. *Black Panther* #8 (2016).
37. Jordan (2013).
38. *Black Panther* (2018 motion picture).
39. Wiltermuth & Heath (2009).
40. Reddish et al. (2013).
41. *Black Panther* #5 (2016).
42. Cohen et al. (2014).
43. Mar et al. (2006).
44. Mumper & Gerrig (2017).
45. Salmon & Reese (2016).
46. Coman et al. (2016).
47. Gallagher & Tollefsen (2017).
48. *Black Panther* #5 (2016).
49. Jordan (2018).
50. *Black Panther* #20 (2000).
51. *Black Panther* (2018 motion picture).
52. Bargh & Chartrand (1999).
53. Lakin et al. (2003).
54. *Black Panther* (2018 motion picture).
55. *New Avengers* #21 (2014).
56. *Black Panther* (2018 motion picture).
57. *Black Panther* (2018 motion picture).

# 7

# WAKANDA AND THE WORLD

## LOOKING AT THE BENEFITS TO THE
## INDIVIDUAL AND THE GROUP

Travis Adams

*"The future of humanity can be assured only through the balance of scientific progress and spiritual maturity."*

—scientist/entrepreneur Kazuo Inamori[1]

*"You let the refugees in, they bring their problems with them."*
—W'Kabi[2]

National price is a common trait throughout the world, but when does it become a burden? Does sharing an idea with others make it more or less impactful—especially if that idea may help others across the planet? These questions plague T'Challa and the people of Wakanda,[3] torn between keeping their knowledge and scientific discoveries to themselves or sharing them with the world to make it a better place.[4] Within

the borders of Wakanda, people prioritize the survival and betterment of Wakanda.[5] Through a collectivistic mindset, the
people of Wakanda have been able to advance their technology
far past that of other nations,[6] but they define their collective
more narrowly, as they keep vibranium, and the technology it
produces, as the exclusive resource of the Wakandan people.[7]
When T'Challa opens up Wakanda's information and technology to the world,[8] was that best for his people, the world,
or both? Who will benefit the most, both externally in their
environment and internally with regard to their psychological
well-being?

## INDIVIDUALISM

An *individualistic culture* holds that individuals are responsible
for only themselves before all others.[9] While their relationship
with the world around them is important, the main goal of the
society is to promote the well-being of the individual.[10] In the
film *Black Panther*, Wakanda itself is a single unit in comparison to the world, the Wakandan people are bonded to their
tribes, and the tribes are loyal to their king.[11] For centuries
they have kept the highly valuable and useful mineral vibranium to themselves and have been able to surpass the world
in technology through its many uses.[12] Instead of sharing their
technology with the world, they chose to keep its advantages
to themselves, although the king does sometimes choose to
help an ally, such as Bucky Barnes,[13] Agent Ross,[14] and Captain
America.[15] That decision is not always supported by the tribal
council members.[16]

Individualism is basing the identity of the individual solely
on his or her accomplishments through personal effort, with an
emphasis on self-fulfillment.[17] Conversely, when a strategy does
not go as planned or the individual fails to accomplish a goal,
that individual carries the doubt or burden of failure alone.[18]

Other consequences of a society's individualistic approach are lack of support for those who suffer from low self-esteem, those who struggle with their identity, and individuals who are struggling emotionally and making decisions based on emotions rather than logic.[19] In the *Black Panther* film, Erik Killmonger, driven by emotions, spends his entire life training and killing in the armed forces and CIA, not only to avenge his father's death but to take the throne from the family who abandoned him.[20] It is possible that if they had taken young Erik with them to Wakanda, his life path would have been changed dramatically. By viewing an experience as limited to a single individual and ignoring other aspects of the situation, an individual may be left feeling deflated, or may feel overconfident when making future choices, both influencing the individual's perception of his or her capabilities.

## INTERNAL STRUGGLE

Within an individualistic belief system, it is important to be aware of the cognitive impact of internal struggles, and the amount of mental strength and resources required to keep oneself separate from others,[21] to focus on oneself. This is often difficult in many cultural settings and can cause internal conflict by stressing the need for personal time, individual freedom, and personal challenges, which are significant in the individualistic culture.[22] When King T'Chaka leaves young Erik in Oakland, he believes he is doing what's right for the boy. When T'Challa meets with the former kings on the ancestral plane, he accuses them of wrongdoing in relation to Killmonger, stating, "We let fear of our discovery stop us from doing what is right,"[23] separating culture from belief and causing internal conflict to manifest. By focusing on his belief, T'Challa can practice empathy for Killmonger as well as show a willingness to sacrifice himself for the betterment of Wakanda.

Individualists often detach context from situations, choosing actions that are better suited to the well-being of the individual than that of the collective. While the individual strives to situationally better his or her standing within society, emotions often convolute perception and impair judgment.[24] Individualists may experience levels of anger that are higher than those who hold a collectivistic stance, which takes into account the other, or the self in relation to others.[25]

# GETTING INTO A WISE MIND

*Dialectical behavioral therapy*, along with *cognitive behavioral therapy*, examines an individual through three different lenses—the emotional, the rational, and the wise mind. Within each of these mindsets, decisions are made based on how an individual is currently feeling, through his or her logic and reasoning skills, or by the need to do what is right at that moment. Through an understanding and awareness of these mindsets, it is possible to take a step back to ensure that the actions taken are those that will best suit the desired needs or goals at that time.

*Emotional mind* is often distorted by an emotionally charged situation, which may impede reason and logic, resulting in behaviors that are out of character or impulsive.

*Rational mind* is the calculating mind, the mindset in which logic and reason determine actions that may override emotions and desires.

*Wise mind* allows a person to take a step back from the situation, to assess emotions as well as logic to determine the best outcome.[26]

## COLLECTIVISTIC CULTURE

A *collectivistic culture* is one that remains tightly integrated, so that the interests of the individual are aligned with the goals of the society.[27] Throughout Wakanda, each of the tribes helps the others, contributing to the life and longevity of the nation.[28] When T'Challa and other Wakandan warriors charge into battle, the scream of "Wakanda Forever" is a statement that their lives are worth risking for the people and the nation,[29] ensuring a tomorrow through the sacrifice of today.

Communities that take a collectivistic approach are better suited to handle issues that shake the norm; the strength of the group strengthens each group member.[30] When an alien army is attacking in order to try to take the Mind Stone from the Vision, Captain America wants to ensure that the battle stays in front of them. T'Challa orders part of the shield to be lowered and Lord M'Baku (ruler of the Jabari, who has an individual-istic mindset) says, "This will be the end of Wakanda." Okoye (general of the Dora Milaje) responds, "Then it will be the noblest ending in history."[31] These two responses reflect the strength and resolve of those with a collective outlook. When a community has banded together, they are more likely to weather issues that might otherwise be disastrous and approach situations with a positive mental attitude.

### PERCEPTION TO REALITY

Perception of events can generate either a happier and more fulfilling life or a negative and self-defeating future. By reframing one's perception, a person can gain greater life satis-faction with fewer physical illnesses through a positive mental attitude. Positive mental attitudes have been shown to increase longevity, boost desire for survival, and play an important role in healthy lifestyle choices and practices.[32] When T'Challa is dying and Shuri is chosen to become the next Black Panther, she is turned away by the panther god, but allowed to live. As she returns from the realm of the panther god, she realizes that she still must fight to keep Wakanda safe; as a result of this decision, she is given the power of the Black Panther. That is, she chooses to fight for her people and not for her own glory.[33] Where an individualized approach may have an impact on self-esteem and self-worth,[34] sacrifice for the betterment of the collective is what gives Wakanda's greatest warriors the power of the Black Panther.[35] The confidence developed through positive mental attitude allows individuals to change, support one another through difficult times, and break stigmas associated with issues such as mental illness and addiction.[36]

## DUALITY OF A NATION

Because the core unit within a collectivistic society is the group,[37] we can see how Wakanda within its walls operates with this belief. While looking at the countries around the world, Wakanda attempts to alienate and exclude itself from the problems of others, operating like an individual in relation to the rest of the world. This may be due to the implication of trust and how it relates to both individualistic and collective societies. Trust within a society of collective culture must be reserved only for those within the in-group (Wakandans). Others, meanwhile, must be viewed with more caution. By contrast, individualistic communities are more apt to extend a predisposed level of trust to those in the out-group.[38]

Willingness to accept others and readiness to trust in general are important factors to consider when looking at decision making and decisional belief systems in individualistic and collectivistic societies. Through a willingness to accept others outside the norm, one may be able to better one's position in various areas. Going against the status quo is an important factor in the decision-making process as well.[39] Incorporating trust into decision making is essential not only for your outcome but for your self-esteem. Recognizing that not all decisions are intuition-based (nature) or logic-based (nurture), and that most decisions will never be perfect or may come at some cost, an individual is afforded some leeway to make a decision that may not be the best but is the best with the information at hand.[40] In the film *Captain America: Civil War*, King T'Chaka is killed in an explosion with all evidence pointing at the Winter Soldier, Bucky Barnes, as the culprit. Captain America knows this cannot be true and defends Barnes against T'Chaka's son, T'Challa the Black Panther. Black Panther is determined to avenge his father's death until it is discovered that he was wrong about Barnes, and it was a setup to incriminate the Winter Soldier. Had he killed him, T'Challa would have had to live with that decision. Later, Captain America brings Barnes to Wakanda for help and he is accepted by the new king.[41]

The difference in beliefs between T'Challa and the tribal leaders, when it comes to sharing Wakandan resources, may be due to *cultural convergence*. Cultural convergence occurs when a unit (i.e., a person, a business, a community, or a country) can be influenced by those with whom the unit interacts. These influences may affect their decision-making abilities, causing them to adopt views different from those of their communities and cultures.[42] T'Challa and his father, King T'Chaka, as diplomats who travel abroad, see how other countries and leaders handle situations,[43] while the tribal leaders stay within Wakandan borders,[44] primarily interacting with one another. As T'Challa and his father recognize how other societies interact and how the leaders of these countries conduct themselves, that may cause a shift in their individual perspectives and influence their decisions in ways that do not always align with those of tribal leaders.[45]

# DISCOVERY THROUGH QUESTIONS

*Motivational interviewing* (MI) is a communication method health care providers use to encourage individuals to make effective behavioral change. Through questioning, an understanding of how and why to make this change is discussed, and that prompts the individual to opt for a healthier choice in life. Among the choices addressed by this method are addiction, decision-making abilities, lifestyle choices, and the use of emotional reasoning, such as the choice to express anger in inappropriate ways. Motivational interviewing has been effective not only in facilitating a change in individuals, but also in increasing rapport between providers and patients.[46]

MI is a strength-based approach, allowing the individual to pinpoint his or her own value system and to find a personal motivation for change.[47] Through MI, individuals identify aspects of their behaviors they want to change and providers elicit responses that offer personal value and generate commitment. Benefits of MI include not being talked *to* but talked *with* when working with a counselor or provider, and utilizing reflective listening to get at the heart of what an individual desires in life. With a newfound passion for change, individuals may be able to break habits, physical or mental, and live a life that is more personally meaningful and fulfilling for them and their loved ones.

Changes in perspective can also be *primed*. Priming is done when a series of questions and/or tasks lead individuals to a predetermined outcome, which is nonetheless unknown to those being primed. Guiding an individual to a desired outcome through calculated questioning may result in the individual reaching a decision that the person doing the priming is hoping for.[48]

## WAKANDA FOREVER

Choices and decisions are more than words; layers of cultural factors, beliefs, and variables have an influence over outcomes. The weight of a decision does not have to rest on the individual and the rewards of that decision do not have to be shared by the group. There is no one way to make decisions. The intrinsic (internal) value, compared to the extrinsic (external) value, is situation-based and individual-specific. Using all the resources and knowledge that Wakanda has to offer, T'Challa not only lowered the walls to help others with the Wakanda International Outreach Center,[49] but has inspired real-life corporations to donate to organizations that support science, technology, engineering, and math.[50] With life imitating art, how could his decision be wrong?

> *"People have no greater calling than to serve the greater good of humankind and society."*[51]
>
> —scientist/entrepreneur Kazuo Inamori

# MAKING CONTACT:
# AN ANTIDOTE FOR PREJUDICE?

Sarah Rizkallah

Our brains are wired to make judgments about the world, but they don't always make the right decisions. As a result, we often form prejudiced opinions about others—that is, opinions that are not necessarily based on lived experience or reason and that prompt discrimination.[52] After years of these mistakes, our society developed a range of false beliefs and misconceptions that are difficult to tell apart from the truth, and perpetrated injustices based on those false beliefs.[53]

Social contact between individuals from different community groups may play a key role in reducing prejudice.[54] Proponents of the *contact hypothesis*[55] hold that simply coming into contact with people who are different can reduce prejudice and discrimination between two different social groups when conditions are right. Optimally, the groups recognize a need for equal status between them, identify common goals, agree to cooperate, and have the support of legal/political systems. Without this contact, when groups remain isolated from one another, the problems of prejudice and conflict can only spread like a disease.[56]

*Black Panther* highlights the risks of social isolation and the rewards of cooperative contact. As the king of Wakanda, T'Chaka conceals his country from the world to such a degree that members need an inner lip tattoo to regain entry[57] and the true wonder of Wakanda seems like a fairy tale to the few outsiders who know about it.[58] As a result, a range of misconceptions and misunderstandings form both within the American and Wakandan societies about the wealth, technological advancement, and moral codes of the other. By embracing social contact, both T'Chaka's son T'Challa and Everett K. Ross learn to respect each other's differences and work toward a common goal—that is, preventing the distribution of vibranium to those who would use it for destructive purposes. The success of this intergroup contact leads T'Challa to make the history-making decision to end Wakanda's seclusion and to promote contact with the outside world in the future.

## NOTES

1. Quoted by Inamori International Center for Ethics and Excellence (n.d.).
2. *Black Panther* (2018 motion picture).
3. *Black Panther* (2018 motion picture).
4. *Rise of the Black Panther* #1 (2018).
5. *Black Panther* (2018 motion picture).
6. *Avengers: Infinity War* (2018 motion picture); *Black Panther* (2018 motion picture).
7. *Rise of the Black Panther* #1 (2018).
8. *Black Panther* (2018 motion picture).
9. Hofstede (2001).
10. Oyserman et al. (2008).
11. *Black Panther* (2018 motion picture).
12. *Black Panther* (2018 motion picture).
13. *Captain America: Civil War* (2016 motion picture).
14. *Black Panther* (2018 motion picture).
15. *Rise of the Black Panther* #1 (2018); *Avengers: Infinity War* (2018 motion picture).
16. *Black Panther* (2018 motion picture).
17. Hofstede (1980).
18. Oyserman et al. (2002).
19. Oyserman et al. (2002).
20. *Black Panther* (2018 motion picture).
21. Oyserman et al. (2008).
22. Love (2007).
23. *Black Panther* (2018 motion picture).

24. Markus & Kitayama (1991).
25. Markus & Kitayama (1991).
26. Wagner et al. (2015).
27. Van Hoorn (2015).
28. *Black Panther* (2018 motion picture).
29. *Avengers: Infinity War* (2018 motion picture).
30. Love (2007).
31. Avengers*: Infinity War* (2018 motion picture).
32. Paganini-Hill et al. (2018).
33. *Black Panther #6* (2009).
34. Oyserman et al. (2002).
35. *Black Panther #4* (2009).
36. Hynes (2010).
37. Oyserman et al. (2008).
38. Van Hoorn (2015).
39. March (1994).
40. Hastie & Dawes (2010).
41. *Captain America: Civil War* (2016 motion picture).
42. Rollnick et al. (2010).
43. Miller et al. (2009).
44. House et al. (2004).
45. *Captain America: Civil War* (2016 motion picture).
46. *Black Panther* (2018 motion picture).
47. House et al. (2004).
48. Oyserman et al. (2008).
49. *Black Panther* (2018 motion picture).
50. Bromwich (2018).
51. Quoted by Inamori International Center for Ethics and Excellence (n.d.).
52. Abrams & Hogg (2006).
53. Abrams & Hogg (2006); Allport (1954).
54. Miller & Brewer (2013); Rose (1999); Williams (1947).
55. Allport (1954).
56. Brameld (1946); Pettigrew & Tropp (2006).
57. *Black Panther* (2018 motion picture).
58. *Black Panther* (2018 motion picture).

# 8

# EXPLORING THE HIDDEN KINGDOMS OF ASSUMPTION

## INTERVIEW WITH WRITER CHRISTOPHER PRIEST ON BLACK PANTHER, CULTURE, AND THE ART OF CHANGING MINDS

### J. Scott Jordan

*"The Avengers are my friends, among whom there can be no issues of protocol. And as for why, it seemed the prudent and reasonable thing to do given the potential threat these people posed to the kingdom."*
—T'Challa[1]

*"This power of generalizing . . . gives men so much the superiority in mistake over the dumb animals."*
—Victorian novelist George Eliot[2]

**D**id we all mishear you?" a surprised Captain America asks after Black Panther indicates that his reason for joining the Avengers was to study them. "No. You did not,"[3] T'Challa says. Captain American is clearly taken aback. For years, he had assumed their relationship was based on friendship, not politics. In the next scene between the two, T'Challa finds Cap working out his frustration on a punching bag, mask removed, as if to reveal the personal-level sense of betrayal he is experiencing.[4] Clearly, Black Panther's revelation has violated one of Cap's deeply help assumptions.

Where do these assumptions come from? It turns out the brain generates them constantly.[5] How many times have you found yourself walking down a flight of stairs, suddenly starting to fall because you *assumed* you had reached the floor, but there was still another stair to go? While you *consciously* felt surprised, you didn't experience the fact that your brain was continuously making unconscious assumptions about what you *should be* feeling as you walked down the stairs.[6] The brain generates these predictions—that is, creates assumptions—all the time, about what *should happen next* in our actions, perceptions, and thoughts.[7] Since these assumptions are unconscious, however, we don't consciously *feel* ourselves making them. Rather, we experience them *intuitively*;[8] that is, automatically, without conscious effort, as if things just *should be* a certain way. Thus, when Black Panther reveals his initial reason for joining the Avengers, Captain America's immediate response is surprise. In a sense, he suddenly finds himself falling down a cognitive staircase, because, all along, he *unconsciously* assumed his relationship with Black Panther had nothing to do with politics.

## ASSUMPTION AND SURPRISE

When reading Christopher Priest's run as author of the *Black Panther* comic book (1998–2003), it becomes clear, rather quickly, how deeply Priest understands the important roles that assumption and surprise play in our daily lives. From the actions and thoughts of his characters, to the structure and arcs of his stories, he takes us on an often funny, occasionally heartbreaking exploration of the kingdoms of assumption we collectively create and live in, every day.

**Scott Jordan:** You were very careful about when you'd let Black Panther be surprised. Why was that important for him as a character?

**Christopher Priest:** Because when I started writing the character, I went back to Stan, I went back to the Fantastic Four, and I said, "Who is this guy? Or who did Stan intend this character to be?" You have the hunters and the hunted, right? He was a hunter. He was always a hunter. Over the years, a lot of writers mishandled him, and I don't think it was because he was Black. I think it was because he didn't have any superpowers, and a lot of writers think comic book fans are excited about "Can the Hulk beat the Thing?" Things like that. So when you have a guy like Black Panther, they didn't think he was sexy and he didn't really excite them as writers, and so kind of lamed-out on him. I want to be very careful about excepting Don McGregor from that idea. I didn't agree with everything he did with the character itself, but he certainly built that world, he constructed that world very expertly and invested in it. So I started to think, "Well, if he's like a jungle cat, you can't sneak up on a jungle cat." It's not just that they're fast and they're lethal. They're smart. They're incredibly smart. Any kid who has ever watched *Jurassic Park* and saw the velociraptors figuring out how to open the door to the kitchen,[9] I thought that's the kind of character this guy

is. I wanted to be very careful about that. It takes a lot
to fool him. It takes a lot to surprise him.

In addition to surprise being important to Black Panther's
identity, it also played a major role in how Priest developed his
story arcs. His tales were often told from the point of view of
Everett K. Ross, who is a Caucasian government liaison assigned
to escort Black Panther during his visit to the United States.[10]
Ross recounts his experiences with Black Panther to his girlfriend Nikki and does so out of sequence, often starting near the
end of the story, then filling in backstory details as his recounting
progresses. By unfolding his stories in this manner, Priest led the
reader to generate assumptions about what might be happening
in the arc, only to violate those assumptions later and surprise
the reader as more backstory was revealed. It turns out that in
addition to surprising the readers, Priest himself was often surprised by how certain critics regarded his use of surprise.

> **Priest:** Almost every story arc I wrote, the first couple
> of chapters I would get hate mail and get beat up on.
> And then they'd read chapter 3 and chapter 4, where
> all these reversals and reveals would come out and the
> Black Panther would start snapping all the mousetraps
> shut, and they'd realize, "Oh, this was his plan all along.
> Oh! Oh! Priest is great!" But then, like, two issues later
> they're back to "Priest sucks" because it would be the
> beginning of the next story arc, where it looked like
> I didn't know what I was doing. And I'm like, "Have
> a little faith!" How many times does Dr. House have
> to pull off some miraculous, lifesaving strategy, before
> the hospital administrator would trust him in the first
> place?[11] Why don't you trust him from chapter 1 and
> just go along for the ride, rather than assume I'm some
> sort of idiot? But that's kind of the seesaw that it was.

Regardless of his critics, Priest consistently used Black
Panther as a means of surprising readers into becoming aware
of their own unconscious assumptions. I asked him what it was
like to have that level of artistic freedom, referring to one of
his very first arcs in which the demon Mephisto is tricked into
visiting the mystical realm of the Black Panther god and is then
promptly consumed by the collective throng of Black Panther
spirits.[12]

> **Jordan:** In the first five issues, you go through the
> Mephisto arc, and it ends with this great scene with
> the Black Panther spirits consuming Mephisto. It felt
> like you were saying, even at the metaphysical level,
> that Wakanda is way better than any culture that gave
> rise to Mephisto, that Black Panther lives in a better
> culture.
>
> **Priest:** That was Marvel Knights.[13] We were free to do
> stuff like that. What's happening now, you're seeing
> a lot of free speech constrained and stomped out, not
> necessarily even by conservatives, but liberals. "You
> can't say that!" "You can't do that!" "You can't write a
> story about that!" And a lot of stuff that we got away
> with in those days, it wouldn't fly now. Ross said a
> lot of racist things. They weren't overtly racist. It was
> his internal monologue. He's talking to his girlfriend,
> Nikki, right? So, they're having this private moment
> and he's letting his hair down, and he's saying incred-
> ibly racist things, like, "I went up to the ghetto, you
> know, and I was told there'd be singing. I was lied to."
> Which is incredibly racist, and Joe Quesada allowed
> me to not necessarily make Ross a racist per se but
> write him realistically, as a hardened New Yorker who
> clearly doesn't have a lot of Black friends, who is being
> thrown into the deep end of the Wakandan pool and is

having an honest reaction to it. Now, you're supposed to write that reaction honestly, without having to clean it up for the censors.

**Jordan:** I'm wondering if you knew at the time you were dabbling in what we now call *microaggressions*.[14]

**Priest:** No. What are microaggressions?

**Jordan:** Microaggressions are like walking up to an African-American woman with braids and saying, "May I touch your hair?"

**Priest:** Oh, right. Okay. Yeah.

**Jordan:** There's this great scene where Black Panther shows up at Avenger's mansion. There was only one Avenger there, and he almost calls Black Panther, "Falcon."

**Priest:** *(Laughs heartily.)* Was it Justice?

**Jordan:** Yeah. He's trying to remember his name, and he doesn't.

**Priest:** That sounds like something I would write *(continues to laugh)*.

**Jordan:** And there's a great scene where Black Panther's leaving, and Justice says to himself, "Falcon? Oh my God, I would have never lived that down!"

**Priest:** It was issue #13, I think.[15] It was Sal Velluto's first issue. Was it the one where some guy was filling up a plane with water?

**Jordan:** Yeah. Nowadays, we refer to statements like that as microaggressions. You were drawing our attention to them almost 20 years ago.

While Priest's use of surprise could often be very funny, it also produced poignant moments of beauty and empathy. In one particularly moving scene, Everett Ross is traveling on a Wakandan monorail with Queen Divine Justice, a Chicago girl of Wakandan descent. While witnessing the diversity of urban and rural Wakandans peacefully riding together on the monorail, the two have strikingly different reactions. Ross's experiences as government operative lead him to assume that such diversity could explode into conflict at any moment.[16] I asked Priest about a scene in which he and an African-American woman generate strikingly different assumptions upon seeing Wakanda (described in chapter 6), and what he was trying to accomplish with this use of simultaneous-yet-different surprise.

**Priest:** It was supposed to be cultural. You see, the first couple years of the series, it was about Everett K. Ross, the State Department handler. It was about his cultural awakening. And I was writing him pretty much as a jerk. It wasn't that he was uninformed. He was lazy. He didn't really embrace this culture. He figured, "This guy's coming over for a weekend. I'm just gonna have to, like, babysit him. Show him around town. I'll check him into the Waldorf Astoria, you know, he'll order up some ribs, that'll be the end of that. Right?" Everett was written to be the point-of-view character for the reluctant Marvel reader. He's supposed to be the voice of these fans that we would have to work really hard to earn, because Black comics, particularly, just never sold. So by the time we moved past year one into year two, I was like, "Well, now what we need to do is go and earn the lapsed comic reader or the lapsed comic fan or the urban comic fan, whether it's Black or Latino, whatever, and do a point-of-view character on that." So now we're having this girl who's based on several kids that I actually know who aren't really invested in African culture. She [Queen Divine Justice] was meant to be that voice. What I wanted to do was to have that kid that I know, that kid that I'd grown up with, have a religious experience of sorts, with African culture.

I mentioned a scene in which Black Panther and Captain American are standing atop a building in New York, trying to figure out how they are going to work together to ensure that people get home safely from the throng who have assembled to see Black Panther in the flesh.[17]

> **Priest:** What's amusing about that—and it's another thing I'd forgotten about until you just brought it up—was that you skip ahead 15 years or whatever it was, and now it's Barack Obama in Berlin and people are going, "We can't believe these people came out to see Barack Obama." Then you go years beyond that and it's the *Black Panther* film that opened so big. I couldn't believe who went out to see the Black Panther film, so it was like what I was writing at the time was this kind of phenomenon where the people of Harlem, or wherever that was, it was a mythic persona that had come to visit them. Not Captain America. Black Panther.

## A LIFE OF SURPRISE

Assumption and surprise permeate our daily lives.[18] And it's an absolute delight to let Christopher Priest take you on a guided tour of the kingdoms of assumption we generate and live in every day. By taking such a journey, one is made increasingly aware of just how dangerous and misleading faulty assumptions can be. Maybe in the end, the point is not so much to avoid making assumptions, as it is to become aware of just how ubiquitously they shape and constrain our thoughts. By doing so, one might be inspired to continually challenge one's unconscious assumptions, cultivate a life of surprise, and, maybe, on occasion, change one's mind.

# NOTES

1. *Black Panther* #8 (1999).
2. Eliot (1871), p. 844.
3. *Black Panther* #8 (1999).
4. *Black Panther* #9 (1999).
5. Friston (2010).
6. Jordan (2013).
7. Koziol et al. (2012).
8. Haidt & Joseph (2004).
9. *Jurassic Park* (1993 motion picture).
10. Beginning in *Black Panther* #1 (1998).
11. *House* (2004–2012 television series).
12. *Black Panther* #5 (1998).
13. An experimental line of Marvel Comics titles often telling darker, more mature stories.
14. Levchak (2018).
15. *Black Panther* #13 (1999).
16. *Black Panther* #20 (2000).
17. *Black Panther* #6 (1998).
18. Bargh & Chartrand (1999).

# III

# DEADLIEST OF THE SPECIES

Women of Wakanda are strong because women are strong, called "the deadliest of the species" sometimes as a caution against underestimating them.[1] Among feline species, it is frequently the females who hunt most for prey.[2] In the land whose people worship a panther god, the goddess Bast, they know what mighty warriors their women can be—each fully warrior and fully woman.[3]

**NOTES**

1. Skeem et al. (2005).
2. Bradshaw (2017); Dohner (2017).
3. *Black Panther* #1–6 (2009).

# 9

# BLACK GIRL MAGIC

## BLACK WOMEN AS LEADERS OF WAKANDA

### Apryl A. Alexander

*"The empowerment of black women constitutes therefore the empowerment of our entire community."*

—race scholar Kimberlé Crenshaw[1]

*"We are the Dora Milaje! Cherished by no man, but adored by the goddess herself!"*
—Dora Milaje pledge[2]

**M**edia representation of diverse and dynamic Black figures has been largely absent. Further, Black women remain largely underrepresented in the media and are often relegated to stereotypical tropes.[3] The media may serve as an agent of gender socialization, especially for Black youth.[4] Black adolescents tend to view more media than non-Black adolescents.[5] Adolescents with homogenous families and communities may be missing important narratives in navigating their social lives.[6] Media can provide youth with an opportunity to safely explore their identity and how others socialize. Therefore, it is important for media to be truly representative, diverse, and devoid of stereotypes, and to present dynamic and diverse Black women across all media (e.g., television, movies, theater).

*Black Panther* has long been lauded for its portrayal of Black characters in the comics. The presence and abundance of Black women and their contributions in Wakanda are notable throughout the series. Its women hold leadership roles, are not background characters, and contribute significantly to the story. For instance, the Dora Milaje are bold, strong protectors of King T'Challa. However, their introduction to the *Black Panther* series was controversial, as their portrayal can be viewed as misogynist. Those concerns are later remedied, and the Dora Milaje are given more agency and independence.

## DEFYING TROPES

The Dora Milaje, the Adored Ones, are strong, resilient warriors of Wakanda. They are King T'Challa's bodyguards, often referred to as his "concomitants," whom he trusts to protect him and fight alongside him.[7] In the film *Black Panther*, the Dora Milaje are fierce, powerful warriors who are crucial to the final battle against Erik Killmonger.[8] Wakandan society displays gender egalitarianism in showing that both men and women have the physicality, intellect, and strength to serve as warriors and in positions of power. Moreover, the portrayal of the Dora Milaje aligns with *Afrofuturist feminism*, "the shared central tenets of Afrofuturism and black feminist thought and reflects a literary tradition in which people of African descent and transgressive feminist practices born of or from across the Afrodiaspora are key to a progressive future."[9] *Afrodiaspora* or *African diaspora* refers to people of African descent involuntarily dispersed during the transatlantic slave trade.[10] Afrofuturist feminism centers Black women from across the Afrodiaspora and their experiences while rejecting heteropatriarchy.[11] Indeed, Afrofuturists attempts to redefine notions of blackness and gender through science fiction and fantasy. *Black Panther* depicts its female characters' narratives, strengths, flaws, and internal and external conflicts while highlighting empowerment and dignity.[12]

The art and styling of the Dora Milaje also incorporates Afrofuturism. Images of Black women dressed in Afrocentric attire with their hair in its natural state is one demonstration of pushing against Eurocentric beauty standards. Throughout their appearances, the Dora Milaje are adorned with their hair in its natural state and in African (or African-inspired) clothing. In the West, Black hair has long been politicized and sometimes criminalized. In the last few years, braids, afros, and locs have been banned from schools, sports, and even the military in the United States. Thus, depicting the Dora Milaje and other Black female characters proudly wearing their natural hair is an act of defiance and resistance. There are rare moments where their hair is straightened, or they are dressed in more Westernized clothing (typically when they are situated in the United States). For instance, during their initial appearance in the series, the Dora Milaje dress in tight red dresses with their hair straightened or relaxed.[13] The moment when Okoye removes her wig while in her red gown is significant in further rejecting Western, Eurocentric beauty standards.

What makes the Dora Milaje unique is that their depiction does not follow the typical tropes of Black women in media. Film historian Lisa Anderson has noted that depictions of Black women in media have given them limited range and harmful tropes. From the "mammy" (the happy-go-lucky caregiver of others but not herself) to the "jezebel" (the sexually aggressively woman) to the "angry Black woman" (one who is loud, aggressive, and sassy), these tropes have been pervasive throughout media. Black female characters or actresses are typecast into these tropes, which continue to perpetuate negative stereotypes about Black women. The Dora Milaje are warriors, fighters, leaders, and protectors. When the comic book antagonist Man-Ape reminisces about the benefits of old, tribal ways and traditions, American–turned–Dora Milaje Chanté Giovanni Brown (also known as Queen Divine Justice) chimes in, "Where women were enslaved and mutilated," reflecting on the patriarchal traditions.[14] Defiance of these tropes is a welcome change from other media representations of Black women, which often rely on the stereotypical tropes that have been long established.

What about the "strong Black woman" (SBW) trope? This trope reflects a perception that Black women are naturally strong, resilient, and self-sacrificing. In the idealized stereotype of the SBW, she is a self-sacrificing individual because of her high level of caregiving responsibility, not complaining or showing weakness because of her desire or need to put others—typically her family, friends, and work—before herself.[15] While the SBW trope and stereotype appear positive on the surface level, it is detrimental to Black women. This trope has also become a stereotype in real life, including among Black women. Holding the SBW stereotype has been found to be linked with negative physical and mental health outcomes and psychological distress.[16] Additionally, research has found that Black college students who endorse SBW appear to be less likely to seek therapy when they need it.[17] Emotional suppression associated with SBW can result in negative coping strategies, such as excessive drinking and eating, and contribute to adverse health consequences in Black women (e.g., disproportionate rates of cardiovascular disease).[18] Researchers have also found that while Black women endorse the Strong Black Woman stereotype, non-Black people do as well. For instance, White people perceive Black people as more tolerant of pain.[19] In fact, this phenomenon extends to the medical sports field where Black athletes undergoing medical treatment are less likely to receive pain medications, receive fewer pain medications when they do receive them, and are less likely to receive analgesics for fractures in emergency rooms.[20] Essentially, this stereotype and media trope are harming actual Black women.

Are the Dora Milaje "strong Black women" in the negative sense? Perhaps. Historically, their main loyalty was to King T'Challa and their identity was tied to protecting him. They are portrayed as strong and fearless, and display few moments of weakness and vulnerability. In later issues, the Dora Milaje bond together through training, which incorporates a lot of socio-emotional learning and emphasis on expression. The Dora Milaje benefit from having strong bonds and a sisterhood. Group therapy with Black women or "sister circles" have been found to be successful in discussing the multiple roles Black women have to hold, including the SBW. This allows for space to address strengths and setbacks Black women have to face in mainstream culture, and difficulties encountered related to racism, sexism, classism, and other forms of oppression. During the Dora Milaje initiation ceremony, Queen Shuri states, "From this moment forward, we fight together, we work together, we learn together, and we love together."[21]

## ENCOUNTERING MISOGYNOIR

Although the Dora Milaje largely defy the traditional tropes centering on Black women, there have been problematic themes related to the Dora Milaje throughout the *Black Panther* series. They are portrayed and viewed as wives-in-training for T'Challa, and T'Challa and the Dora Milaje address each other as "beloved." They speak only to the Black Panther and each other in Hausa. They are also frequently referred to as children, even if they are adult women.[22] Despite their frequent portrayal as "wives-in-training," mixed messages are sent about this title. The series also notes that this is simply a ceremonial title and T'Challa never engages in romantic or intimate relationships

with the Dora Milaje. However, tension develops when Nakia
begins having romantic feelings for T'Challa.[23] Okoye reminds
her, "We are the king's concomitants and shall remain pure
until we are released from our vow."[24] It is not entirely clear
when the Dora Milaje are released to have independent relationships or families. Nakia becomes infatuated and obsessed with
T'Challa and once he does not reciprocate her affections, she
becomes Malice and betrays T'Challa by aligning herself with
Erik Killmonger.[25] In referring to Nakia's infatuation, T'Challa
states, "A severely unbalanced child, one of my Dora Milaje,
became possessed by her emotions."[26] These historical portrayals
undermine the Afrofuturist feministic viewpoints discussed earlier. Given their loyalty to T'Challa, he is the center of their lives
and they have little agency outside of their duties to him.

The term *misogynoir* describes the anti-Black racist misogyny
and problematic intraracial gender dynamics that Black women
experience, particularly in popular culture.[27] The term's origina-
tors noted, "Racism ending without sexism ending does not help
Black women."[28] When the Dora Milaje first appear in the comics,
they have long, straight hair and dress in tight, short, red dresses or
bathrobe-type outfits with stiletto heels.[29] They are initially sex-
ualized, and misogynist remarks are made about their appearance
and their relationship to T'Challa by male characters. For instance,
Everett Ross says, "They were Amazonian teenage karate chicks
from two Wakandan tribes. Keeping them in his family as potential wives somehow kept the peace between the city dwellers and
the tribal factions of the client's kingdom. Which, no matter how
you looked at it, made the client the luckiest guy on the face of
the Earth."[30] In a later issue, he says, "If I had two gorgeous high
school karate chicks to play with, I'd be like a fat kid with ice
cream."[31] These comments undermine their intellect and ability
to serve as essential warriors for the Black Panther.

Author and columnist Ta-Nehisi Coates has remarked on the
concerning historical portrayal of the Dora Milaje in the comics.

In an interview, he said, "I was uncomfortable with the notion of the Dora Milaje—a scantily clad troop of female bodyguards devoted to the Black Panther. It felt like a male fantasy, they seemed to me almost to be jewelry for the Black Panther."[32] Thus, in Coates's *Black Panther* stories, he countered the historical portrayal of the Dora Milaje. The artists maintained their beauty without sexualizing them. Additionally, Coates depicts a lesbian relationship between Aneka and Ayo, two former Dora Milaje, in his first issue.[33] Ayo and Aneka offer resistance to the Dora Milaje's patriarchal system. *Black Panther: World of Wakanda* further shifts the narrative of the Dora Milaje to a less patriarchal and misogynist lens, citing in its first page, "An ancient tradition originally designed to help keep the peace among the rival tribes, the Dora Milaje used to also be potential wives-in-training for the king, but that aspect has since fallen by the wayside."[34] In the film, Okoye has to struggle between loyalty to her husband and loyalty to her country. In other contexts, where she would be forced to submit, she does not. Same with Nakia—does she continue to be an activist for the marginalized individuals and other African countries, or remain in Wakanda serving T'Challa's wishes? In later issues of the comics, the Dora Milaje and other female characters shift their loyalties and alliances from specific men (mainly T'Challa) to the country of Wakanda itself. Mistress Zola notes, "What we just did—severing our ties with T'Challa—breaks with centuries of tradition. This decision was as unprecedented as it was necessary. We are in a difficult place, you who are the fiercest women of Wakanda. I will not offer you easy, empty words. But I will say that as Dora Milaje we are more than servants to any one man or woman—we serve Wakanda."[35]

## LEADERSHIP AND BLACK GIRL MAGIC

One character says of T'Challa's sister Shuri, "She is the child of T'Chaka, the former king of Wakanda, and one of the greatest to ever don the habit of the Black Panther. She has enjoyed the same upbringing, education, and training as T'Challa. Had he not claimed the mantle first, we would doubtlessly be addressing her as Black Panther today."[36] Even after Shuri becomes Black Panther, people in the real world and in the comics continue to refer to her as Shuri while calling T'Challa the Black Panther.[37]

The term *Black Girl Magic* was popularized by CaShawn Thompson in 2013 "to celebrate the beauty, power, and resilience of Black women."[38] *Black Panther* depicts a technologically advanced African nation where the women—Princess Shuri, Queen Ramonda, Okoye, and the Dora Milaje—represent the very definition of Black Girl Magic.[39] The term has developed beyond just a catchphrase and has been incorporated into the Black feminist movement, as a way to recognize the accomplishments, successes, and leadership of Black women. As previously noted, gender egalitarianism allows for the women of Wakanda to serve in leadership positions and be well-respected members in their society.

Princess Shuri, daughter of King T'Chaka and Queen Ramonda and younger sister of T'Challa, is depicted as a super-genius. She is the chief science officer of Wakanda; her intellect and training in technology have led her to create many inventions used in Wakanda. Not only is she intelligent, but she is a skilled fighter and highly witty. Her intellect, training, and royal status allow her to take on the mantle of the Black Panther when T'Challa is critically injured by Doctor Doom.[40] Her path to the mantle Black Panther does not go unquestioned, however. Many doubt her capability as leader, including her own mother and herself. This is not far removed from experiences of Black women in leadership. *Imposter syndrome* refers to a situation when individuals find it hard to believe that they personally deserve credit for their achievements or are convinced that they are frauds and others will discover this despite their competence. This phenomenon frequently occurs with women leaders and has been noted as a frequent experience of Black women in leadership. Further, persistence has been found to be an important variable that influences success and achievement.[41] Shuri eventually begins to find her strength in holding the mantle of the Black Panther and forge her own legacy.

Media incorporating an Afrofuturist perspective is often political.[42] The *Black Panther* motion picture changed the narrative for Nakia from being a member of the Dora Milaje who falls for T'Challa in her comic book depiction to an activist who is focused on protecting those in need, rather than pursuing a relationship with T'Challa. In the film, Nakia is portrayed as an activist who is introduced as rescuing a group of captive women and girls in another African nation. Though she returns to Wakanda to help T'Challa mourn and support his transition as new ruler of Wakanda, she continues to discuss her wishes to help refugees of other countries. Some have remarked that her activism reflects that of the #BringBackOurGirls movement, following the capture of young women by the Boko Haram.[43] In the film portrayal, it is apparent that T'Challa is enamored of her and values her principles. Again, although she returned to Wakanda to support her home country, she makes it clear that she will only be a queen (and his wife), if it is her choice. The writers of the movie may have deliberately incorporated a more Afrofuturist feminism framework in their choices, as one of the key tenets of feminism and Black feminism is the ability to choose one's path in life, relationship, and work.

## REPRESENTATION MATTERS

*Black Panther* stories provide a narrative that Black women are dynamic and multidimensional. Women can be strong warriors and leaders. Tropes that have long been supported through various forms of media are beginning to shift. The representations of Black women in Wakanda not only debunk common stereotypes but offer viewers to see aspects of black-ness that are multidimensional and allow Black girls and women see themselves in these representations. Afrofuturist feminism does not reinforce racism, sexism, and heteronorma-tivity and Afrofuturism examines the current problems faced by Black people and provides critical interpretations of the past and future.[44] The notion of Afrofuturist feminism and Black Girl Magic in media helps create fictional role models and a diverse array of figures to admire and aspire to. Additionally, it allows viewers to see Black women successfully navigate lead-ership. Despite discrimination, stereotypes, and biases, women of color have made huge strides in terms of career achieve-ment and leadership in the last several decades.[45] There has also been a growing number of women as heads of state across the diaspora, including Jamaica, Brazil, Trinidad and Tobago, and Costa Rica. With the movie grossing over $1 billion world-wide at the box office, more people have exposure to *Black Panther* and the women of Wakanda than ever before. Despite the underrepresentation of women of color in leadership roles, women of color leaders can promote positive changes in insti-tutions and organizations with their unique skills, values, and perspectives.[46] Afrofuturist feminist depictions, such as *Black Panther*, demonstrate the importance of representation in the media, particularly for Black adolescents who are in greatest need of these depictions for their own identity formation.

## NOTES

1. Crenshaw (1992).
2. *Black Panther* #3 (2016).
3. Ellithorpe & Bleakley (2016).
4. Anyiwo et al. (2018).
5. Ellithorpe & Bleakley (2016).
6. Ellithorpe & Bleakley (2016).
7. *Black Panther* #1 (1998).
8. *Black Panther* (2018 motion picture).

9. Morris (2012), p. 154.

10. Harris (1982/1993).

11. Morris (2012).

12. Faithful (2018).

13. *Black Panther* #1 (1998).

14. *Black Panther* #34 (1998).

15. Beauboeuf-Lafontant (2007).

16. Watson-Singleton (2017).

17. Romero (2000).

18. Watson & Hutner (2016).

19. Hoffman & Trawalter (2016); Trawalter & Hoffman (2015); Waytz et al. (2015).

20. Druckman et al. (2017).

21. *Black Panther: World of Wakanda* #1 (2016).

22. *Black Panther* #35 (1998).

23. *Black Panther* #3 (1998).

24. *Black Panther* #11 (1998).

25. *Black Panther* #24 (1998).

26. *Black Panther* #15 (1998).

27. Bailey & Trudy (2018).

28. Bailey & Trudy (2018).

29. *Black Panther* #1 (1998).

30. *Black Panther* #2 (1998).

31. *Black Panther* #6 (1998).

32. Gray (2016).

33. *Black Panther* #1 (2016).

34. *Black Panther: World of Wakanda* #1 (2016).

35. *Black Panther: World of Wakanda* #3 (2016).

36. *Black Panther* #2 (2008).

37. e.g., *Shuri* #1 (2018).

38. Wilson (2016).

39. Allen (2018).

40. *Black Panther* #3 (2008).

41. Vasquez (2013).

42. Yaszek (2006).

43. Allen (2018).

44. Morris (2012).

45. Vasquez (2013).

46. Vasquez (2013).

# 10

# WOMEN IN COMBAT

## THE DORA MILAJE AND THE IMPACT OF MILITARY LIFE

### Travis Adams & Jenna Busch

> *"I do not believe in using women in combat,*
> *because females are too fierce."*
>
> —anthropologist Margaret Mead[1]

*"You are so much more than your service."*
—Ayo to Aneka[2]

The history of the world has been molded through war and conflict, and, for most of that history, women have been excluded from fields in military service. While gender roles have often kept women from progressing in their careers, many militarized nations have kept women from specific military occupational specialties involving direct combat. Historically, women have been given more traditional roles, such as cooks, nurses, and personnel in charge of laundry and administrative tasks.[3]

Despite some people's objections to the role of women in

a combat zone, history has shown that not only do women have the abilities required for combat, but that many women have borne the scars of war for centuries. Poems of a Warrior-Queen go back as far back as 3500–1800 BCE,[4] paintings of women brandishing weapons within fortress walls, in the 1400s a 16-year-old woman led the French in victory over the English,[5] and in 1998 Wakanda's special forces composed of women known as the Dora Milaje debuted in *Black Panther.* The Dora Milaje, a reflection of a real-life group of women called the Dahomey,[6] protect the king of Wakanda. Today, why does anyone still find it hard to believe that women have the skills, abilities, and mental resources required for combat?

## FAMILY AND SUPPORT

In the US military, there are approximately 2 million active-duty and reservist men and women, with 3 million dependents, more commonly known as spouses and children. The family is often uprooted every two to three years and must realign their lives to the military's stance on rotation of orders. These moves have been shown to have a significant impact on the family system development within active-duty and reserve families.[7] Moving, along with the uncertainty of their parents' safety, has a direct effect on children's psychological makeup, which could impact the way they view others, their intimate relationships, how they handle conflict, and if their relationships are adaptive, enmeshed, or disengaged.[8]

### CHILDREN

*Ecological systems theory* suggests that each child has a direct relationship with the various environments in which he or she is placed.[9] The smallest reciprocating environment is the *microsystem*, the smallest system. Within this system a child's family, school, and neighborhood have an influence on how the child behaves as well as how the people within this system react to the child—a *bidirectional influence*.[10] When a parent is taken out of the system for a deployment and returns months or years later, a strain is placed on the family system.[11] Reunion of families have been shown to have an effect on higher rates of anxiety, marital stress, and sometimes physical violence.[12] This can also happen when the parent doesn't return from combat. A very young Killmonger's life changes when his father is taken out of the picture. Killmonger later speaks about how T'Chaka should have taken him back to Wakanda and how that support would have made a difference in his life. King T'Chaka, who is Killmonger's uncle in the film version, expresses the same concerns.[13]

Ecological systems theory expands past the family unit and encompasses community, religious organizations, and even the period in which one lives. As the systems expand outward, the bidirectional influence expands as well, the *mesosystem* (connections), *exosystem* (indirect environment), *macrosystem* (social and cultural views), and *chronosystem* (era and changes over time), all have a direct influence on one another.[14] When T'Challa addresses the United Nations, he understands that people, places, and countries have an impact on the surroundings in which we live. As he decides to share the Wakandan intellectual wealth with the world for the betterment of all, he simply states, "More connects us than separates us."[15] As the system grows, the bidirectional influence interaction follows along, the mesosystem has a direct impact on the exosystem as well as the microsystem, and so on and so forth.[16] Because these systems are bidirectional, we may see two children of the same family react differently over time as their personality traits, temperament, and even biological factors impact how they are treated and how they treat others, as is the case with T'Challa and his sister Shuri. When looking at the new Black Panther suits Shuri makes for T'Challa, they reference his design and how her designs have gone above and beyond what he thought possible.[17] Although she is a fighter, we see where each of their strengths lie throughout the *Black Panther* movie.

When looking at children of service members, an understanding of connection and rapport has eased and reduced tension to aid them in their transition.[18] Programs have been designed to ease students' transitions, acclimating them to new schools and cities or sometimes new countries. These programs also develop trainings for staff who work within these communities, with an emphasis on trainings in grief, resilience, coping, and the impact of PTSD on children of military households.[19] In the *Black Panther* comics, we find the women of the Dora Milaje becoming a support system for each other. They even refer to the Queen Mother Ramonda as Mother.[20] As Mistress Zola says to the Dora Milaje, "We are in a difficult place, you who are the fiercest women of Wakanda. I will not offer you easy, empty words. But I will say that as Dora Milaje we are more than servants to any one man or woman—we serve Wakanda. And let us not forget, we also serve each other. Together we will always rise."[21]

## SUPPORT

Approximately 38 percent of active-duty military members have children, while roughly 42 percent are married.[22] Unlike the US military until the repeal of its "Don't Ask, Don't Tell" policy in 2010 and the Dahomey Amazons whom the Dora Milaje reflect,[23] the Wakandan ruler's all-female guard freely have relationships with both men and women.

While deployed, the family unit faces multiple uncertainties and health issues arise. Since 2001, the US military has realized that military life, along with combat experience, not only takes a toll on the service member but on the entire family. Spouses often report struggles with depression, sleep problems, anxiety disorders, adjustment issues, and acute stress.[24] Programs have

# WOMAN IN COMBAT:
# INTERVIEW WITH MARINE VETERAN TARA BACHMAN

Marine Corps veteran Tara Bachman spoke with us about being a woman in a largely male military unit. We began with how combat experience has impacted her life.

**Tara Bachman:** As far as being a woman and coming back home, war has affected me. I'm really strong-minded, set in my ways. I was in the Marine Corps for 15 years. I never got disrespected. I earned my respect with a lot of the men I've worked with and served with over there and it's really affected my life . . . When a woman is very independent, and kind of knows herself very well, it seems to come off. It's affected me when I didn't think I was going to come home to my daughter because my daughter was in kindergarten when I went over and I was 30, my life was in jeopardy when I was over there and it was an experience.

**Busch:** What changes would you like to see happen for women in the military?

**Bachman:** I think they need to really look past the physical side and into the mental side, the things that I did while I was in the service I was able to hold my own and do my thing because of that strength. But I can also put myself in other people's shoes, or other women's shoes, and see the difficulties. I would like to see women be integrated in training and boot camp.

been developed to aid the family system before, during, and after deployment.[25] The Department of Defense Educational Activity, along with nonprofits and other government agencies, have implemented programs to aid families of service members with their transitions and during times of parents' deployment and/or to help them positively cope with frequent moves.[26] Culture inside and outside the military impacts the family's lives just as much as the service member's,[27] such as when duty causes stress between W'Kabi and Okoye[28] or when Aneka defies her military duties to save her beloved Ayo.[29]

Implementing programs that aid in connecting others with similar experiences have been shown to benefit the spouses and children of service members;[30] however, those programs have been mainly designed for spouses who are wives, not husbands.[31] While the intent is to bring spouses and families together, male spouses have been found to feel ostracized from the community as they are the minority of military spouses.[32] This exclusion shows a reduction in esteem, sense of belonging, and possibly even has an effect on the spouses' self-worth.[33] This may account for the discrepancy in dissolved marriages of male and female service members. Male service members who deploy are 2.6 percent likely to return to a dissolved marriage whereas 6.6 percent of female service members return to a marriage ending, with a direct correlation to the longer a deployment the higher the likelihood of divorce will occur.[34]

Stressors of the military and multiple deployments, coupled with responsibilities at home, have had a tremendous impact on service members and significant others as well. Marital dissolutions, or divorces, may occur in any relationship; however, divorce rates following combat deployments have been shown to be significantly higher than divorce rates among civilians or service members who did not deploy in direct combat. When a military service woman is discharged from the military, she is three times more likely to become a single parent, compared

# Interview with Ruth E. Carter,

## Academy Award® Winner for
## Best Costume Design for *Black Panther*<sup>35</sup>

Jenna Busch

Ruth E. Carter, the costume designer for the Marvel film *Black Panther*, spoke with us about creating armor for the Dora Milaje, the female warrior troop that protects the ruler of Wakanda.

**Ruth E. Carter:** We had the opportunity to use vibranium and the concept to vibranium, so it was used as a thread throughout their costumes, their arms, their chest, their legs. It was a woven piece. So it was like your chain mail might be. If you look at the Dora Milaje and you see the striations on their arms and legs to mimic scarification, it also lets you know that these metal elements are woven into the fibers of the costume and its vibranium is the strongest metal known to man. So that's our concept here. It's mostly soft sculpture that would be molded pieces. I know a lot of armor in the past for women has been molded, handcrafted to the female form and then worn, but we didn't go down that route. The pieces were molded out of rubber so the stunt people can actually do their work.

She continued speaking about making the armor functional, as opposed to some of the armor you see in fictional scenarios for women.

**Carter:** I just felt that our women were completely covered. When our women go into battle, they have functional armor. When women [on-screen] have traditionally gone to battle, they don't have functional armor, they have armor that is not functional, they have heels on, they just aren't dressed appropriately for battle. When you're a superhero, I guess that's okay—when you're Wonder Woman. When you're Dora Milaje, you have to protect the king. We wanted the look and feel of it to feel more serious. And, therefore, we covered them from head to toe. But we also made it beautiful by giving them the jewelry under the armor: We left the high sheen on the armor so that it would feel like jewelry. And we designed the harness that wraps around the body to wrap around the body in a very sensuous and sexy way, but not to disrupt what they needed to do, and make it even feel like it's possibly a harness that could be used for climbing. I just feel like it was more effective and that it was still sexy and beautiful. They still look like women but they could seriously kick some ass.

to active duty.[36] Females returning from war are more likely
to receive a diagnosis of depression, compared to their male
counterparts, who would receive a diagnosis of posttraumatic
stress disorder.[37] In the film, we see Okoye, who is a general in
the Dora Milaje, in a romantic relationship with W'Kabi. They
face issues over whose side they're on. Okoye puts her military duty above her relationship, as we see when W'Kabi says,
"Would you kill me, my love?" Okoye answers, "For Wakanda?
Without question." Her service causes a rift between them.[38]

## RETURNING FROM WAR

The impact trauma has on the family has a direct correlation to the service members' ability to reintegrate into society
and relationships following deployments.[39] Conversely, the
more service members distance themselves from their support
system, the more difficult they find life post-deployment to be.
Among the areas in the life of a veteran/service, returning from
war, that have been shown to be major stressors for themselves
as well as their support system are interpersonal relationships,
deployment- or military-related items, health concerns, death
of a loved one, daily needs (financial, housing, transportation),
and employment or school.[40] Family support is a key component of service members' ability in recovery and their level of
reintegration into a healthy lifestyle.[41] In the comics, a beaten
Shuri, who has been the Black Panther and Queen of Wakanda,
finds her support system in the spirits of her female ancestors, all
of whom were warriors and leaders.[42] Reintegration is essential
to the deployment cycle for active-duty service members and
impacts their ability not only to be a strong role model and to
parent but also to be an effective soldier.[43]

## MILITARY ROLES

Women, who were given the ability to serve in the US military before they got the right to vote,[44] have played integral roles in the military Since 1901, women have been officially encouraged to fulfill ranks within the military.[45] Although women serving in the armed forces were primarily support staff, some women were moved to the front lines as nurses, while others disguised themselves as men pushed their way to combat.[46] In 2015, Defense Secretary Ashton Carter announced a policy removing the ban on combat military operation specialties for women, allowing women to serve in combat roles in the US armed forces.[47] The Dahomey Amazons, one of the inspirations for the Dora Milaje, served as far back as the 19th century in the Republic of Benin as the primary bodyguards for the king, beginning their training as teens.[48]

Many service members view women in the military and in a post-military setting through the lens of gender roles.[49] In the film *Black Panther*, we see this gender role expectation being used as an advantage. The general population still doesn't look at women as a physical threat. In the club scene, Nakia and Okoye are discounted as agents, whereas those looking for them spot General Ross and the henchmen of Ulysses Klaue quite quickly. That allows the Dora Milaje to gain the advantage.[50] Conversely, in America, many of the studies currently being done focus directly on males who have served in a combat zone, neglecting the women who are directly or indirectly placed into combat and the important roles they can play,[51] while also overlook the fact that women have had direct combat exposure since the Revolutionary War. Some critics argue that if women were incorporated fully into military service, that would take away from the warrior mentality and cause future wars to be lost.[52] We see this in the comics in the introduction of the Dora Milaje, wearing clothing that initially marks them as women at a party rather than warriors ready to fight.[53]

## BREAKING DOWN THE WALLS

With women still relatively new to active combat roles in the American military, there are issues that need to be addressed, from the expectation of gender roles to support for husbands who stay at home to designing armor for women's bodies. If we continue to shine a light on these issues, they're more likely to be taken seriously. Although women have been a part of US military history since the Revolutionary War, and over the past few years they have been able to join any occupational specialty, there is still a long way to go before female service members gain full equality and family support. With the heightened roles of fictional women in combat, issues are being brought more deliberately into the public eye; thus these fictional representations are bringing more attention to what needs to be addressed. By talking to women veterans about their military experience, it could actually cause a discussion that leads them to the help that they want and need.[54]

*"We will continue to serve, but from this day forth,*
   *our eyes will be open.*
*We will serve, but we will also think and act for ourselves,*
   *and what we think best."*
—Ayo to Aneka[55]

## NOTES

1. Mead & Métraux (1979).
2. *Black Panther: World of Wakanda* #2 (2017).
3. Cook (2006).
4. Kaul et al. (2014).
5. Vale et al. (2018).
6. Coleman (2018).
7. Ruff & Keim (2014).
8. Rothbaum et al. (2002).
9. Skinner (2012).

10. Ryan (2001).
11. Snyder et al. (2016).
12. Lester et al. (2010).
13. *Black Panther* (2018 motion picture).
14. Ryan (2001).
15. *Black Panther* (2018 motion picture).
16. Vélez-Agosto et al. (2017).
17. *Black Panther* (2018 motion picture).
18. Capuzzi & Stauffer (2015).
19. Francisco & Gorman (2010).
20. *Black Panther* #1 (2016).
21. *Black Panther: World of Wakanda* #2 (2017).
22. Sayer et al. (2010).
23. Coleman (2018).
24. Gewirtz et al. (2011).
25. Murdoch et al. (2006).
26. Masten (2013).
27. Sheppard et al. (2010).
28. *Black Panther* (2018 motion picture).
29. *Black Panther* #1 (2016).
30. Gewirtz et al. (2011).
31. Southwell et al. (2016).
32. Southwell et al. (2016).
33. Williams et al. (2016).
34. Southwell et al. (2016).
35. Deb (2019).
36. Kelley (2006).
37. Maguen et al. (2010).
38. *Black Panther* (2018 motion picture).
39. Yan et al. (2013).
40. Yan et al. (2013).
41. Smith et al. (2013).
42. *Black Panther* #1 (2016).
43. Doyle et al. (2005).
44. Hughes (2018).
45. McNulty (2012).
46. Jensen (2008).
47. Rosenberg et al. (2015).
48. Coleman (2018).
49. Elnitsky et al. (2013).
50. *Black Panther* (2018 motion picture).
51. Yan et al. (2013).
52. DeGroot (2001).
53. *Black Panther* #1 (1988).
54. Murdoch et al. (2006).
55. *Black Panther: World of Wakanda* #2 (2017).

# 11

# SHURI

## A HERO ASCENDS

### Craig Pohlman

*"Moved earth and heaven, that which we are, we are,*
*One equal temper of heroic hearts,*
*Made weak by time and fate, but strong in will*
*To strive, to seek, to find, and not to yield."*
—poet Alfred, Lord Tennyson[1]

*"I've dreamed about this my whole life. I thought it*
*would be glorious, a moment of great joy and excitement . . .*
*not one filled with so much pain and loss."*
—Shuri[2]

What is a hero? There are criteria and definitions, to be sure. In fact, the field of heroism science has emerged to formally study heroism.[3] Heroes have traits such as resilience and selflessness, and they provide inspiration.[4] But like many things in the world, such as an obscenity or a duck, we know a hero when we see one. When we look at Shuri, we see a hero—someone who ascends to the level of heroism.

Heroes are those whom others judge to have behaved heroically.[5] This circular logic captures the subjective nature of heroism. Those around the would-be hero decide whether or not her actions match up with what we seem to intuitively know as heroism. When we look at Shuri, what do we see?

## HEROISM EXPLAINED

A narrow definition of a hero is someone who chooses to take physical risks on behalf of others, despite the possibility of suffering severe consequences or death.[6] This definition has been expanded because physical risk does not apply to everyone we consider to be heroic,[7] even though physical peril tends to be more heavily weighted in perceptions of heroism.[8] The phrase "banality of heroism" was coined to express the notion that heroic deeds can be performed by anybody at any time, not simply by an exceptional few.[9]

Heroism takes many forms, each with its own definition and set of criteria. Twelve subtypes have been identified, with only two involving risk of physical peril: civil (courageous civilians) and military/martial.[10] Unlike military heroism, civil heroism lacks a clearly defined code of conduct.[11] Even though Shuri may not always operate within Wakanda's formal defense apparatus, she is connected to her nation's warrior history and code. She does not fit the mold of courageous civilian.

Thought leaders have yet to settle the issue of compensation for heroic actions and duty.[12] Is heroism about *self-actualization*, a pinnacle state of being, and the best in human nature? Does earning money or manifest reward for acting heroically diminish the heroism? Is it even possible for any action to be devoid of reward?

Numerous subtypes of heroism that do not involve immediate

physical danger are known collectively as *social heroism*, which promotes and defends ideals. Social heroes face significant non-physical risks, including loss of social status, sometimes to the level of ostracism[13] (think whistleblower or someone whose thinking is ahead of her time). A subtype of social heroism is scientist,[14] which certainly applies to Shuri in her role as technologist for T'Challa and Wakanda.[15] Prototypical features of heroes include bravery and moral integrity, and one peripheral feature is intelligence.[16] Social heroes strive to preserve a value or standard that is under duress, like a community or nation unraveling.[17] Considering the high ideals that could be at stake, the social hero can be perceived as even more heroic than one engaging in more physical forms of heroism.[18] As the ascendant Black Panther,[19] Shuri represents both military and social heroism. She is an inspirational keystone for a nation and a people.

## HEROISM EXPLORED

Heroism is a social activity.[20] The actions of the hero must, in some fashion, benefit at least one other person. So however brave, for example, a lone castaway may be on a deserted island, fighting for his survival, he is not technically a hero (if he ever makes it off the island and his story provides inspiration to others, that's a different story). An action-taker becomes a hero when five criteria are met:

1. Actions are in service to others in need or in the defense of an ideal, such as when M'Baku's people rescue the wounded T'Challa despite previous friction between them.[21]
2. Actions are voluntary. Shuri acts voluntarily, and against the orders of T'Challa, when she investigates dangerous seismic activity in Wakanda's vibranium mine.[22]
3. The action-taker recognizes possible risks and costs of the

actions. Zuri and W'Kabi hold off Morlun, knowing they must risk their lives to buy time for Shuri and protect the comatose T'Challa.[23]

4. The action-taker is willing to make anticipated sacrifices. When the Avengers must stop Proxima Midnight from destroying the world, Shuri knowingly faces certain doom so that others might escape, and she does get killed[24] (not knowing she will return to life years later).[25]

5. The action-taker does not anticipate external gain at the time of the actions.[26] This tends to fit most superheroes and their heroic allies.

Much of Shuri's service to others is in the arena of science and technology. The motion picture establishes her as the head of research and development, serving the interests of her royal family and, of course, the people of Wakanda and all that her nation represents. When the chips are down, she steps up to help her brother reclaim the throne, including by engaging in military combat.[27] But her heroism primarily is propelled by her intellect, which greatly benefits those around her. Her talents include medical training (healing the critical gunshot wound sustained by CIA officer Everett Ross) and psychology (unscrambling the mind of Bucky Barnes). She repeatedly and unflinchingly takes actions to help others in need, even when those needs represent significant challenges to her scientific know-how.

No one has to twist Shuri's arm. Actually, she chomps at the bit to get into the action. She aspires to become the Black Panther by stepping into the ring during the annual challenge rite.[28] But her birthright presents an interesting angle. As royalty, how much choice does she really have about her life path? How voluntarily can she act when she has the expectations of generations of rulers, and an entire country, upon her?

The *exclusive model* of heroism looks at a narrow range

of extraordinary behavior, including the heroic leadership demonstrated by exceptional individuals (such as T'Challa) and outstanding examples of regular citizens' volunteerism.[29] The *inclusive model*, on the other hand, presents heroism as integral for ordinary living, looking at everyday life and widespread volunteer participation as setting norms for people to follow. About 20 percent of adults surveyed in the United States reported having carried out heroic acts in some form.[30] That number surely would be much bigger in Wakanda, where heroism is woven into the traditional fabric of society. So there is good reason to think that Shuri would be a heroic scientist even if she had just been a genius born into a non-noble family.

Heroes do more than act voluntarily. They do so even when danger, in some form, is on the table. Shuri plays an important role in the South Korea car chase, remotely driving a car for her brother who surfs it in pursuit of Ulysses Klaue. But as helpful as she is, she pilots from the safety of her lab back in Wakanda. She faces no physical danger herself, but any mistakes on her part would put her brother's life in jeopardy. Shuri faces much higher risks when the final battle with Killmonger erupts, sporting panther-shaped blaster gauntlets. She does risk the integrity of her equipment by allowing Ross to use her tech unsupervised. The comic book version of Shuri is even more pursuant of risk. She ascends to the throne of Wakanda when her brother is out of commission. As monarch, she leads Wakandan forces against the invading Atlanteans and Namor the Sub-Mariner, culminating in an epic counterassault on Atlantis.[31]

Heroes become even more heroic not only when they recognize risk, but also when they accept that they might need to make sacrifices. Shuri certainly appears to be there for her brother and her nation, helping to stave off a global race war in the process. She also accepts sacrifices, including the possibility of unforeseen loss. When Klaue attacks Wakanda, she uses the Ebony Blade to defeat Radioactive Man in physical combat.[32]

# SISTERHOOD OF SCIENCE

Gender stereotypes in science are real, including significant differences in experiences, attitudes, and perceptions of schooling and careers. Boys report more experiences with paraphernalia like electric toys, fuses, and microscopes. Girls report more experiences like knitting and planting. Interests of male students veer more toward computers, x-rays, and other technology. Female students are more likely to report interest in animal communication, rainbows, and weather. More females than males report that science is difficult to understand, and more males report that science is dangerous and more suitable for boys.[33]

With perceptions like that, the gender gap in science is not surprising, with a male to female ratio that can be as high as 3 to 1.[34] What factors likely contributed to Shuri's affinity and gift for science? Cultural socialization is immensely important. She probably has had more opportunities to tinker with scientific devices. This would have sparked curiosity and creativity, as well as normalized scientific inquiry across genders. Boys' more positive attitudes toward science are most pronounced for general science,[35] so Shuri would have been well-served to get early discipline-specific instruction, such as in physics, chemistry, or code-writing.

Good teaching would have made a difference. She probably had highly engaged learning experiences, lots of personal support and mentoring, and strong positive relationships with peers (though not necessarily in a single-gender setting). A quality teacher would have innovated and contextualized concepts.[36] Field trip to the vibranium mine, anyone? Males are drawn to career factors such as control over other people, fame, and wealth. Females, more than males, want to help others with their career paths.[37] Shuri likely had mentors who modeled science as a heroic calling.

The encounter traumatizes her and she requires counseling and mentoring from T'Challa to recover. So she sacrifices a portion of her innocence and her emotional well-being. If Shuri had known that slaying an opponent could so negatively affect her, and she still chose action, would that have made her actions even more heroic?

Shuri as scientist helps others on a wide scale. She does more than just equip her brother with kinetic energy–absorbing, nanite-controlled body armor. She takes on monumental tasks, such as designing the advanced infrastructure for Wakanda's vibranium mining operation.[38] Her inventions and technology benefit her country and its global diaspora. That heroic work may well have required sacrifices in terms of her personal life. When asked to surgically remove the Mind Stone from the Vision, she accepts risk in terms of the impending attack of the Outriders.[39] Sacrificing the Vision, comrades, or herself might be necessary. She acts knowing that the fate of the galaxy is in her hands.

## HEROISM EXEMPLIFIED

Heroes take action for selfless reasons. They don't act with the expectation of external gain. We do accept heroes earning modest compensation, such as law enforcement officers, first responders, and military personnel. Their salaries in no way detract from their heroic actions. But someone who reaps considerable reward, financial or otherwise, for heroic actions is in stark contrast with someone who draws no significant benefit.

What are the potential external gains for Shuri? She fights Killmonger[40] for the well-being of her family and friends. She recognizes that many innocent people will die or suffer if her side loses. She is defending a set of ideals about Wakanda's place in the world and its leadership role in advancing it. Heroes influence emotions, thoughts, and behavior along various dimensions, such as hidden or exposed, weak or strong, short-term or long-term, and limited or widespread.[41] As scientist and some-times-warrior, her influence may be hidden from the world at large, but it is strong, long-term, and widespread.

The ascendant Black Panther struggles with external gain. With T'Challa incapacitated, Queen Ororo taps Shuri to meet the panther god for judgment.[42] During the ensuing trials, she sneers at the difficulty level of the tasks she must pass, such as dodging arrows and meditating for six hours in a scorpion pit. Her overconfidence stems from her arduous, lifelong training and her perceived birthright. She acknowledges being over-confident but also tells herself that she was born for this and that Panther-status is hers by right. She's also driven to disprove the doubts of her mother.[43] So there are plenty of eternal gains to be had.

Shuri then tells the panther god Bast that she is ready to step out from her brother's shadow and embrace her destiny, which is a bad move on her part. Not surprisingly, Bast mocks her declaration of worthiness and turns her away, telling her that the mantle of the Black Panther is not about entitlement but sacrifice, about putting the greater good ahead of personal glory.[44] Bast has no use for external gain.

Those who face Bast and are deemed unworthy supposedly are killed, and yet Shuri is spared. She does not understand why. Reeling from her failure and without the mantle of the Panther, including the inherent powers and boosted self-confi-dence, she leads the attack against Morlun, facing him alone. In so doing, she passes Bast's ultimate trial, showing her worthi-ness by rallying without the mantle and selflessly heading into a likely suicide mission.[45] She becomes a Black Panther without expectation of external gain.

Shuri meets the five criteria of heroism: service, volun-teerism, risk-recognition, sacrifice, and action sans external gain. She also fits into three categories of heroes. *Transfigured heroes*, like Amelia Earhart and Robin Hood, are constructed in that they are molded or emerge from circumstances.[46] Becoming Panther is no cakewalk for Shuri. She has to earn it with years of training and pain, and by overcoming tremendous self-doubt. *Transformational heroes*, such as Nelson Mandela and Mahatma Gandhi, effect positive change on a societal level.[47] She is a savior of Wakanda and, likely, the greater world. Finally, *transcendent heroes*, like Abraham Lincoln and Harry Potter, ascend above all other heroic categories.[48] Even in a relatively progressive society like Wakanda, a female Black Panther transcends as a role model.

Heroes act as physical shields, protecting the defenseless. They also are psychological shields, protecting human dignity.[49] Shuri hits the mark as both kind of shield. She is in harm's way, kicking butt and taking names to keep others safe. She's also a social hero who inspires fellow Wakandans, not to mention vast audiences and countless readers.

## NOTES

1. Alfred, Lord Tennyson (1842).
2. *Black Panther* #6 (2009).
3. Efthimiou & Allison (2017).
4. Allison & Goethals (2011).
5. Allison & Goethals (2013).
6. Becker & Eagly (2004).
7. Martens (2005).
8. Franco et al. (2011).
9. Franco & Zimbardo (2006).
10. Franco et al. (2011).
11. Zimbardo (2007).
12. Franco et al. (2018).
13. Glazer & Glazer (1999).
14. Franco et al. (2011).
15. *Black Panther* (2018 motion picture).
16. Kinsella et al. (2015).
17. Franco et al. (2011).
18. Peterson & Seligman (2004).
19. *Black Panther* #6 (2009).
20. Franco et al. (2011).

21. *Black Panther* (2018 motion picture).
22. *Black Panther* #4 (2005).
23. *Black Panther* #5 (2009).
24. *New Avengers* #24 (2014).
25. *Black Panther* #8 (2016).
26. Franco et al. (2011).
27. *Black Panther* (2018 motion picture).
28. *Black Panther,* episode 1–01, "Pilot" (November 15, 2011).
29. Zimbardo et al. (2013).
30. Zimbardo et al. (2013).
31. *New Avengers* #8 (2013).
32. *Black Panther* #6 (2005).
33. Jones et al. (2000).
34. Osborne et al. (2003).
35. Osborne et al. (2003).
36. Osborne et al. (2003).
37. Jones et al. (2000).
38. *Black Panther* (2018 motion picture).
39. *Avengers: Infinity War* (2018 motion picture).
40. *Black Panther* (2018 motion picture).
41. Allison & Goethals (2013).
42. *Black Panther* #2 (2009).
43. *Black Panther* #3 (2009).
44. *Black Panther* #4 (2009).
45. *Black Panther* #6 (2009).
46. Allison & Goethals (2013).
47. Allison & Goethals (2013).
48. Allison & Goethals (2013).
49. Franco & Zimbardo (2006).

# IV
# TEMPERED
# BY
# TROUBLES

The adage, "What doesn't kill you makes you stronger,"[1] oversimplifies suffering to the point of being a lie.[2] Stress and trauma can exercise our mental faculties and make us stronger, but they can also weaken people to the point of altering personality, making life less satisfying, and causing both physical and mental illnesses.[3] When, then, do our troubles build us up? And are some people, not just those who eat heart-shaped herbs, more predisposed to recovering from them?

**NOTES**
1. Derived from "That which does not kill us makes us stronger."
   —F. Nietzsche.
2. Shpancer (2010).
3. Lovallo (2015).

# 12

# WORDS CAN HURT YOU

## DISCRIMINATION THROUGH
## NON-PHYSICAL AGGRESSION

### Brea Banks, Leandra Parris & Eric D. Wesselmann

*"Prejudice has not genuinely declined—*
*it has merely become more indirect and insidious."*

—clinical psychologist Scott O. Lilienfeld[1]

*"Guns—so primitive!"*
—Okoye[2]

**M**any forms of aggression and violence exist in both the real and fictional worlds. *Black Panther,* like many superhero stories, is ripe with intense eruptions of violence that include assault, physical attacks, murder, and wars waged with a variety of weapons. Other aggressive acts are not so readily apparent, though. These forms of violence can be subtle, overlooked, or so normalized by society that they are not always recognized as "real" aggression. Yet these everyday acts of aggression represent an insidious set of behaviors that, for some people, creates a much longer-lasting negative impact on the victim than outright violence without ever raising a weapon. Indeed, sometimes social weapons are far less sophisticated means of aggression than words and smaller, but more pervasive and ongoing, aggressions. Why expend the energy of weaponized aggression when silence or simple words will, in fact, hurt you? In the world of *Black Panther,* this means that while our heroes experience violence on a much larger scale, it may in fact be these everyday aggressions that truly wear down their overall functioning and well-being.

This is particularly true given that the majority of characters hold marginalized identities, which puts them at greater risk of experiencing these forms of aggression. Since *Black Panther's* creation, writers and artists have used this world to tell stories from the perspective of individuals whose voices were not traditionally heard, and were at times completely excluded, in comics. When readers pick up comics, they escape into fictional worlds that represent the social culture in which they live. The inability to do so for Black individuals can be experienced as a form of systematic ostracism, the mainstream culture ignoring their stories, perhaps even a form of cultural aggression. The story of T'Challa the modern Black Panther and those around him provides an opportunity for the writers to portray characters having experiences that are normal and nonheroic, such as microaggression, social exclusion, and bullying. From snide remarks about Wakanda as a country to the outright relational bullying Storm experiences after marrying T'Challa, the narrative of the *Black Panther* illustrates that physical violence is not always necessary to cause harm to another.

# REPRESENTATION AS SOCIAL INCLUSION

Ryan Coogler, director and co-writer of *Black Panther*, has described the importance of T'Challa as an example of a hero who shares his racial/ethnic background.[3] In addition to being historically underrepresented in media, when Black characters are featured, typically they are negatively stereotyped.[4] For much of comic book history, not only are Black characters stereotyped but they are also often presented as comic relief or sidekicks to the main (usually White) characters.[5] As Coogler explained, "I wanted to find a comic book character that looked like me and not just one that was on the sidelines."[6] Psychological research has found that exposure to negatively stereotyped Black characters relates to negative self-esteem among Black individuals (this pattern also occurs for other persons of color).[7]

Additionally, a *lack* of representation also may negatively impact Black individuals. When someone does not see any characters that look like them, they may feel ignored or invisible. When individuals consistently feel ignored, they also feel socially isolated and devalued, as if unwanted or unnecessary to society.[8] Both comic artists and scholars have argued that Black individuals' experiences have been ignored in comics.[9] Black artists, scholars, and fans have noted their feelings of excitement and validation when they saw Black heroes, such as the Black Panther, in part because the similarity made it easier to relate to these heroes.[10] These anecdotes parallel psychological data suggesting that media with Black main characters may provide a boost to Black adolescents' self-esteem.[11]

## MICROAGGRESSIONS

Individuals holding marginalized identities have long reported experiences with interpersonal exchanges that highlight the stereotypes that exist for their social groups, and psychologists have conducted research to understand these experiences. Given that individuals of color are today less likely to report experiences of blatant racism, as compared to the Jim Crow era between 1877 and the 1950s, psychologists have investigated the prevalence and impact of subtle forms of racism on persons of color, which seems to have become a more common experience.[12] Research suggests that even though these subtle behaviors may be unintentional and seem innocuous, they are still harmful. For example, when persons of color interact with a White person who makes comments suggesting racial diversity is unimportant or that "I don't see race/color," they experience various negative outcomes (e.g., decreased cognitive performance, feelings of invalidation).[13]

Many researchers are studying *microaggressions*, insults or slights that are perpetrated unknowingly by often well-intended individuals who are engaging in conversation, attempting to initiate small talk, meaning to give a compliment, or intending to tell a joke.[14] Those on the receiving end, however, do not interpret these verbal, or in some cases nonverbal behaviors, as flattering. For example, when T'Challa and Storm fill in as Fantastic Four members while Mister Fantastic and the Invisible Woman take a second honeymoon, the Thing refers to T'Challa as "T'Charlie."[15] Regardless of whether or not the Thing intends this as a joke, researchers have identified mispronunciations of names as microaggressive.[16] The psychology literature identifies three types of microaggression: microassaults, microinsults, and microinvalidations.[17]

*Microassaults* are comments or behaviors that are meant to be harmful to individuals holding marginalized identities.

Although, labeled as *micro*, these comments and behaviors are best interpreted as macro-level aggressions, as the purposeful and intentional nature of these slights clashes with the very definition of *micro*aggression. For example, during the Cannibal's visit to the Vatican to recruit the Black Knight, the priest who has arranged the meeting calls the Wakandans "a bunch of animal-worshiping pagans."[18] Once in combat with the Wakandans, the Black Knight further perpetuates this view of the Wakandans, as he refers to a Wakandan pilot as a "heathen" and the T'Challa as a "savage," both of which are meant to be intentionally slurring and not technically microaggressive, because microaggression refers to behaviors and comments that are perpetrated unintentionally.[19] That said, these types of experiences unfortunately are common for persons of color.

For the other two types of microaggressions, the offending individual often does not intend harm to a specific person. *Microinsults* convey rudeness or insensitivity surrounding an individual's group identification. For example, in response to learning of Wakanda's restricted airspace during a briefing at the White House, a general uses a racial slur when asking where Africans "get off telling us they've got a 'no-fly' zone over their hatched hut?"[20] This comment is loaded with problems. The character's use of a racist term represents the higher-level macroaggression, or what researchers define as a microassault.[21] However, if one were to ignore the use of the blatantly racist slur, one would find that Wallace views Wakanda's refusal to allow the United States to fly where they please as absurd, because he interprets Wakanda as a small, poor country, instead of the most technologically advanced country in the world, which has never succumbed to foreign influence.

After receiving nonverbal feedback from others in the room in the form of silence and blank stares, Wallace recognizes that Secretary of State Dondi Reese (who is Black) is present and offers his apologies for his language, not for his view that Wakanda has no right to implement a no-fly zone. Wallace continues to put his foot in his mouth, as his apology to Reese is also microinsulting: "I'm sorry! You know I don't mean *you* when I say . . . I mean, they're nothing like you." This exchange between Wallace and Reese aligns perfectly with the following statements that have been identified in the microaggression literature: "You're not like the rest of them," "You're different," "If only there were more of them like you," "We have never been around a black person this friendly," or "I could hang with you, you are not intimidating to me."[22] Wallace's comments directed at Reese *may* have been intended to be benign or reassuring, but instead communicate insult to Reese—more specifically, that Wallace views her social group unfavorably. Even though her brown skin puts her in the same racial group as Wakandans, Wallace does not view her as *other*, likely because of her education, citizenship, and status as the secretary of state. In assuming that Reese will interpret his follow-up comments favorably, he further negates the fact that she is in fact Black and has not been exempt from the Black experience.

Another type of microaggression, called *microinvalidation*, constitutes behaviors that invalidate the experiences of individuals with marginalized identities. Microinvalidations include statements that serve to dismiss, nullify, or exclude the thoughts and feelings of someone[23]—such as asking someone, "How did you learn to speak English so well?," as though someone from his or her background is assumed to struggle with language acquisition. Another example would be the emphasis on the need to "just work hard" to succeed, which negates the very real barriers that often exist for marginalized populations. After T'Challa's announcement that Wakanda will begin sharing culture and resources with the rest of the world, he is met with some skepticism. One United Nations representative asks, "With all due respect, what can a nation of farmers offer the rest of the world?"[24] This is a clear example of invalidating the experiences and relevancy of Wakanda.

Although much of the psychological literature on micro-aggressions has focused on race, such insults can be relevant to any identity that a person holds. Further, microaggressions are not enacted for one identity at a time, as they often occur at the intersection of the identities a person holds. Hudlin's portrayal of two of the main female leads illustrates this well. Shuri and Storm hold several identities in the series that at times lead to inner conflict and impact the way they are treated by others. Storm, a mutant woman born to an American father and a Kenyan princess, is orphaned at an early age, survives by operating as a thief, and becomes a member of the X-Men, all before marrying T'Challa. Her marriage to T'Challa creates more identity conflicts, as Storm assumes the role of queen of a country that sees her as a foreigner, a mutant, and a global power among superheroes. Specifically, before speaking to a crowd of rural Wakandans, Storm expresses concern regarding the way she will be received, as she feels that she "will be the American who stole the heart of [the] king for a while yet." Although she is reassured by the woman escorting her, her sentiments are valid, as many Wakandans do not approve of the marriage between her and T'Challa. Microaggressions surrounding Storm's marginalized identities are prominent in Wakandan barbershop discussion after the announcement of their engagement, when people comment that "He does not recognize the beauty of *our* women," wonder whether Storm can bear his children ("Do their genes match enough?"), or suggest that "Storm should submit to DNA testing before the ceremony occurs."[25] One might argue that these comments are not intended to harm but are only offered within the context of striving to protect the future of Wakanda. Nonetheless, they insult and invalidate Storm's experiences as an African and mutant woman.

Shuri is also at the receiving end of microaggressive comments that denigrate her age and gender. When Killmonger sends Nigandan men into her jail cell, they make comments about her physical shape ("just the way I like it, nice bottom girl") and her hair ("She needs a weave"), both of which represent microaggressive themes that have been identified by Black women in the literature.[26] In the film, M'Baku takes issue with Shuri's leadership position, insulting her on Challenge Day and later when she visits Jabari to ask for help with Nakia and the Queen Mother; this criticism could refer either to her age, her gender, or both.

## SOCIAL EXCLUSION

*Social exclusion* occurs when something happens to make someone feel physically or emotionally separated from others.[27] One form of social exclusion, *ostracism*, occurs when someone is ignored or left out of a group, either intentionally or unintentionally. This may occur in multiple ways, such as someone refusing to make eye contact or not providing salient social information (e.g., wedding announcements), using the silent treatment, or refusing to invite the individual or group to social gatherings.[28] Shuri often experiences ostracism by being kept to the fringes of decision making, such as when T'Challa refuses to consider her request to investigate the vibranium caves after an earthquake.[29] In the film, T'Challa and Okoye ostracize Everett Ross by conversing in Xhosa, knowing he cannot understand them. Interestingly, individuals still report negative reactions to ostracism even when it comes from strangers (instead of close others) or when being ostracized is to the individual's benefit,[30] such as when the Queen Mother has Shuri locked in her rooms to keep her away from the combat ritual.[31]

Another example of ostracism comes from Wakanda itself. Within Wakanda, the Jabari tribe has separated from the others and over the years the divide has resulted in ostracism by both sides. Though the Jabari tribe are the ones who have broken away, M'Baku reminds T'Challa that Wakanda has allowed this isolation through statements such as "Us? You are the first king to come here in centuries and you speak of 'us'?"[32] As a society, Wakanda has a self-imposed isolation from the rest of the world. As a people, they withhold technological and medical information from the rest of the world. This is done as a means of protecting themselves, but is clearly perceived negatively by the rest of the world.[33] Wakanda not only rebuffs the rest of the world in very meaningful ways, but at times outright rejects their offers of aid[34] or offers of trade, as they see other nations as "sullen teenagers."[35]

These examples represent another form of social exclusion, *rejection*, which can either be explicit (e.g., refusal to include someone in a group, not allowing someone to participate in an activity)[36] or implied through behaviors such as dehumanizing language or offensive jokes.[37] Klaw's ancestor uses dehumanizing language when referring to Wakandans as a type of simian.[38] Disparaging jokes are another form of social rejection, such as when Klaw says of a villain called the Rhino, "God help us if he had a brain."[39] These diverse examples illustrate ways in which people can use social exclusion as a means of *othering* individuals or groups: setting up the idea that there is an "us" and a very clear, different "them." While ostracism is a lack of attention, rejection includes the use of negative attention. When examining the continuum of nonphysical forms of aggression, rejection is the point at which behaviors move from possibly unintentional to certainly deliberate.

# Expanding Beyond Wakanda's Moral Borders

Director Ryan Coogler said that a key question in the film *Black Panther*'s story is the question, "Am I my brother's keeper?"[40] Does Wakanda have a moral responsibility to use its advanced knowledge and resources to build a better world for everyone? The answer to this question may involve how we determine our *moral boundaries* (i.e., the limits of what a society considers to be permissible actions by its citizens):[41] Which individuals (and groups) do we consider worthy of moral consideration and whom do we exclude? These boundaries are driven in part by our social identities; we protect those we consider part of our in-groups and not those who are members of our out-groups.[42]

T'Challa struggles with his moral boundaries throughout the film.[43] He begins with the traditional, isolationist viewpoint held by his father T'Chaka—Wakanda is all that matters. T'Challa's perspective is challenged by both Killmonger and Nakia. Killmonger believes that Wakanda has forsaken Africans outside of Wakanda, indeed anyone with African heritage across the world. Killmonger's moral border is focused on racial/ethnic heritage. Nakia, however, has a more inclusive moral border than Killmonger. Nakia consistently calls on T'Challa to rule differently than his predecessors and share Wakanda's resources with the world, for the betterment of all nations. Nakia's in-group boundary transcends national and racial/ethnic affiliations to include humanity broadly. T'Challa's perspective on social identity eventually moves closer to Nakia's, motivating him to open Wakandan outreach centers in other countries and calling on everyone in the United Nations to care for each other as "one tribe."

## BULLYING AND CYBERBULLYING

Whether intentional or not, microaggressions and social exclusion may occur as isolated incidents that may only occur once. When these behaviors are repeated, we then start to conceptualize these behaviors as *bullying*—a situation in which someone who is socially or physically more powerful than someone else intentionally engages in repeated aggressive behaviors that are perceived by the victim to be distressing or threatening.[44] Note that bullying is largely determined by the *perception* of the victim as having actually been victimized. So even if we, as readers, interpret some character's actions as bullying, it's only if the victim appears to interpret those actions as humiliating or hurtful that counts. For example, when T'Challa invites the Fantastic Four to Wakanda, the Thing lifts the Human Torch's chair overhead, resulting in the Torch retaliating through name-calling.[45] As an outsider, if we didn't know the relationship between these two characters, such actions might constitute bullying if they occur multiple times. However, based on later interactions between the two, it does not appear that either seems hurt or distressed by their interaction.

Bullying may be verbal, relational, cyber, or physical in nature.[46] *Verbal bullying* includes repeated use of derogatory humor, name-calling, and verbal threats.[47] When Everett Ross shares information about Wakanda at the White House, General Wallace becomes hostile and resorts to name-calling and statements meant to degrade another's social standing ("Since when has beating the French meant anything?").[48] Another example would be the Nigandan prime minister, who makes repeated verbal jabs at T'Challa by saying things such as "Was the crown weighing too heavy on your swollen head, young king?"[49] *Relational bullying* includes spreading rumors about someone, ostracism, social rejection, and any other repeated use of social power to threaten or attack someone's social standing.[50] M'Baku demonstrates the use of both verbal and relational bullying. Throughout the film, he undermines others through name-calling (such as calling Shuri a child), interrupting others (grunting at Ross until he stops speaking), and using degrading humor as a means of gaining social power ("I will feed you to my children"). Another example would be the way in which Wakandans discuss Storm when it is revealed that she will be the next queen. While most discussions may be one-off remarks, together the invalidating statements undermine her social power and call into question her ability to function within that role. Closely associated with relational bullying is *cyberbullying*, which is the repeated use of electronic devices to threaten or cause distress for the victim.[51] If the Nigandan prime minister had texted his degrading comments to T'Challa multiple times, or if the Wakandan people posted reports or comments on social media that called into question Storm's social validity as a ruler, this would constitute cyberbullying.

*Physical bullying* includes behaviors such as hitting, kicking, tripping, and other physical expressions of aggression that are not severe enough to constitute assault.[52] Typically, these behaviors are ways to cause embarrassment or as a show of power, rather than to cause significant physical injury, such as when Klaw or Doctor Doom shoves an underling who does not feel free to strike back.

## IMPACT AND TREATMENT

The socially aggressive behaviors discussed above have negative effects on the victim. For example, all three forms (microaggression, social exclusion, and bullying) are associated with increased depression, anxiety, social distress, loneliness, and increased substance use among victims.[53] Threats to basic psychological needs, such as a feeling of connectedness to others, control, self-esteem, and a meaningful existence are also found among victims of these behaviors.[54] Further, particularly in the case of bullying, victims may engage in revenge behaviors or begin to bully or aggress against others in an attempt to regain social power or a sense of control.[55] This is similar to Killmonger justifying his attacks on Wakanda because of the injustice and cumulative stressors of his childhood.[56] As Okoye points out, over time Killmonger's heart becomes "so full of hatred."[57]

When working with individuals who experience behaviors ranging from microaggression to bullying, it is important to help them overcome the negative impact and thrive. Often, validation and social support are the most effective tools for helping individuals with these experiences.[58] Providing social empowerment, increasing self-esteem, and bolstering feelings of control in social situations helps to directly mitigate the outcomes of aggressive behaviors and improve the lives of individuals who hold marginalized identities. It is possible that if someone or enough people had provided Killmonger with these forms of social validation while he was growing up, he would not feel the need to take revenge on T'Challa in an effort to regain control and a sense of belonging. This is further evident through the spirit of Wakanda itself, which is full of social validation and employment for its citizens. Even their battle cry of "Wakanda forever!" is a rallying to come together. Even T'Challa comes to recognize the need to give and receive social support as a means of combating social isolation and rejection, deciding that Wakanda will no longer "watch from the shadows."[59]

## NOTES

1. Lilienfeld (2017).
2. *Black Panther* (2018 motion picture).

3. Coogler, R. (2018). Interviewed for the introduction to the film *Black Panther*, "Page to Screen" roundtable discussion, *Black Panther* Blu-ray Disc bonus feature.

4. Behm-Morawitz & Ortiz (2013); Li-Vollmer (2002); Mastro & Greenberg (2000); Monk-Turner et al. (2010); Williams et al. (2009); Wohn (2011).

5. Duffy & Jennings (2010); Foster (2005); (2010); *Robert Kirkman's Secret History of Comics*, episode 5, "Color of Comics" (December 4, 2017).

6. Greene (2018).

7. Browne Graves (1999); Rivadeneyra et al. (2007); Ward (2004).

8. Wesselmann et al. (2016); Williams (2009).

9. Duffy & Jennings (2010); Foster (2005; 2010).

10. Brown (2000); Foster (2005; 2010); Ghee (2013); *Robert Kirkman's Secret History of Comics*, episode 1–05, "Color of Comics" (December 4, 2017).

11. Ward (2004).

12. Dovidio (2001).

13. Holoien & Shelton (2012); Sue et al. (2007a; 2007b).

14. Sue et al. (2007b).

15. *Black Panther* #26 (2007).

16. Kohli & Solórzano (2012).

17. Sue et al. (2007b).

18. *Black Panther* #3 (2005).

19. Lilienfeld (2017).

20. *Black Panther* #1 (2005).

21. Sue et al. (2007b).

22. Solórzano et al. (2000); Von Robertson & Chaney (2017).

23. Nadal et al. (2016).

24. *Black Panther* (2018 motion picture).

25. *Black Panther* #14 (2006).

26. Lewis et al. (2013).

27. Seidel et al. (2013).

28. Wesselmann et al. (2016); Williams (2009).

29. *Black Panther* #4 (2005).

30. Nexlek et al. (2012); Williams (2009).

31. *Black Panther* #2 (2005).

32. *Black Panther* (2018 motion picture).

33. *Black Panther* #3 (2005); *Black Panther* (2018 motion picture).

34. *Black Panther* #6 (2005).

35. *Black Panther* #3 (2005).

36. Blackhart et al. (2009).

37. Wesselmann et al. (2016); Wesselmann et al. (2018).

38. *Black Panther* #2 (2005).

39. *Black Panther* #3 (2005).

40. "Page to Screen" roundtable discussion, *Black Panther* Blu-ray disc bonus feature.

41. Lauderdale (1976).

42. Bandura et al. (1975); Crimston et al. (2016; 2018); Jordan & Wesselmann (2015); Opotow (1990); Opotow et al. (2005); Reed & Aquino (2003).
43. *Black Panther* (2018 motion picture).
44. Olweus (1994).
45. Fantastic *Four* #52 (1966).
46. Hinduja & Patchin (2007); Olweus (1994).
47. Olweus (1994).
48. *Black Panther* #1 (2005).
49. *Black Panther* #5 (2005).
50. Olweus (1994).
51. Hinduja & Patchin (2007).
52. Olweus (1994).
53. Lemstra et al. (2012); Reijntjes et al. (2010); Reiter-Scheidl et al. (2018).
54. Williams (2009).
55. Marsh et al. (2011).
56. *Black Panther* (2018 motion picture).
57. *Black Panther* (2018 motion picture).
58. Wesselmann & Parris (in press).
59. *Black Panther* (2018 motion picture).

# 13

# A PANTHER'S PATH

## THE POWER OF BIOPSYCHOSOCIAL INFLUENCES

### Asher Johnson & Billy San Juan

> *"Such harmony may be disrupted at any level,*
> *at the cellular, at the organ system, at the whole person*
> *or at the community levels."*
> —psychiatrist George L. Engel[1]

> *"The world took everything away from me!"*
> —Erik Killmonger[2]

**W**arrior, hero, champion . . .

These terms conjure images of an athletic build, stalwart resolution, and focused demeanor. T'Challa, rightful king of Wakanda and bearer of the Black Panther mantle, fits them all. However, so does his rival Killmonger. They are similar in many aspects, yet chose different paths in life. Their reasons for choosing these paths are varied, but can be categorized and perhaps understood.

# Intrapsychic Conflict

The distinction between heroism and villainy may depend on two things: the method of processing intrapsychic conflict, and whether the related action is driven by selfishness or selflessness. T'Challa consistently processes his intrapsychic conflict regarding his roles. As he puts it, "Two men are forever warring within me—the man I am called to be, and the man I truly am."[3]

*Intrapsychic conflict*—the experience of having conflicting or opposing thoughts, needs, impulses, or desires within one's mind—can amount to an internal war between good and evil.[4] This makes it necessary to consider not only one's actions, but also where the action comes from—such as the good or evil side—because a good deed done by the unrighteous mind can still end in disaster. The mind supposedly regulates intrapsychic conflict through a number of variables, such as one's upbringing, morals, priorities, ability, and current situation.

When Everett Ross gets shot in a battle with Killmonger, T'Challa is faced with a decision: Preserve the Wakandan traditions of isolation from outsiders or bring Agent Ross to Shuri for healing. T'Challa brings Ross to his country for healing in an arguably heroic, though controversial, choice. Conversely, a pivotal scene shows Killmonger facing Ulysses Klaue after Klaue has taken Killmonger's girlfriend hostage. Killmonger may experience conflict, but chooses his mission over his girlfriend's life.[5]

The experiences and obstacles T'Challa, Killmonger, or any individual will each face along their respective paths can be biological, psychological, or social in nature, according to the *biopsychosocial model* of personal development.[6] This model explores how biological, psychological, and sociological factors both operate separately and interact to shape us into who we become. So it might explain how these variables could merge to pave paths that lead one person to become a heroically compassionate ruler[7] while another becomes a feared, albeit tragic, warmonger.[8]

## BIOPSYCHOSOCIAL THEORY

Biopsychosocial theory holds that people are influenced by biological, psychological, and social dimensions that influence human thought, feelings, and behavior.[9] Our lives are not determined by a single factor, but rather by these three dimensions forming a beautiful spectrum of character, much as three primary colors can combine to create an array of vibrance. Choosing what to do with a wallet full of cash becomes more difficult as the reasons behind our behavior intensify in their level of opposition. T'Challa's and Killmonger's experiences, and the interactions of those experiences, fall into these dimensions and can explain their decisions. The decisions, in turn, are influenced by their strengths and vulnerabilities.

### BIOLOGICAL FACTORS

A long lineage of royalty precedes T'Challa's reign of Wakanda.[10] According to Wakandan lore, in an era "a long time forgotten,"[11] a shaman warrior named Bashenga sees a meteorite containing vibranium crash on Wakanda, and, as ordered by Bash, the Panther God, Bashenga establishes the royal line in Wakanda as well as the first Black Panther.[12] This royal bloodline enables T'Challa to partake of the heart-shaped herb, a plant mutated by vibranium. The heart-shaped herb provides for T'Challa the capability to take on panther-like qualities, including enhanced hearing, smelling, vision, and feeling, and increased physical strength, speed, and agility—anyone not of this bloodline or not worthy can die if they eat it.

Killmonger's biological profile is perhaps his strongest protective factor, and the reason he was able to achieve his goals. The cinematic version of Killmonger is a descendant of Wakandan royal blood and T'Challa's first cousin. His biological factors are similar to T'Challa's, shown by his ability to eat the heart-shaped herb and gain superhuman powers. In comics, the herb is poisonous to him because he is not of royal blood, but he can use a synthetic version to empower himself.[13] Whether because his lineage on film entitles him as a royal heir or because traditions in the comics allow any Wakanda to compete for the title, he has the opportunity to become the Black Panther. Killmonger's body is also conditioned for combat due to his Special Forces military training.[14] Personnel in the Special Forces comprise a psychologically and physiologically distinct subset of soldiers who undergo more intense and specialized training than the average service member.[15]

## PSYCHOLOGICAL FACTORS

When T'Challa introduces himself to the Fantastic Four as the wealthy Wakandan chieftain, he explains, "But, it was not always so! My tale is one of tragedy—and deadly revenge!"[16] During this historic meeting, he describes the trauma of watching his father's murder by Klaw during a raid for vibranium.[17] T'Challa displays patience and engages in careful planning, waiting a decade before he is prepared to avenge his father's death. The eventual defeat of Klaw could lead to a void of purpose and an intrapsychic struggle unless T'Challa has sufficient purpose elsewhere in his life. For people with internal motivation for goal achievement, feeling a sense of emptiness after achieving their goal is not uncommon.[18] The Fantastic Four eventually help T'Challa find a new purpose as a fighter against injustice by informing him that the world is in need of his superpowers.[19] This type of *cognitive restructuring*, as well as the support provided by the Four, is a resiliency factor that guides T'Challa toward a path of heroism.

A few years later, T'Challa experiences emotional conflict upon returning to a Wakanda ravaged by Killmonger.[20] Rage engulfs him, and he struggles against the desire for vengeance.[21] His identity suffers,[22] he experiences self-doubt,[23] and he begins to feel the burden of his duties as king weigh upon him.[24] However, his compassion for the innocent outweighs his urge for revenge.[25] T'Challa eventually acts on patience, and acknowledges his people's feelings of abandonment.[26] He chooses to rise against Killmonger in a manner true to his values.[27] Thus, he stays true to the heroic path he has chosen to follow in life.

## SOCIAL FACTORS

T'Challa is raised with high social status and economic privilege, surrounded by the support of loved ones.[28] This promotes a secure attachment style, which allows children to manage stressful situations in a healthy fashion.[29] This type of attachment also predicts a higher likelihood of altruistic behavior, which is evident in T'Challa's method of leadership.[30]

The deep-rooted culture of Wakanda may contribute to T'Challa's strong social development, grounded in its societal values and moral codes.[31] This includes the warrior traditions in which T'Challa grows up. The Black Panther mantle is decided by the tradition of defeating the current Black Panther in ritualistic combat.[32] This ritual symbolizes the Black Panther's duty to be the strongest warrior in the land, whose duty is to be Wakanda's protector.[33] The Black Panther spirit is very sacred, and closely tied into the spiritual beliefs of the Wakandans.[34] The tradition of being Wakanda's protector is a social status that T'Challa chooses to continue and embody.

The cinematic version of Killmonger is raised in America.

His father tells him stories of their homeland, Wakanda, and the boy yearns to see its sunset. However, the child experiences the trauma of having his father killed by T'Chaka, king of Wakanda and T'Challa's father. Such a childhood experience could cause the child to suffer anxiety as well as emotional and behavioral difficulties.[35] He is then abandoned by his people, leading to an intrapsychic crisis of identity. Erik's mother is in prison, where she eventually dies. Children with incarcerated parents have a higher chance of experiencing adversity, social stigmatization, unstable upbringing, and developing antisocial behaviors by the time they reach adolescence or early adulthood.[36] This may further explain the antisocial traits Killmonger displays, especially when considering the intense trauma of finding his father murdered.

Killmonger eventually joins a military special operations force, where he is given his moniker due to the high number of his confirmed kills. These are done to prepare for a coup of Wakanda's throne; however, he is also now desensitized to death. This desensitization is highlighted when he readily murders his girlfriend for the sake of his goals.

The comic book depiction more obviously shows that Killmonger's violence is guided by his greed and ego; his political ideology is self-centered, he takes pleasure in murder, and any act of kindness is instrumental for his future gain.[37] Killmonger also displays a high level of intelligence, with the ability to plot several schemes and carry them through to fruition.[38] Both versions of Killmonger demonstrate *antisocial personality disorder* characterized by a consistent pattern of indifference toward and violation of others' rights, which can be demonstrated with remorselessness, irritability and aggressiveness, nonconformity to social norms, deceitfulness, impulsivity, and lack of regard for safety for self and others.[39]

Social factors related to Killmonger are similar in both cinematic and comic book storylines. Killmonger lacks the emotional regulation abilities gained from protective societal factors typically learned in childhood. He experiences displacement upon returning to Wakanda. Unlike T'Challa, he does not have family members to reinforce a set of values or morals.

In the comic book stories, Killmonger studies at a university as a youth, where he meets Horatio while defending Horatio from bullies.[40] He relates to Horatio, stating that he knows how it feels to be an outsider, and promises Horatio that he will take him to Wakanda where he will be accepted. The ability to connect with Horatio indicates that Killmonger's sociopathy might not have been organic but rather a result of the psychological and social experiences that he endures.

## OVERCOMING FACTORS: CHOOSING A PATH

The circumstances surrounding a person's life are oftentimes not controllable. T'Challa and Killmonger do not choose their birthrights, nor the deaths of their fathers, nor many other of the biopsychosocial factors they experience. Yet, T'Challa resonates as a hero due to the choices he makes despite these factors. Meanwhile, Killmonger's trail of bloodshed is the result of his decision to embrace an inner darkness. All humans hold agency to make choices based on their chosen morals, despite uncontrollable factors affecting their body, mind, and environment. Though this may be frightening, knowing that we all have the possibility of becoming a bloodthirsty warrior like Killmonger also means we can choose to be king.

## NOTES

1. Engel (1979), p. 162.
2. *Black Panther* (2018 motion picture).
3. *Black Panther* #6 (2016).
4. Jung (1953/1999).
5. *Black Panther* (2018 motion picture).
6. Sperry & Sperry (2012).
7. *Fantastic Four* #53 (1966).

# THE SUPERHERO AND THE SUPERORDINATE

Victor Dandridge, Jr. & Travis Langley

Unity is a basic tenet for advanced civilizations in the Marvel Universe. Extraterrestrial empires such as the Kree, Skrulls, and Shi'ar each appear to be, as a whole, relatively free of the internal conflicts that would disrupt their advancement,[41] whereas Earth-based populations such as the Inhumans and especially the Wakandans all show a wide range of both cooperation and infighting. This impression could merely be an illusion of *out-group homogeneity,* in which members of *out-groups* (groups we are not in) appear to be more similar to one another than they really are. This parallels *in-group differentiation,* in which we recognize variety and inconsistency in our *in-groups* (the groups we belong to and identify with).[42]

Wakandan tribes and cults clash at times over resources such as vibranium,[43] the uneven distribution of which creates a power differential between groups. Unequal power breeds unequal status, and unequal status breeds prejudice, discrimination, and intergroup conflict.[44] The Wakandan groups sometimes unite as a nation, though, when threatened by outside forces.[45] Under the right circumstances, a higher-order, *superordinate goal* can prompt opposing groups to cooperate in instances when working together will benefit everyone and the need is great.[46] In the comics, M'Baku and his isolationist Jabari tribe join a Pan-African gathering in Wakanda when the world's superhumans are threatened, and, in film, he and the Jabari back other Wakandans against Killmonger.[47]

8. *Jungle Action* #6 (1973).
9. Sperry & Sperry (2012).
10. Markus (2018).
11. *Black Panther* #167 (2017).
12. Markus (2018).
13. *Black Panther* #61 (2003).
14. *Black Panther* (2018 motion picture).
15. Banks (2006).
16. *Fantastic Four* #52 (1966).
17. *Fantastic Four* #53 (1966).
18. Deci & Ryan (2001).
19. Fantastic Four #52 (1966).
20. *Jungle Action* #6 (1973).
21. *Jungle Action* #6 (1973).
22. *Jungle Action* #10 (1974).
23. *Jungle Action* #15 (1975).
24. *Jungle Action* #8 (1974).
25. *Jungle Action* #6 (1973).
26. *Jungle Action* #14 (1974).
27. *Jungle Action* #7–8 (1974).
28. *Black Panther* (2018 motion picture).
29. Mikulincer & Shaver (2016).
30. Shaver et al. (2016).
31. *Fantastic Four* #53 (1966).
32. *Black Panther* #167 (2017).
33. *Black Panther* (2018 motion picture).
34. *Fantastic Four* #53 (1966), p. 8.
35. Whetton et al. (2011).
36. Murray et al. (2012).
37. *Jungle Action* #7 (1973).
38. *Black Panther* (2018 motion picture).
39. American Psychiatric Association (2013).
40. *Jungle Action* #7 (1973).
41. *The Official Handbook of the Marvel Universe—Deluxe Edition* #3 (2006).
42. Fiske (2002); Gonsalkorale & Williams (2007); Ostrom & Sedikides (1992); Tajfel (1970).
43. *Doomwar* #1–6 (2010). Script: J. Maberry. Art: W. Conrad, K. Lashley, S. Eaton, P. Neary, A. Lanning, R. Campanella, J. Mendoza, & D. Meikis.
44. D'Exelle & Riedl (2013); Grant (1991); Kahan & Rapoport (1975); Rapoport et al. (1989).
45. e.g., *New Avengers* #7–12 (2013).
46. Sherif (1966).
47. Respectively, *Civil War Battle Damage Report* #1 (2007), and *Black Panther* (2018 motion picture).

# 14

# DIVIDED BY OUR FATHERS

## TRANSGENERATIONAL TRAUMA IN *BLACK PANTHER*

### Larisa A. Garski & Justine Mastin

*"Long before Africans were brought to this country as slaves, they belonged to tribes descended from ancient civilizations on the continent of Africa. This legacy is rich in custom and mythology."*

—clinical psychologist Nancy Boyd-Franklin[1]

*"Heavy is the head, they say. That proverb does no justice to the weight of the nation, of its people, its history, its traditions."*
—T'Challa[2]

We tend to think of *inheritance* as a positive event, a gift in the form of property, history, title, or duty that is given by past generations to future generations to help them survive and, if they are lucky, flourish. It is the way in which humanity's grasp may equal its reach. But not only do we pass down the physical, we also pass down the psychological. Current research into the impact of epigenetics—processes that change a gene's activity, without changing the sequence of DNA and is then passed down to the next generation of biological progeny[3]—has only confirmed the powerful impact that environment, in general, and parental behavior, in particular, wield on the growth and maturation of the generation that follows.[4] For T'Challa, this inheritance is both genetic and metaphysical, since becoming the Black Panther involves embodying both the values and traditions taught to him, as well as those awakened within when he imbibes the heart-shaped herb.[5]

But what happens when the story being passed down from generation to generation is not one of triumph and wonder, but rather one of horror and pain? Erik Killmonger née N'Jadaka, cousin[6] (in film, not comics) and long-standing nemesis (in both film and comics) of Black Panther, inherits a lineage of betrayal, loss, and bondage: "You and your father's reign have taken too much from me already. Your line of descent ends with you and you'll take nothing from me ever again!"[7] Both N'Jadaka and T'Challa inherit expectations and limitations that they do not choose, begging the question with which psychotherapy continues to wrestle: Can one be released from transgenerational trauma or is it instead a life sentence?

## A PAINFUL HISTORY

*Transgenerational trauma*—the process by which trauma is passed down from the first generation of survivors in a family system to subsequent generations within that same family system—was a concept brought to the fore in the 1960s to describe the phenomenon observed in the descendants of Holocaust survivors who demonstrated symptoms of depression, anxiety, and/or posttraumatic stress disorder that could not be explained by the environmental factors of their present circumstances.[8] Today, we understand transgenerational trauma to have both a genetic and systemic component; not only are children influenced by their family system *(nurture)*, they are also influenced by their family's genes *(nature)*. Within the context of the Wakandan tribe, this passing on of both trauma and glory is foundational to the continuation of both their system of government and their protector, Black Panther. T'Challa explains: "War is our nation's trade. It has been so for generations. We will not be terrorized. We are terror itself."[9]

Often equally as important in terms of traumatic legacy is the way that cultural leaders, teachers, and core caregivers or parents represent the story of trauma to up-and-coming members of their social group or family. This practice in effect ensures that the traumatic event lives on in the emotional psyche of the social group long after the victims of the trauma have died.[10] This *transgenerational transmission of chosen trauma,* in which a group continues to reexperience and relive a painful occurrence generations after the actual event occurs, can just as easily ensure that a social group retains the hard-won knowledge culled from pain as it can ensnare the group in the unhealthy reenactment of trauma.[11] Both possibilities merge in the Wakandan cultural practices surrounding their leader and protector, the Black Panther. The very existence of the Black Panther is founded upon the tribes' early participation and witnessing of the devastating violence and tyranny that swept through the African continent in general and the assaults of Ulysses Klaue in particular.[12] As the inheritor of the Black Panther legacy, T'Challa both benefits and suffers as a direct result of decisions made by his forbears. This decision to retell the stories of the threats to the Wakandan way of life woven throughout Wakandan culture[13] result in T'Challa's central struggle with how to relate to the outside world: Should he help where he can or protect the family secret of vibranium at all costs instead? As is often the case with transgenerational trauma, this legacy of secret keeping causes strife for T'Challa

# DIFFERENTIATION

*Differentiation* signifies a state of existence in which an individual is both separate from and connected to the important people in their lives—friends and family.[14] Murray Bowen, the psychiatrist who first used this term, described this process as often taking years for an individual to achieve and theorized that it might never be possible to fully actualize.[15] Rather, it was best understood as a continuous state of perpetually becoming autonomous while maintaining ties to loved ones, both biological and chosen.[16] The concept of differentiation offers a unique way forward for those struggling with transgenerational trauma, as it speaks directly to a way that they might maintain ties to their family while separating themselves from the history of pain that has haunted both past and present generations. For T'Challa and Erik Killmonger, this process is further complicated because they feel duty-bound to right some of the wrongs of the past.[17] Particularly in his later years, T'Challa makes strong steps toward differentiation: He goes against his forefathers' wishes to maintain the secrecy of Wakanda's prosperity and chooses to reveal Wakanda's true identity, thereby paving the way for Wakanda to increase its own connection to the rest of the world.[18] Killmonger exemplifies the ways that differentiation can prove tortuous, as his own personal pain caused by abandonment and the early loss of core caregivers fuses with the history of his father's own betrayal to tragic ends.[19]

in both personal and public arenas: He struggles to maintain his commitments to both the Avengers and the Wakandans[20] while nearly losing the affection of his childhood love, Nakia. "You can't let your father's mistakes define who you are. You get to decide what kind of king you're going to be."[21]

Yet, his dual role as king and protector of Wakanda gives T'Challa a powerful sense of purpose. "Too many people warp the word *heritage*," T'Challa observes. "They use it to mean superiority when it is only meant to give one identity!"[22] T'Challa's living connection to Wakandan culture, history, and family helps him to understand himself, informing both his personal and public selves. The importance of being both connected to, and separate from, one's family group enables one to be open to the restorative aspects of family while maintaining perspective on maladaptive family habits. As T'Challa's father reminds him: "The elders will tell you that you must master the arts of manhood. But if you learn them at the expense of childhood, my son, you will learn only self-deception."[23]

## A LONE AVENGER

If we understand transgenerational trauma to be something that we inherit both culturally and genetically from our forebears, then we might assume Erik Killmonger to be less prone to transgenerational woes as he is reared outside of Wakanda with minimal connection to its culture and traditions.[24] Transgenerational trauma need not be witnessed for it to be passed on and thus experienced by forthcoming generations. There is evidence to suggest that this trauma is conveyed via attachment, or rather lack of attachment, with core caregivers.[25] Children are acutely attuned to their caregivers, and when their caregivers are acting from a place of trauma, the child also perceives and experiences this trauma often without having words to frame the experience as such.[26]

Killmonger bears the struggle of both of his parents—an African-American mother who came of age in Oakland in the 1960s and a Wakandan father who betrayed his family and his country—without any of the benefits of parental teaching or guidance.[27] Killmonger's mother, as an African-American woman, has both the transgenerational trauma passed on by her ancestors who were forced into slavery and the trauma that comes from systemic racism of people of color in the United States. "To be Black and poor is to live in fear."[28] Killmonger himself also experiences the trauma of life in his community and speaks to this when he meets his father on the ancestral plane: "Everybody dies. It's just life around here." As an adult, he struggles to find a place to put "this empty space"[29] where conscious understanding of traumatic memory would reside and thereby fill the hole where both his identity and family would flourish. Denied the latter, he struggles profoundly with the former, leaving carnage in his path. Though he escapes the binds of Wakandan dictums that plague T'Challa, he also loses a cultural framework in which to understand his personal pain within the context of a larger purpose. As an adult, this loss results in him becoming "an outcast . . . and bitter like an almond."[30] Bereft of his own tribe, the man who calls himself Erik Killmonger seeks to fashion his own, gathering the outcasts of other nations and cultures and using the tools of chosen trauma to rally them to fight against an imaginary oppressor: T'Challa, the Black Panther.[31]

## HEALING FROM GENERATIONS OF LOSS

Both T'Challa and N'Jadaka experience trauma via inheritance and lived experience. But healing from a history of such devastation is no small task. Recent work related to posttraumatic transformation—as opposed to posttraumatic stress disorder—via either *posttraumatic growth* or *posttraumatic resilience* points to the possibility of recovering from trauma with either an intact

# POSTTRAUMATIC GROWTH

*Posttraumatic growth* is perhaps best understood as a potential alternative to posttraumatic stress disorder.[32] Both are by-products of severe loss and pain, but one involves a turn toward growth and positive change while the other involves a turn toward maladaptive coping patterns and destructive tendencies.[33] Factors that increase the likelihood of posttraumatic growth are supportive community, meaning-making activities, constructive rumination (reflection), and spirituality.[34] T'Challa has both the benefit and privilege of many of these protective factors, including supportive community, spirituality, and the Black Panther myth itself, which gives him not only purpose but a framework within which to understand his pain, since it is only through the death of one Black Panther that another may ascend and thus maintain the power of Wakanda. Killmonger is denied these privileges. Bereft of both family and his birth rite, he has neither community nor spirituality to help him understand his loss within the framework of a greater purpose or potentially positive change.[35] As a young boy, he attempts to create meaning from Wakandan relics left by his now deceased father—a journal, his father's ring, and his war dog tattoo—using them to feel both connection and potential hope for the future. He is also able to find meaning through his education and the military, but his strongest driving force for growth was less than ideal—the hope for eventual revenge. Though he demonstrates the skill of rumination, he uses it to create a purpose, casting himself as the sole avenging agent against a sea of misfortune. Certainly, both T'Challa and Killmonger change as a result of their trauma. But it would appear that only one of them has the support necessary to use their trauma as an opportunity for growth and metamorphosis.

or positively changed identity.[36] While both possibilities seem to be at play for T'Challa at different stages of his life,[37] Erik Killmonger displays early signs of posttraumatic resiliency or the ability to return to the way one behaved prior to the traumatic event or events.[38] For years, it appears that he has survived his traumas with resilience and minimal damage: Despite the trauma of losing first his mother and his father at a young age, Erik graduates from a prestigious university and goes on to achieve in the military.[39] Ultimately, however, he chooses a path of pain for himself and those around him.[40]

T'Challa seems to seek harmony between his personal pain and painful lineage whereas Killmonger seeks dominion over both. These differing responses suggest something almost Freudian—dare we say Jungian—as this battle is similar to that between the conscious and unconscious mind.[41] In his early years, T'Challa's response to both his inherited trauma and his new mantle of leadership were characterized by almost authoritarian action: "T'Challa saw only the beneficial things technology could bring his land. Perhaps he chose to ignore anything that threatened his dream. Or else convinced himself that he could overcome any setback that might arise."[42] His actions mirror Killmonger's rash desire to take back what he perceives as his rightful place at the top of Wakandan leadership, attempting to use power to keep both his transgenerational trauma and his personal suffering over a lost home and a lost family at bay. Psychoanalytic therapists have long believed that suppressing the terrors of the unconscious can only cause increased suffering both for the patient and for those close to him or her.[43] What T'Challa attempts as he grows into his dual roles as both leader of Wakanda and Black Panther is *individuation*, or an integration between his disparate traumas, using both personal (conscious) and transgenerational (unconscious) narratives/events/stories to re-forge his identity and destiny into one that more closely mirrors his twin desires to lead and to heal.[44]

## THIS IS NOT THE END

There are a number of ways that trauma may be passed down through generations: via genetics, attachments, and witnessing caregivers' pain. And while inheriting this trauma can contribute to someone being more prone to having his or her own mental health challenges, the evidence suggests that people are able to make changes to improve their circumstance. That is, just because trauma has been passed down does not mean that the recipient has to accept this unfortunate gift without a fight. There is certainly the opportunity for healing not only oneself, but the circumstances of future generations moving forward. But one must first acknowledge that the generational trauma is present and take mindful steps toward changing for healing to take place.

Sadly, N'Jadaka does not have the chance to find out what healing looks like. As Killmonger, he dies at T'Challa's hand,[45] a direct result of the acting out of the generational trauma to which they were both heirs. N'Jadaka's genetic line ends with him and we do not know what changing the legacy of himself might have meant for him and any future children. T'Challa does decide to change his fate from his father's and therefore the Wakandan royal family's legacy. He chooses to alter the cycle that was handed to him, and with that he changes the course of his own future, his children's future, and the future of Wakanda. While the legacy that these cousins inherited is one of fractured relationships stemming from generational trauma, that does not have to be the end of the story. As T'Challa himself says: "What happens now determines what happens to the rest of the world."[46]

## NOTES

1. Boyd-Franklin (2003), p. 6.
2. *Black Panther* #2 (2016).

3. Weinhold (2006).
4. Salberg (2015).
5. *Jungle Action* #8 (1974); *Black Panther* (2018 motion picture).
6. *Black Panther* (2018 motion picture).
7. *Jungle Action* #6 (1973).
8. Rakoff (1966).
9. *Black Panther* #4 (2016).
10. Volken (2001).
11. Volkan (2001).
12. *Jungle Action* #7 (1973), #16 (1975); *Black Panther* (2018 motion picture).
13. *Jungle Action* #11 (1974), #13 (1975).
14. Skowron (2004).
15. Skowron & Dendy (2004).
16. Skowron & Dendy (2004).
17. *Jungle Action* #10 (1974).
18. *Black Panther* (2018 motion picture).
19. *Black Panther* (2018 motion picture); *Jungle Action* #16 (1975).
20. *Black Panther* #6 (2016).
21. *Black Panther* (2018 motion picture).
22. *Jungle Action* #8 (1974).
23. *Jungle Action* #15 (1975).
24. *Black Panther* (2018 motion picture).
25. Salberg (2015).
26. Salberg (2015).
27. *Black Panther* (2018 motion picture).
28. Boyd-Franklin (2003), p. 273.
29. Salberg (2015).
30. *Jungle Action* #8 (1974).
31. *Jungle Action* #8 (1974), *Jungle Action* #11 (1974); *Jungle Action* #12 (1974).
32. Calhoun & Tedeschi (2006).
33. Van Slyke (2013).
34. Van Slyke (2013).
35. *Jungle Action* #16 (1975); *Black Panther* (2018 motion picture).
36 Calhoun & Tedeschi (2006).
37 *Black Panther* (2018 motion picture).
38 Klasen et al. (2010).
39 *Black Panther* (2018 motion picture).
40. *Black Panther* (2018 motion picture).
41. Jung (1963).
42. *Jungle Action* #15 (1975).
43. Salberg (2015).
44. Jung (1963).
45. *Jungle Action* #17 (1975); *Black Panther* (2018 motion picture).
46. *Black Panther* (2018 motion picture).

# 15

# MOURNING THE KING

## VULNERABILITY, RESILIENCE, LOSS

### Brittani Oliver & Billy San Juan

*"Everything can be taken from a man but one thing: The last of the human freedoms—to choose one's attitude in any given set of circumstances, to choose one's own way."*

—existential psychiatrist Viktor Frankl[1]

*"A man who has not prepared his children for his own death has failed as a father."*
—King T'Chaka[2]

T'Challa loses everything—his father in an unexpected murder, his country to a bloodthirsty warrior, and his faith in the traditions that have kept Wakanda hidden from the world. These losses cause him tremendous pain, and yet he finds meaning in his suffering and redefines the mantle of the Black Panther. Finding or making meaning out of trauma may be key to coping and subsequently growing as a person.

N'Jadaka loses everything, too—his father in an unexpected murder, his identity when he grows up unconnected to anyone else, and his humanity in his search for vengeance. He makes meaning of his own, though in a very different way.

Grief and loss play a tremendous role in the stories of the Black Panther and his rival, Erik Killmonger. The choices they made are strongly influenced by their reactions to grief. Two people can journey down radically different paths as they manage intense emotions related to loss and reach destinations that are far apart.

## TRAUMA-CONTEXTUAL GRIEF

Human beings often experience events that are perceived as physically/emotionally harmful, or even life-threatening. These *traumas* may produce lasting adverse effects on the individual's mental, emotional, social, physical or spiritual functioning or well-being.[3] During a traumatic event, the individual's ability to integrate his/her emotional experience is overwhelmed. Should the trauma be linked to the death of a loved one, further complications may arise.[4] When an individual experiences death, particularly the death of a parent, he or she may have additional concerns with issues such as navigating the world, losing unique connections, confronting mortality, and constructing identity.[5] The death may also cause complications in the regulation of emotional and behavioral reactions, such as difficulty trusting others, acting out behaviors, and increased risk-taking (such as using drugs or self-harming).

## GRIEF VERSUS BEREAVEMENT

Though often used interchangeably, there is a difference between the terms *grief* and *bereavement*. Bereavement is an objective situation of having lost someone or something and often includes the death of an individual.[6] Grief is the emotional and affective response to bereavement.[7]

## BEREAVEMENT

Complex and debilitating behavioral and emotional implications from bereavement have been seen in up to 10 percent of the US population.[8] Individuals who experience complex bereavement are more likely to have increased levels of depression and anxiety, and have decreased regulation and overall emotional and cognitive functioning.[9] A bereavement event or situation can alter an individual's homeostasis and alter his or her perceptions of the world and life as he or she knows it.[10] Bereavement can undermine attachment bonds, physical health, and conceptualizations of life's purpose or meaning.[11]

Although both T'Challa and N'Jadaka lose their fathers, N'Jadaka's bereavement is complicated by several factors. N'Jadaka is still a child at the time, with limited cognitive ability to process his situation. The death is wholly unexpected, unlike T'Challa's father's death during a political ceremony where a certain level of danger is often assumed. Finally, N'Jadaka does not have a strong social support network to help him cope with the loss of his father, whereas T'Challa mourns with his surviving family members. These complications may explain why N'Jadaka follows a path of aggression and bloodshed.

## GRIEF

Individuals in the grief process may exhibit social, behavioral, and cognitive impairments as a result of bereavement.[12] Common responses include cognitive delays, acting out, isolating from friends/family, and difficulty with emotions. Mourning is characterized by social expressions or acts by the practices of society or a cultural group. These "grief rituals" may include emotional responses similar to those of PTSD and depression, such as prolonged guilt, sadness, shame, and anger.

Several biopsychosocial reactions accompany grief. Physically, there may be intense sensations of shortness of breath, tightening in the chest, or a "hollowed-out" feeling. Psychologically a person may *ruminate* (dwell) on the details of the death event. The person may find difficulty focusing, or even experience strong spikes in negative emotion. Socially, a person may begin to isolate from friends and family. Inversely, a person may reach out to seek help.[13]

## SEEKING ISOLATION VERSUS SEEKING SOLACE

Individuals who have experienced traumatic loss or grief and bereavement may be reluctant to reach out for social support, due to the stigma associated with seeking emotional assistance in the Western world. In this, individuals in the Western world hold a belief of high resilience and "moving on" when grieving. It is common in the Western world to have limited "bereavement days" from work and employment, and oftentimes the society functions as "moving forward and getting over it." This creates dissonance in individuals who have or are experiencing grief and bereavement. Due to this, there is less value in commemorating the loss and experiencing the totality of the loss and more value in "moving forward," regardless of whether the individual is capable of doing so. More attention should be paid to those who have experienced a death and are currently experiencing grief and bereavement in order to rectify or conceptualize the loss.[14]

T'Challa's grief is assuaged by strong ties to Wakandan culture, royal traditions, and the values instilled in him by his
father. His emotional reactions are anchored by the knowledge
of socially appropriate context. N'Jadaka does not have these
regulating factors. His primary motivators in life are survival
and vengeance, and thus his grief is channeled through these
two lenses. These factors, which help regulate and structure
reactions to grief, are known as resilience factors.

## RESILIENCE FACTORS

An individual's resilience is directly influenced by internal and
external structures, protective factors, and influences that protect against risk factors. These promotive or *resilience factors* help
individuals adapt to adversity and stress they may experience.
Although death is an event that is inevitable, the experience of
the loss can greatly influence an individual's ability to adapt.
Intrinsic and extrinsic resilience factors are utilized in individuals who cope successfully through the grieving period. Such
resilience factors include some organic personal factors as well
as other subjective environmental factors.[15]

Personal factors that influence resilience in the context of
grief and loss include personality traits, gender, age, and previous history of loss.[16] Individuals who present with higher
levels of distress after the death of a loved one often present
with higher levels of anxiety and depressive symptoms. Gender
also influences depressive episodes, as men have historically
had less opportunity to seek social supports culturally and are
more likely to withhold grief expressions, such as sadness and
guilt. As men are more likely to internalize their grief experiences and narratives, they are more likely to respond through
behavioral communication, such as anger and isolation.

Although the loss of a parent in older adults may cause an
upsurge of dormant attachment feelings and a review of goals

and identity,[17] T'Challa has intrinsic resilience to adapt to the loss of a parent due to age in comparison to a younger adult. As T'Challa experienced the death of his father later in life, he was able to better conceptualize the meaning and outcome of his father's death, due to his emotional maturity. Additionally, the Black Panther lineage is rooted in the inherent understanding that its mantle will pass through the defeat and eventual death of the previous Black Panther.[18]

T'Challa's understanding of death is complemented by the various social systems in his life. From the intimate relationships within his family to the support of the Wakandan people, T'Challa is able to frame his grief in an appropriate and healthy context. Although the death of T'Challa's father was tragic and unplanned, the citizens of Wakanda cradled their new prince in his grief experience and celebrated the crowning of a new king; this resulted in increased adaptability to the loss. T'Challa, as prince of Wakanda, also lived within a social status that afforded him access to care and support. In addition, he was also shown to take part in cultural rituals, which may have allowed him to grieve within a religious context.[19] An individual's external support structures are critical in his or her ability to adapt after the death of a parent or loved one. These environmental resilience factors may include, but are not limited to, social supports, positive family functioning, mode of death, socioeconomic status, and religiosity.[20] As few as 20 percent of individuals who come from unstable homes with inconsistent social supports are able to perceive a positive future after the death of one parent.[21] Moreover, how a family can reorganize and come together after the death of a parent is the highest predictor in overall adaptive functioning.[22]

T'Challa exhibited a variety of resilience factors that Killmonger lacked. Conversely, Killmonger experienced several *risk factors* that put him at danger for difficulty in managing grief in a healthy manner.

## RISK FACTORS: KILLMONGER

*Risk factors*, variables that place someone at risk for a negative condition, arise when limited resources are available to combat maladaptive responses and problematic outcomes. Loss of a parent as a child causes intense and persistent grief, including negative social/cognitive/behavioral issues.[23] This may include but are not limited to difficulty regulating emotions, isolating behaviors, hypersomnia, difficulty maintaining attachments, impulsivity, higher levels of substance abuse and other risky behaviors, as well as difficulty concentrating and racing thoughts about the deceased.[24] Individuals who have experienced the death of a parent are less likely to cultivate and maintain social and emotional functioning in their age-appropriate counterpoints. For example, for individuals who have experienced the death of a parent in adolescence, behavioral and emotional responses, such as isolating behaviors, acting-out behaviors, and anger or resentment have occurred. For individuals who have experienced the untimely death of a parent or a life span–normative death of a parent in adulthood, additional emotional and behavioral responses of fear of death or dying, issues with interpersonal relationships, and lower overall functioning have also been found. Just as there are internal and external resilience factors, there are also risk factors that influence an individual's ability to adapt after a death.[25] Killmonger experienced several risk factors that acted as a catalyst for his maladaptive grieving responses.

Risk factors that greatly influenced Killmonger's emotional and behavioral responses to the death of his father include level of maturity, situation surrounding death, social support, socioeconomic status, and geographical dissonance. Individuals who experience the death of a parent during childhood have been found to view the death as one of the single most difficult experiences in their lives and are less likely to respond positively throughout life.[26] The age at which Killmonger experienced the death of his father serves as a risk factor because of his internalization of the death and his inability to process and conceptualize his loss due to his level of emotional maturity.[27] Moreover, due to the nature and circumstances of his father's death—both finding his father murdered in his home and without justice or reasoning for the death—Killmonger was also unable to process his grief in a healthy, adaptive manner. Sudden and tragic traumas and deaths such as these are more highly associated with negative emotional and behavioral responses for the surviving family members.[28] At the time of his father's death, Killmonger was living in an urban community with low socioeconomic status that may have fewer social supports and prevented him from processing his loss in totality as well. Unlike T'Challa, Killmonger also did not have the financial stability to help him cope with the death of his father. There was no palace, no kingdom, and no family to help him cope with his grief. Because Killmonger was not part of the Wakanda community at the time of his father's death, he had access to only limited cultural and community resources and rituals, which increased his overall risk factors. As he did not have the Wakandan rituals for mourning, he was not able to frame the loss of his father in a specific context that allowed for increased ability to process and conceptualize the loss.

## FROM DEATH COMES LIFE

Grief, above all else, is a process and cannot be reduced to a simplistic and universal singular response. Instead, similar to that of the ebb and flow of kinetic energy of vibranium, grief has boundless power over the way in which people conceptualize the world around them. The death of a parent does not prevent the sun from rising, but it can change the course of one man's life. It is in the most difficult of times that individual strengths and weaknesses are illuminated. We do not choose when death comes; it makes the choice itself and it alone has the power to defeat great men standing in its path. When faced with great adversity, individuals can succumb to risks along their journey or seek to find their own resilience. The story of T'Challa and Killmonger is the story of the human condition, in which we are influenced by circumstance, chance, and who we are as people. Death takes all people, while grief serves all people, with little room to choose.

## NOTES

1. Frankl (1946).
2. *Black Panther* (2018 motion picture).
3. Stroebe & Schut (2001).
4. Xu et al. (2015).
5. Barry (1969).
6. Stroebe & Schut (2001).
7. Stroebe & Schut (2001).
8. Barlé et al. (2015).
9. Hayslip et al. (2015).
10. Barlé et al. (2015); Stroebe & Schut (2001).
11. Bowlby (1969).
12. Silverman et al. (1992).
13. Barlé et al. (2015); Edwards (2006); Stroebe & Schut (2001).
14. Stroebe & Schut (2001).
15. Stroebe & Schut (2001).
16. Stroebe & Schut (2001).
17. Morris (2010).
18. Morris (2010).
19. Stroebe & Schut (2001).
20. Stroebe & Schut (2001).
21. Stroebe & Schut (2001).
22. Stroebe & Schut (2001).
23. Barlé et al. (2015); Chowns (2008).
24. Xu et al. (2015).
25. Stroebe & Schut (2001).
26. Lawrence et al. (2005).
27. Bowlby (1969).
28. Hayslip et al. (2015); Stroebe & Schut (2001).

V

# A
# SOURCE
# OF
# INSPIRATION

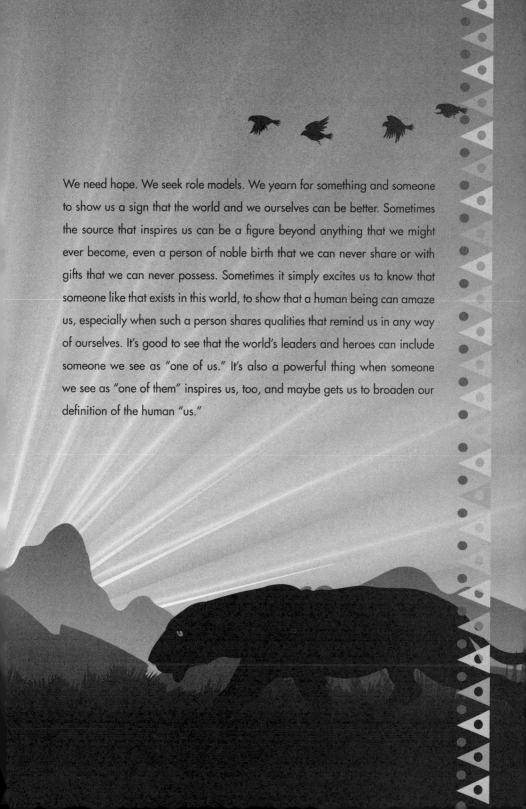

We need hope. We seek role models. We yearn for something and someone to show us a sign that the world and we ourselves can be better. Sometimes the source that inspires us can be a figure beyond anything that we might ever become, even a person of noble birth that we can never share or with gifts that we can never possess. Sometimes it simply excites us to know that someone like that exists in this world, to show that a human being can amaze us, especially when such a person shares qualities that remind us in any way of ourselves. It's good to see that the world's leaders and heroes can include someone we see as "one of us." It's also a powerful thing when someone we see as "one of them" inspires us, too, and maybe gets us to broaden our definition of the human "us."

# 16

# THE POSITIVE PANTHER, A HEALTHY HERO

## Travis Langley

*"This guy who was always two steps ahead of the world . . ."*
—Everett K. Ross, regarding T'Challa[1]

*"That person who helps others simply because it should
or must be done, and because it is the right thing to do,
is indeed, without a doubt, a real superhero."*

—Black Panther co-creator, writer Stan Lee[2]

The success of fiction about dark, angry, tormented heroes can give the misguided impression that heroes must be grim and have tragic backgrounds. An emergency or potential misfortune might create the circumstances under which someone steps up to do the heroic thing, but that does not mean the hero does so because of prior misfortune or inner conflict. People may choose to do the right thing because of values they've learned, and empathy for others may be the greatest determinant of who will step up in a crisis.[3] Before his father's murder,[4] T'Challa is already a good person who has learned the importance of looking out for others, and even though he sets out to avenge his father, vengeance is not where he finds purpose in life. Real-life heroism tends not to be motivated by a single, driving tragedy. Concerned that people might learn the wrong lesson from his own cinematic productions about a dark, brooding hero,[5] producer Michael Uslan stressed that their success does *not* mean all superhero stories must be dark, gritty, and set in contemporary America,[6] and the box office triumphs of the motion pictures *Wonder Woman, Black Panther,* and *Captain Marvel* appear to back him up.[7]

The abundance of heroes with catastrophic origin stories and the treatment of them as broken people within fiction also reflect a long-standing criticism of psychology, that the field often focuses so heavily on the worst parts of human experiences that it overlooks the best. Echoing the psychologist who created Wonder Woman,[8] American Psychological Association president Martin Seligman began promoting "psychology's forgotten mission,"[9] the need to understand normal, healthy behavior, often neglected by therapists and researchers fixating on the abnormal, unhealthy parts of human nature. Out of Seligman's concerns grew the area known as *positive psychology*, which examines the characteristics and values behind the best of human activity and mental health.[10] Heroic individuals possess many of those qualities,[11] and the ideal person to become a new Black Panther would embody them all.

## CHARACTER STRENGTHS AND VIRTUES

As a counterpart to the *Diagnostic and Statistical Manual of Mental Disorders* (DSM or DSM-5),[12] which categorizes and describes mental illnesses, Seligman and a colleague developed a "manual of the sanities,"[13] a positive psychology guide called

*Character Strengths and Virtues: A Handbook and Classification* (CSV).[14] The CSV outlines six core *virtues*, individual human traits widely recognized as signs of good character and mental health. Because inner virtue alone makes little difference in the external world, the manual also describes empirical findings regarding the *strengths* that enable people to take action.

Each Black Panther is Wakanda's champion, chieftain, and religious leader. Chosen through a series of ritualistic challenges, each must prove himself (or, eventually, herself)[15] to be worthy to serve in every one of those roles and to lead their people. Human beings oversee most of the process, but the goddess Bast is the final arbiter.[16] While this may seem a bit removed from real-world democratic elections or hereditary monarchies, it reflects real traditions in which leaders of many kinds prove themselves through rituals and can be challenged by others who wish to usurp their positions, even if most don't answer to a company president who also happens to be a god. Because the Black Panther serves so many roles, the ideal candidate for this title would be someone who embodies all the virtues and many of the strengths studied by positive psychology.

## WISDOM AND KNOWLEDGE

*Creativity, curiosity, open-mindedness, love of learning, perspective (wisdom).*

Wisdom is a characteristic explicitly valued in a Black Panther. In the superhero Civil War conflict, both movie and comic book versions,[17] many fans view T'Challa as the only character to show wisdom in the end, certainly more than Iron Man and Captain America.[18] Even on the brink of death, when the cosmic entity Death poses as the spirit of his father, T'Challa is still wise enough to see through its charade.[19] Queen Ramonda, the stepmother whom T'Challa views as mother, describes T'Challa: "He plans for everything, and the everything-spinning of those plans. He is not like us, I tell you. How, you ask? By thinking two steps ahead of his enemies. And three steps ahead of his friends."[20] T'Challa's sister Shuri may be the smartest person in their world,[21] but despite her vast knowledge and cleverness, she is younger and has a lot of wisdom yet to gain.

The strengths studied by positive psychology are not simply about ascribing to someone the inner quality of a psychological virtue, but they are also about making sure the individual can put those virtues into action in the world. Even though T'Challa's enemy Erik Killmonger shows insight, making excellent points about Wakanda's isolationism and its failure to help individuals of African descent elsewhere in the world,[22] emotion and selfish motivations often supersede his wisdom. When he orders the destruction of the heart-shaped herb that would allow an eventual heir to become the next Black Panther, Killmonger shows that he values his anger at the world over his people's future. Dark emotions get in the way of his own wisdom, whereas T'Challa will even consider the words of an enemy as he comes to see that Wakanda must change.[23]

Having the wisdom to understand what needs to be done and the knowledge necessary to find a solution, though, does not accomplish much unless the individual also possesses the courage to put them into effect.

## COURAGE

*Bravery, persistence, integrity, vitality.*

Heroic stories are replete with examples of *courage*, emotional strength involving the exercise of willpower to fulfill goals in the face of internal or external opposition.[24] Almost by definition, the superhero is brave and vital, and despite overwhelming odds, the superhero repeatedly wins the day through persistence.[25] Despite the fact that modern world leaders tend not to leap into dangerous situations and act as their own champions, warrior-kings and warrior-queens throughout history have earned great respect by fighting their own battles while leading fellow citizens in combat, conquest, and missions of mercy. Perhaps it is not so illogical, then, for the people's leader to face danger repeatedly if the people would prefer a short-lived hero over a long-lived coward.

Even compared to other superheroes, T'Challa is particularly courageous. He has moments of weakness, of course, because he is a human being. For example, when Killmonger shows up at the royal palace and pushes T'Challa to say who Killmonger really is, that he is of royal blood, T'Challa shows neither the wisdom nor the courage to handle that better and acknowledge the truth.[26] His courage never wavers when he needs to stop Killmonger, though. He fears for others more than for himself, and he is brave enough to take action to try to help.

Villains can also show many courageous qualities, though, including persistence to the point of obsession. Among the strengths that promote the virtue of courage, *integrity* (being authentic and honest, as well as true to oneself and one's personal values) may be the one that more often separates heroes from villains. Despite his frankness in some situations, Erik Killmonger betrays people, double-crosses allies, and prioritizes his anger at the world above ideals he espouses. He is right about many things and offers a perspective that others need to hear, but his hatred and desire for personal power impair his integrity when it comes to promoting that perspective himself.[27]

Integrity does not distinguish all villains from heroes, though, because some of the greatest villains possess great integrity. Doctor Doom is renowned as a man of honor who will not break his solemn word. Knowing this, T'Challa has at times extended courtesies to Doom as a fellow monarch that he would not likely provide to some other world leader who has also been his enemy, such as providing Doom with sanctuary while deposed from the Latverian throne.[28] Providing a safe haven to someone who has tried to conquer the world[29] takes bravery (or foolishness, but T'Challa is no fool), but the calculated risk is based on Doom's own integrity.

If the virtues of wisdom/knowledge and courage do not adequately distinguish hero from villain, the difference may have more to do with underlying motives.

## COURAGE BEFORE THE STORM

Courage is not always obvious. When T'Challa exerts his official authority and one-sidedly annuls his marriage to Storm after a conflict between Avengers and X-Men wrecks Wakanda,[30] is he bravely prioritizing his people over his own heart or does he fail to show the courage necessary to stay true to his marital pledge, even in the face of conflict? As a human being, T'Challa can make a hasty decision and let emotions cloud his judgment and intrude on his ideals. Perhaps he annuls his marriage as an emotional reaction when distraught over the devastation in Wakanda and then *rationalizes* that decision (convinces himself of a rational-seeming, better-feeling explanation). He is normally a level-headed man and, unlike Killmonger, T'Challa will reflect on his own imperfections and inconsistencies, and he will strive to make amends to others. He manages to salvage his deep friendship with Storm, which calls for courage on both their parts.[31] Storm comes to his aid in times of need, such as when she joins Black Panther's crew to combat villains sowing dissent in Wakanda.[32]

## HUMANITY

*Love, kindness, social intelligence.*

When people judge whether an action is *altruistic* (helping others without expectation of reward and with risk to oneself)[33] or *heroic* (helping others when it's most dangerous[34]), we consider the motivations behind the behavior. Because a mercenary saves a kidnap victim in order to collect a hefty paycheck, that rescue is not altruistic and the mercenary might be considered less heroic than a rescuer who risks life and limb merely out of concern for others or a need to do what's right.

Killmonger possesses "an acute grasp of human nature,"[35] which gives him some psychological advantage when he seeks to manipulate, intimidate, or persuade others to see his point of view. He therefore possesses considerable *social intelligence*, the understanding of human nature,[36] but he has no love or kindness in his heart. An empathetic person does not murder hundreds of human beings, often one at a time. The psychopath or sociopath devoid of empathy is unlikely to understand the better side of human nature as well as he understands the worse.[37]

T'Challa's half-sister Shuri wants to become the first female Black Panther, a worthwhile goal. Breaking such a glass ceiling would be important for herself personally and significant for all Wakandans. When the time comes for her to become Black Panther in T'Challa's absence, though, the panther goddess Bast deems her unworthy because of her self-serving motives. Only when Shuri shows a willingness to die fighting for the sake of her people, finally putting her love for them ahead of her own ambitions, does Bast give her blessing for Shuri to assume the Black Panther role.[38]

"I always saw T'Challa as a leader who tried to represent all his people. He was a king who cared and understood," comic book writer Don McGregor wrote when reflecting on how he

wrote the character.[39] So T'Challa's love for his people influences how he tries to lead them.


## JUSTICE

*Citizenship, fairness, leadership.*

Why would any country want a leader who is also a superhero?
Maybe it is because they want a leader who is brave, but it might
also be because they want to feel more confident that their leader
is just. Out of all the virtues outlined by positive psychologists,
one more than any other goes to the heart of what a superhero is:
*justice*, the pursuit of what is right, fair, and equitable for everyone.
As a monarch, T'Challa strives to govern with fairness, justice,
and consideration for everyone's needs, without dominating the
people as a tyrant.[40] As a hero, he pursues justice every day.


## TEMPERANCE

*Forgiveness and mercy, humility/modesty,*
*prudence, self-regulation.*

Unlike another hero who repeatedly relives his parents'
deaths[41] or one who starts doing good deeds out of guilt because
he failed to stop the burglar who soon kills Uncle Ben,[42]
T'Challa does not let his own father T'Chaka's murder determine what he does as a hero. He wishes to avenge his father, to
be sure, but does not make that his heroic *raison d'être*. In fact,
some characters even criticize him for following a more positive
path. When Iron Man fights Captain America because of how
the movie version of T'Chaka's killer has manipulated them
all, Black Panther realizes that he should not let anger and hate
govern him: "Vengeance has consumed you. It's consuming
them. I'm done letting it consume me."[43] Soon, Erik Killmonger
derides T'Challa for not being more revenge-minded, and yet
T'Challa nevertheless offers to save his enemy's life.[44]

## TRANSCENDENCE

*Gratitude, hope, humor, spirituality, appreciation of beauty and excellence.*

Comic book stories tend to avoid addressing whether superheroes hold religious beliefs. T'Challa, though, is one of comics' more openly religious and spiritual superheroes.[45] The Black Panther holds a position as head of the state church of their panther god, Bast. Institutional authority, however, does not confirm inward religiosity.[46] Also, a person can accept the principles of a religion cognitively without appreciating them emotionally. The personal virtue of *transcendence* goes beyond mundane existence "to embrace part or all of the larger universe,"[47] a sense of interrelatedness that provides meaning and value through purpose and faith. Its key strength is *spirituality*, feeling connected to nonmaterial nature or to universal, sacred, or divine nature, involving faith and purpose. Other transcendent strengths such as gratitude and hope not only are able to help the person find meaning and value but can also help someone escape, overcome, or persevere by providing reasons to keep going. These qualities boost resilience and promote mental well-being.[48]

T'Challa often shows a transcendent view of the world, with an appreciation of the beauty and majesty in everything around him. An early girlfriend, Monica Lynne, notes, "I think you have a touch of the poet yourself, T'Challa."[49]

Transcending the mundane world can give someone an otherworldly or distant quality. In T'Challa's case, this may be reflected in how modern writers tell his stories through other characters' perspectives more frequently than with other superheroes—not always, to be sure, but certainly more often. For example, throughout most of author Christopher Priest's issues of *Black Panther*, the American character Everett Ross is telling the story to the comic book audience, so the narrative and dialogue do not get into the title character's head the way most Spider-Man stories do.[50]

## THE PERFECT IMPERFECT

T'Challa embodies all the virtues that positive psychologists consider to be indicators of mental health and adjustment—not perfectly so, of course, because he is truly human. Where a humanistic psychologist might view him as an example of a *self-actualized person*, someone who has taken his potentiality and turned it into actuality while still continuing to grow,[51] the positive psychologist might note that personal potential is more complicated than that and does not so neatly fit the mold of what the founder of humanistic psychology considered to be the ideal person. Even T'Challa's enemies show many of the strengths and virtues as well. Admittedly, they show fewer of them because his enemies tend to be driven by motives most people would consider to be less than positive. The movie and the comics depict T'Challa at different points in his Black Panther journey, and so the different stories also show him at different stages in his development of these virtues and strengths.

## NOTES

1. *Black Panther* #37 (2002).
2. CyberSpacers (2004).
3. Batson et al. (2002), Coke et al. (1978); Goldberg & Michaels (1985); Hoffman (2000).
4. Committed by Helmut Zemo in *Captain America: Civil War* (2016 motion picture) and by Ulysses Klaw in a flashback first shown in *Fantastic Four* #53 (1966).
5. Starting with *Batman* (1989 motion picture).
6. Uslan (2011) and many personal communications.
7. Box Office Mojo (n.d.).
8. Marston (1928). Under the pen name Charles Moulton, he later created Wonder Woman, who debuted in *Sensation Comics* #1 (1941).
9. Seligman (1998), p. 1.
10. Bolt & Dunn (2004); Park et al. (2004); Peterson & Seligman (2004).

11. Allison & Goethals (2011).
12. American Psychiatric Association (2000 at the time; 2013 as of this writing).
13. Easterbrook (2001), p. 23.
14. Peterson & Seligman (2004), similarly described by Langley (2017).
15. *Black Panther* #1–6 (2009).
16. *Black Panther* #60 (2003), #2 (2005).
17. *Black Panther* #23–25 (2007); *Captain America: Civil War* (2006 motion picture).
18. e.g., Monique (2018).
19. *Black Panther* #4 (2009).
20. *Black Panther* #168 (2017).
21. Arvedon (2018); Chapman (2018).
22. *Black Panther* (2018 motion picture).
23. *Black Panther* #10 (2017); *Black Panther* (2018 motion picture).
24. Peterson & Seligman (2004).
25. Coogan (2006).
26. *Black Panther* (2018 motion picture).
27. *Black Panther* (2018 motion picture).
28. *Fantastic Four* #311–312 (1988).
29. And sometimes has become ruler of the world (e.g., *Super-Villain Team-Up* #14, 1977; *Marvel Graphic Novel* #27, 1987) or of the multiverse's remnants (*Secret Wars* #2, 2015).
30. *Avengers vs. X-Men* #9 (2012).
31. *A + X* #3 (2012).
32. *Black Panther* #6 (2016).
33. Batson et al. (2002), Coke et al. (1978); Goldberg & Michaels (1985); Hoffman (2000).
34. Allison & Goethals (2011).
35. Wiacek (2018), p. 38.
36. Thorndike (1920).
37. Hare (1996); Patrick et al. (2009).
38. *Black Panther* #3–6 (2009).
39. McGregor (2018), p. 7.
40. *Black Panther* #12 (2017).
41. *Detective Comics* #33 (1939) revealed the murder of Bruce Wayne's parents (his father Thomas and his not-yet-named mother Martha Wayne).
42. Spider-Man does not learn that great responsibility must accompany great power until the end of his origin story in *Amazing Fantasy* #15 (1962).
43. *Captain America: Civil War* (2016 motion picture).
44. *Black Panther* (2018 motion picture).
45. Kramer (2017).
46. Dennett & LaScola (2015).
47. Peterson & Seligman (2004), p. 519.
48. Ong et al. (2006); Sun et al. (2014); Wu (2011).
49. *Jungle Action* #16 (1975).
50. *Black Panther* #1–29 (1998–2001), 34–45 (2001–2002), 48–49 (2002).
51. Maslow (1967, 1971).

# 17

# WAKANDAN SURROGATES

## HEALING TRAUMA THROUGH PARASOCIAL RELATIONSHIPS

### Janina Scarlet & Jenna Busch

*"Learn from the pain."*
—T-Challa[1]

> *"Connection is why we're here; it is what gives purpose and meaning to our lives."*
> —social work researcher Brené Brown[2]

At a time when real-world tragedies can be too difficult to bear, fictional stories can help people find a way to cope, manage, and heal. People who witness violent events, such as hate crimes, tragic deaths, and school shootings, may develop anxiety or trauma-related stresses.[3] In addition, people who lose loved ones in a violent way are likely to experience post-traumatic reactions, such as guilt and isolation. Social isolation can further increase people's distress and symptoms, as well as slow down their recovery.[4] On the other hand, social connections can help many individuals to improve their mental health functioning even after traumatic events.[5] This kind of social connection can be seen when Black Panther's bodyguards, Ayo and Aneka, are attacked by Namor, the Prince of Atlantis. After the attack, Ayo and Aneka support one another, helping each other to get through that experience.[6] Although some individuals may not feel comfortable creating meaningful social connections with people in real life, they may instead form friendships with fictional characters, such as the Black Panther. Can such relationships with fictional characters be helpful in managing one's trauma symptoms?

## ISOLATION AND CONNECTION

People who experience a traumatic event often undergo feelings of guilt, anger, and regret. We see this in the way T'Challa is hesitant in dealing with Killmonger after dealing with the loss of his father.[7] In addition, individuals who experience trauma may struggle when it comes to reaching out to others. These individuals are likely to isolate themselves at a time when they are in most dire need for support.[8] In the process of saving his country from Doctor Doom, T'Challa destroys the source of the nation's wealth and power it.[9] Remorseful over this, T'Challa leaves his title and riches behind to go fight crime instead in Hell's Kitchen, where no one knows him and he has no friends. He even isolates himself from his then-wife, Ororo Monroe.[10]

*Social isolation* can take the form of withdrawal from others, canceling meetings, dates, or appointments, as well as emotional flatness, or the avoidance of confrontation with other people.[11] Trauma survivors might withdraw from some or all sources of social support, such as family, romantic partners, and friends.[12]

Alternatively, they may minimize their emotional distress, pretending that they are unaffected by the traumatic experience.[13] Erik Killmonger sheds no tears for his father as a child when he finds his body. When he has a flashback of that time, the vision of his father asks him why he is unable to cry for him. In response, Killmonger shrugs and says, "Everybody dies."[14]

On the other hand, receiving *social support* can alleviate symptoms associated with trauma, anxiety, and depression.[15] In fact, seeking out and accepting continuous support can serve as a form of resiliency. Specifically, after a traumatic event, social connection can become a buffer against mental health disorders, such as posttraumatic stress disorder (PTSD) and depression.[16] Examples of this include M'Baku of the Jabari tribe helping to calm T'Challa's mother and sister when two believe that T'Challa is dead[17] or when, in the comics, attorney Foggy Nelson helps T'Challa enter the United States after Daredevil leaves Hell's Kitchen.[18]

## PARASOCIAL RELATIONSHIPS

Human beings have an innate need to experience a sense of belonging. Such a sense of belonging can be obtained when an individual is willing to be vulnerably transparent with themselves and others.[19] T'Challa is open with his wife, Ororo Monroe (Storm of the X-Men), about the fact that he needs to test himself as a normal person without powers. He admits his vulnerability to her and, in turn, her acceptance of his desire allows him to process what he goes through after his battle with Doctor Doom.[20] Although a sense of belonging is typically thought of as having a real, in-person connection with others, scientists are finding that connections with fictional characters, such as the Black Panther, can also create a sense of belonging.[21] A relationship with fictional characters is called *parasocial relationship*.[22]

## JOINING THE WAKANDAN TRIBE

Reading passages about beloved characters, or watching movies or TV shows featuring one's favorite characters can lead to people experiencing lower rates of loneliness and isolation.[23] In fact, when establishing parasocial relationships, people often adopt the characters' culture, phrases, and actions.[24] Hence, connecting to characters such as T'Challa and his people can encourage real individuals to feel and act as if they were a part of the Wakandan family, while potentially boosting their sense of belonging and connection. Such a connection can help people feel better about themselves and potentially improve their mood and performance.[25] In fact, some athletes demonstrate significantly improved performance after thinking about (i.e., being primed with) Black Panther or performing the "Wakanda forever" salute.[26]

Parasocial relationships can serve as social surrogates for people at a time of emotional distress. Such relationships can take the place of surrogate friend groups, family members, or even romantic partners. These relationships can allow people to fulfill their need to belong through fictional characters by allowing the individual to have social support without the risk of social rejection.[27]

Because many individuals who experience trauma may struggle with social connection, and because social connection is beneficial when it comes to recovering from trauma-related disorders, it stands to reason that finding safe ways for individuals to understand their traumatic experiences can be helpful in recovery.[28] On more than one occasion, T'Challa speaks to his father T'Chaka in the spirit world.[29] Viewing such connections with deceased family members through the lens of fiction can help viewers to process and understand their own grief.[30]

At a time when real-life social connections may be challenging or inaccessible, parasocial relationships can take the form of surrogate social support systems for people who experience trauma. In fact, relationships with fictional characters, such as Black Panther, appear to increase mental well-being for individuals who experience traumatic events. Furthermore, individuals with a traumatic history appear to be more drawn to establishing parasocial relationships than individuals without a trauma history.[31]

## RETELLING OF THE TRAUMA NARRATIVE THROUGH PARASOCIAL RELATIONSHIPS

Traumatic experiences can lead trauma survivors to develop unhelpful narratives. For example, people like T'Challa, who lose a loved one in a violent manner, may believe that that they should have somehow been able to prevent the traumatic event or that the world is a dangerous place.[32] After his father is killed in an explosion, T'Challa chooses to keep Wakanda's technological advancements from the outside world, believing the world to be too dangerous to have access to it. Despite Nakia and W'Kabi's insistence that their help could make a difference in the world, T'Challa chooses to stay isolated from it. Only after he faces the repercussions of this decision does T'Challa change his mind, deciding to share Wakandan technology with the world.[33]

Some trauma survivors may struggle with coping with their experiences because they have difficulty conceptualizing what happened to them. Most individuals are not taught how to label and identify their emotions. Hence, when a traumatic event takes place, people may not be able to understand their experiences, or trauma reactions.[34] After finding his father's lifeless body, Killmonger puts his anger and hurt into the art of killing. Specifically, he makes a game of how many people he can kill while in the armed forces.[35]

Parasocial relationships can assist trauma survivors by teaching them how to understand and report traumatic events to the proper authorities.[36] For example, by learning about a fictional character's assault experience, viewers/readers can learn to understand and label their own assault experiences, as well as learn how to ask for help.[37] When T'Challa has to face becoming a king after his father's death, he asks Nakia to be with him, as well as his mother and his sister Shuri.[38]

In addition, case studies and recent research studies show that when people establish meaningful connections with social surrogates, such as the Black Panther, they are more willing to commit to therapy.[39] The most helpful therapy interventions in treating trauma-related disorders, such as PTSD, include an *exposure* to one's traumatic event (retelling one's trauma story until it becomes less triggering). Many people may avoid treatment because of fear of doing an exposure in therapy. However, parasocial relationships appear to strengthen the individuals' willingness to participate in exposures and adhere to treatment.[40]

## NARRATIVE EXPOSURE THERAPY

During traumatic events, the sounds, smells, and visual cues can become associated with emotional arousal, such as anxiety, fear, and anger (the classic *fight-or-flight response*). In the future, when individuals see, hear, or smell something that reminds them of the traumatic event, they may become triggered and experience a fight-or-flight response again. Memories that trigger fight-or-flight response are called *hot memories*.

# Superhero Therapy

## Janina Scarlet

In many ways, parasocial relationships can serve as examples
of appropriate coping behaviors when someone experiences a
tragic or a traumatic event. As such, fictional characters, especially superheroes such as T'Challa, can serve as active mentors
to the viewers. T'Challa's grief, his coping skills, his honor, and
his commitment to doing the right thing,[41] can inspire the viewers
to engage in similar behaviors.[42]

Superhero therapy refers to incorporating popular culture characters, such as T'Challa, into evidence-based therapy to help
people learn how to become their own version of a superhero
in real life. This treatment can be used to help people manage
depression, anxiety, and trauma-related disorders.[43] This treatment incorporates the retelling of the trauma survivor's origin story
in connection to his or her parasocial relationships. For example,
an individual who experienced a devastating death of a loved
one (his or her origin story) may relate to T'Challa's grief over his
father's passing. This individual may then be asked to consider
what guidance someone like T'Challa may provide for him or
her when he or she is struggling with grief.[44] After going through
the loss of his father, perhaps T'Challa would counsel someone
going through grief to imagine a conversation in which the
deceased comes back to speak to the bereaved. By incorporating T'Challa's mentorship, the trauma survivor would then be
invited to retell his or her origin story from a survivor's perspective,
thus increasing his or her sense of resilience.[45]

In order to reduce the impact of the trauma on the individual, the trauma survivor going through narrative exposure therapy (NET) might be invited to list his or her positive and negative life experiences in chronological order (a *lifeline*). The individual would then be invited to discuss his or her lifeline events over time until the hot memories become less triggering for the trauma survivor.[46]

For example, if T'Challa participated in narrative exposure therapy, he would first write out his lifeline, which would include the birth of his sister Shuri, the death of his father T'Chaka, the rite of passage, and the dissolution of his relationship with Ororo Monroe after his father's death.[47] Other events on his lifeline would include joining up with the Avengers while they battled over the Sekovia Accords,[48] as well as his country being overrun by aliens.[49] He would subsequently go through his lifeline in detail, processing the painful memories with his therapist to help him cope with his own hot memories.

## ASSEMBLING YOUR AVENGERS TEAM

After experiencing a devastating loss, such as losing one's parent, as T'Challa does,[50] some people might struggle with understanding and processing their experiences. Some might minimize their emotional pain, while others might isolate from their support groups.[51] Forming a parasocial relationship with fictional characters, such as T'Challa, can have positive effects for someone going through trauma.[52]

A fictional character, like T'Challa, can become especially relatable to the viewers when he is going through something similar to what they are experiencing. Such parasocial relationships can allow the individual to feel a stronger sense of social connection, and can help promote prosocial behaviors, as well as create a path for healing.[53] Specifically, parasocial relationships can be used in a mental health setting to help survivors to understand and process their traumatic experiences, as well as to find a sense of resilience after a traumatic event. Furthermore, parasocial relationships can encourage people to take courageous steps toward recovery and toward helping others.[54] Therefore, such implementation of fictional characters into counseling can help trauma survivors become their own versions of a superhero in real life.[55]

## NOTES

1. *Marvel Heroes* (2013 MMORPG).
2. Brown (2015), p. 253.
3. Fallahi & Lesik (2009).
4. Wilson et al. (2006).
5. Pietrzak et al. (2009; 2010).
6. *Black Panther* #2 (2017).
7. *Black* Panther (2018 motion picture).
8. Gabriel et al. (2017); Wilson et al. (2006).
9. *Black Panther: The Man without Fear!* #519 (2011).
10. *Black Panther: The Man without Fear!* #519 (2011).
11. Wilson et al. (2006).
12. Tsai et al. (2012).
13. Wilson et al. (2006).
14. *Black Panther* (2018 motion picture).
15. Pietrzak et al. (2009; 2010).
16. Pietrzak et al. (2009; 2010).
17. *Black Panther* (2018 motion picture).
18. *Black Panther: The Man without Fear!* #519 (2011).
19. Brown (2015).
20. *Black Panther: The Man without Fear!* #519 2011).
21. Derrick et al. (2009).
22. Derrick et al. (2009).
23. Derrick et al. (2017).
24. Gabriel & Young (2011).
25. Derrick et al. (2009); Howard & Borgella (2018).
26. Howard & Borgella (2018).
27. Derrick et al. (2009).
28. Gabriel et al. (2017); Tsai et al. (2012).
29. e.g., *Avengers* #21 (2014); *Black Panther* (2018 motion picture).
30. Markell & Markell (2013).
31. Gabriel et al. (2017).
32. Resick & Schnicke (1992).

33. *Black Panther* (2018 motion picture).
34. Elbert et al. (2015); Neuner et al. (2004).
35. *Black Panther* (2018 motion picture); *Rise of the Black Panther* #4 (2018).
36. Garbarino (1987); Scarlet (in press).
37. Garbarino (1987); Scarlet (in press).
38. *Black Panther.* (2018 motion picture).
39. Scarlet (in press).
40. Scarlet (in press).
41. *Black Panther* (2018 motion picture).
42. Scarlet (in press).
43. Rubin & Livesay (2006); Scarlet (2016); Scarlet (in press).
44. Scarlet (in press).
45. Scarlet (in press).
46. Neuner et al. (2004).
47. *Black Panther* (2018 motion picture); *Avengers vs. X-Men* #9 (2012).
48. *Captain America: Civil War* (2016 motion picture).
49. *Captain America: Civil War* (2016 motion picture).
50. *Black Panther* (2018 motion picture).
51. Gabriel et al. (2017); Wilson et al. (2006).
52. Markell & Markell (2013); Scarlet (in press).
53. Gabriel et al. (2017); Scarlet (in press).
54. Rubin & Livesay (2006); Scarlet (in press).
55. Scarlet (in press).

# 18

# WHY BLACK PANTHER MATTERS TO US ALL

## Dave Verhaagen

*"An entire generation of children will now know that a Black
superhero, society, imagination, and power can exist right
alongside Peter Parker, Steve Rogers, and Bruce Wayne. An
entire generation of children will not know what it feels like to
not see themselves reflected back on costume racks, coloring books
or movie screens."*

—writer Tre Johnson[1]

*"Today we are all the Black Panther!"*
—T'Challa[2]

In a rancorous and divisive time in our world, *Black Panther* rose up to become not only the biggest box office film of the year and one of its most critically acclaimed, but also an important cultural landmark. This was a movie about heroes of African origin who were courageous and ingenious and powerful. These were men and women who were proud Africans who fought selflessly to save the whole world.

So important was this film to those of African descent that a man named Frederick Joseph raised over $50,000 through GoFundMe to send the children of Harlem to see the movie in theaters. He challenged other communities to do the same, prompting 600 nationwide campaigns that raised nearly one million dollars for thousands of kids to see the movie. Donations rolled in from all 50 states and 50 countries around the world. "All children deserve to believe they can save the world, go on exciting adventures, or accomplish the impossible," said Joseph.[3]

The film had a special importance for me as the adoptive dad of an African son. Daniel was born in West Africa during a gruesome civil war that landed him and his two sisters in an orphanage. His life in America was far safer, but adopting him allowed me to witness firsthand racial tensions and actions here that I never could have experienced before. It drove me to explore why people often behaved badly toward others who are different. The psychology of bias has some unexpected twists and turns. Those understandings provide us with some reasons why this cultural phenomenon of a film is important to us all.

## WHY BLACK PANTHER MATTERS TO ME

My dad had just started his senior year at Granby High School in Norfolk, Virginia, when administrators padlocked the doors and placed the school under police guard following a state order designed to fight integration. The school closed for the year, forcing around 10,000 White students to lose their senior year, all because the state didn't want to admit 17 African-American kids years after *Brown v. Board of Education* had been decided.[4] My father went to the shipyard to complete a GED and never earned his high school diploma.

Matters of race occupied much of my adult life, both professionally and personally. I spent the first five years of my career working in community mental health agencies that served mostly African-American teenagers. Most of my clients during those years were of African descent, as were most my co-workers.

Race also took center stage in my personal life. After my wife Ellen's diagnosis with ovarian cancer, we built our family through adoption, first with a White kid, then a Hispanic girl born to a Guatemalan woman in Virginia. Years later, long after we thought our family was complete, we learned of a brother and sister living in an orphanage in Liberia, West Africa, who wanted to be adopted by a family in Charlotte near their biological sister. We read their profiles, talked to people who knew them, received letters from them, and spoke with them by phone. We fell in love with these two kids. The four of us (my wife and I and our two original children) decided as a family to adopt these siblings.

Within adoption circles, there is considerable debate about White families adopting children of color, and of families in wealthy countries adopting children from third world countries. The arguments are more complex and nuanced than I'd realized. While I sympathize with the perspective that pulling children out of developing nations is not always the best way to serve those countries, we were not just adopting orphans from a poor country; we were adopting these two particular children. I'd argue we were all meant to be together. And whether you'd agree with this, the fact is we were—and are—permanently together.

As his new dad and advocate, I saw firsthand how Daniel, the boy we adopted from Liberia, was viewed with suspicion and rarely given the benefit of the doubt. More so than his biological sister, Daniel made people uneasy, despite his easy smile and gentle manner. I was present when he was followed by the manager in a drugstore, denied a membership in a rec center, and asked to leave the grounds of an apartment complex for no other reason than his presence made people grilling hamburgers feel uncomfortable. And these are only the experiences I witnessed. No doubt he has experienced dozens more.

One night around midnight, he got pulled over for a DWB (Driving While Black) outside of my house just outside of Nashville. He and a friend had driven over 450 miles to stay with us during their spring break, yet he got pulled over a few feet from his final destination. I saw the blue lights and peeked out the window to see a cop shining his flashlight into Daniel's eyes. I threw on my shoes and sprinted outside.

The officer asked who I was and looked surprised by my answer: "I'm his father."

His eyes narrowed. He explained that he pulled my son over because one of his taillights was out. The only problem was there was no missing taillight. When I pointed that out, he changed his story, claiming he pulled him over because Daniel slowed down as the officer followed him, which provided probable cause. (Doesn't everyone slow down when they see police following them?)

In the end, the officers conferred and let Daniel go with a written warning that read, "WARNING: Lights required—motor vehicles." Notice it didn't say the car had a missing light but only that lights were required, as if the police were pulling over random people to alert them they needed to have lights on their cars.

As of this writing, Daniel has never broken the law, never been a behavior problem at home, and never gotten in trouble at school (except for the time he clobbered a kid who called him the n-word and took a swing at him). Yet he's faced many more indignities before age 25 than I ever have at more than twice his age.

Maybe it's just a coincidence or bad timing when the store clerk greets every White person who comes into the store, but looks down and says nothing when Daniel comes in the door. Maybe it's an oversight when the two tables that got seated after us get waited on before Daniel and I do. Maybe it's bad timing when no one ever comes to help Daniel while he's waited patiently for over 15 minutes to try on a pair of shoes in a sporting goods store. Maybe. But I doubt it.

I seem to observe it more than he does, but maybe he's seeing it all and just keeping silent. After years of such subtle mistreatment, maybe he's learned to keep it in. He remains unswervingly polite.

Imagine coming from a war-torn country where you've been shot at, seen a relative hit with a grenade, watched your father die, faced near starvation, and suffered a thousand other hardships, only to be treated with suspicion and derision in America. Yet he is a remarkably resilient person, letting all the slights and injustices roll off him much better than I ever could.

Into that reality comes *Black Panther*, a magnificent story of an African prince who is also a superhero. Many readers throughout the world had known this story for several decades,[5] but films turned it into a worldwide phenomenon.[6] For a young Black man like Daniel—and his White dad—it's a story that matters. Watching an African superhero command the big screen with dignity and courage and strength mattered a great deal. T'Challa was the hero we needed. He is also a hero who echoes and amplifies the real-life Black heroes who walk among us.

One of those heroes is Congressman John Lewis, a central figure of the civil rights movement, beginning at only age 20, when he became a leader of the sit-ins in Nashville, the city

I now call home. He'd suffered a brutal beating during the Selma march and had been thrown in prison at least 24 times. He knows what it means to sacrifice. John Lewis embodies courage. He and Andrew Aydin wrote a graphic novel memoir trilogy called *March*, chronicling Lewis's life and struggles for equality.[7] This became the first graphic novel to win the National Book Award.[8]

Another of my heroes was the unlikely president of Liberia, the West African country that was the birthplace of Daniel and his sister, Maddie. Ellen Johnson Sirleaf was a major force in the women's movement that turned the tide in the bloody and hellish Liberian Civil War. Along the way, she was imprisoned more than once and even given a 10-year sentence, before being pardoned following the international outcry.

In 2009, I attended an invitation-only movie screening of a documentary called *Pray the Devil Back to Hell*[9] in Charlotte, NC. The film depicted how the women of Liberia had banded together to use nonviolent protests to force peace talks that eventually ended the horrifying conflict that took a quarter of a million lives. The organizers told us there might be a special guest at the end of the screening. As the lights came up, Secret Service agents entered the theater and took their positions. They advised us to stay in our seats.

After a few minutes, President Ellen Johnson Sirleaf entered the room to tremendous applause. Even then, as the first female president of an African country, she was a legendary figure. She was a Harvard-educated economist, the recipient of the Nobel Peace Prize, and one of Forbes's top 100 most powerful women in the world.

After she spoke about the hardships Liberia had faced in the past and the challenges it faced in the future, she took questions, I asked what the state of mental health services in Liberia since the war was like. She answered, "We have a very traumatized country, and we do not have adequate services to deal with all of it. If you would like to come help us, I personally invite you to come."[10]

The following year, I was on a plane to Monrovia, the nation's capital, to meet with leaders from the national medical center there. The hospital, named after JFK, was occupied by rebel soldiers during the civil war and used as a machine gun nest overlooking a major thoroughfare. It had taken substantial damage during the battles and had only been renovated the year I arrived.

As the head of the hospital, her staff, and the special assistant to the president gathered around my iPad, I laid out a proposal for increasing access to mental health services in the form of talks for parents held in local churches. They were enthusiastic about the initiative.

Later that week, I ventured into the bush toward an orphanage, down dirt roads and past massive mud holes that could have submerged our jeep. During the war, this refuge had sponsored the Liberian Boys Choir, a fund-raising effort that allowed some of the boys to leave the war-torn country for periods of time.

During the height of the civil conflict, the boys were performing at a church in North Carolina when they learned that rebel soldiers had overrun their orphanage. They had nowhere to live if they returned to Liberia, so several families in the Charlotte area adopted over a dozen of the boys, creating a true Liberian community around the city. Over time, the community grew, spawning three Liberian restaurants, two Liberian churches, and several other African businesses.

Now, years after the war, the orphanage had been reclaimed and rebuilt, with a wall built around it to keep thieves from looting it as they had for years. Even after the conflict had ceased, the head of the orphanage, an older but powerfully built man, suffered a scar across his palm from a machete strike, having confronted a band of rogues who were robbing the food storehouse. Wielding a metal rod, he single-handedly ran the entire mob off, like an African Daredevil.

When I arrived at the children's village, the kids swarmed me, grabbing my hand, pinching my skin with fascination, yelling out their names so I might remember them. Tears came to my eyes, not only because these little kids were so starved for affection, but because my own African children had lived in that same orphanage.

An experience like that changes you. Africa and its people burrow under your skin and wrap around your heart. When you are touched so deeply, you want nothing more than to see the children of Africa—wherever they now live—to be richly blessed, to feel dignity and respect, and to experience love and acceptance.

So when *Black Panther* arrived and I could watch it with my children, it was much more than another Marvel superhero movie. It was an aspirational vision of Africa with dark-skinned Africans who were scientists and superheroes who moved with grace and acted with valor. It was a story that mattered.

## THE PSYCHOLOGY OF PREJUDICE

*"Y'all sitting up here all comfortable. Must feel good. Meanwhile, there's about two billion people all over the world that look like us, but their lives are a lot harder."*
—Erik Killmonger to Wakandans[11]

Two months after the release of *Black Panther*, a 14-year-old African-American boy named Brennan Walker woke up late and missed his bus in Rochester Hills, Michigan, so he started the 90-minute walk to school. His mom had taken his phone away as a punishment, so when he got lost along the way, he couldn't call for help. He approached a house and knocked on the front door for directions.[12]

"I knocked on the lady's door," Brennan said later, "then she started yelling at me and she was like, 'Why are you trying to break into my house?' I was trying to explain to her that I was trying to get directions to Rochester High." That's when the situation went off the rails. "She kept yelling at me, then the guy came downstairs and he grabbed the gun. I saw it and started to run and that's when I heard the gunshot."

Home security footage showed the woman's husband, a 53-year-old White man, aim and fire a 12-gauge shotgun at Brennan as he fled, missing him. The young boy hid and broke down in tears. Later he said, "I'm happy that I didn't become a statistic."

In the month before I wrote this chapter, I collected at least one story every day of Black men and women being subjected to mistreatment, often with the incident captured on video. Even when Black men were acting heroically, the results have been heart-wrenchingly tragic. Jemel Roberson was a 26-year-old security guard working at a nightclub in the Chicago suburbs when a fight broke out and someone fired shots. He subdued the suspect, but when police arrived, an officer shot and killed Roberson. A similar incident happened in an Alabama mall a week later when 21-year-old E.J. Bradford was shot three times from behind by an off-duty police officer. The autopsy concluded the cause of death was "homicide."[13]

*Black Panther* comic book writer[14] Ta-Nehisi Coates wrote to his own teenage son, "But all our phrasing—race relations, racial chasm, racial justice, racial profiling, White privilege, even White supremacy—serves to obscure that racism is a visceral experience, that it dislodges brains, blocks airways, rips muscle, extracts organs, cracks bones, breaks teeth. You must never look away from this. You must always remember that the sociology, the history, the economics, the graphs, the charts, the regressions all land, with great violence, upon the body."[15]

Racism is perhaps our ugliest, most tenacious sin. At times, it hides in the underbelly of our culture; at other times, it is on vivid display, as we've seen in Charlottesville and in many recorded incidents since then. To be clear, I don't know the hearts of the Starbucks manager, the homeowner who fired at the kid, or the cops who shot the young adults. Perhaps some of them are overtly racist, but perhaps not. Still, the outcome is the same, ranging from humiliating to scary to deadly. Someone need not be an avowed racist or White supremacist to commit acts of injustice, but it does beg the question of why.

Psychology provides us with some answers.

Social scientist Margaret Hagerman spent two years doing in-depth interviews with White children and their families for her book, *White Kids: Growing Up with Privilege in a Racially Divided America*.[16] She found that kids learn about race and racism not just from overt conversations with their parents, but from the decisions their parents make about where they live, who gets invited to picnics, what schools they choose for their children, when they lock their doors, what media they consume, how they respond to racist comments and jokes, and other, seemingly invisible choices. Even if the parents are not expressing overtly racist attitudes—and even if they are outspoken in their support of minorities—these small decisions have a big impact on their children's attitudes toward race and racism.[17] These children grow up to be adults who have internalized all the subtle but powerful racial messages of their youth.

This early priming allows negative media portrayals of Black men to reinforce these unconscious associations, which has awful real-life consequences. One review of the research literature found that negative mass media portrayals were strongly linked to more health problems and lower life expectancy among Black men.[18] Another study concluded that negative media portrayals of Black men affected how police treated them.

Dr. Pamela Valera, one of the authors, said, "Unarmed Black Americans are five times more likely to be shot and killed by police than unarmed White Americans. We believe that media may play a significant role in these disproportionate deaths."[19]

In another study, researchers rapidly flashed two images to 64 college students, telling them to ignore the first picture, which was the face of either a Black or White child. The second image showed either a gun or a baby toy. They then asked the students to identify the object. Researchers found that study participants more quickly identified the second picture correctly as a gun if they had also seen a picture of a Black boy. And here's the kicker: They also inaccurately identified the picture of the toy as a gun if they had previously seen the picture of the Black boy. Two follow-up tests found that participants associated Black faces with guns and White faces with nonthreatening objects, no matter the age of the person in the picture. For their fourth trial, the researchers found that participants were more likely to associate scary words, such as *violent*, *hostile*, and *dangerous*, with Black boys than with White boys.[20]

Besides the subtle (or, for some, not-so-subtle) messages about race that we receive from our families, coupled with the negative portrayals of Black men in the media, there may also be a seemingly benign trait in humans that contributes to racist behavior. To illustrate, let's do a very basic experiment. Look at this row of shapes and rate how uncomfortable it makes you from 1 (not uncomfortable) to 10 (extremely uncomfortable):

Now, look at the next row of shapes and rate how uncomfortable it makes you from 1 (*not uncomfortable*) to 10 (*extremely uncomfortable*):

Was there any increase in your level of discomfort from the first row to the second row? For some people, there might not be the slightest increase, but for many others, there may be anywhere from a little more discomfort to a lot more discomfort.

Why? And how does this relate to racism and social prejudice?

One recent study, conducted by researchers at Yale, provides a surprising insight: People crave patterns and they become uneasy when those patterns are broken. Our brains seek familiarity. From an early age, it's how we learn and make sense of the world. These patterns also help us feel safe. The week I wrote this chapter, one of my clients, a college student at a major university, lamented the stress of going from high school to college. He said, "I used to know everyone and know how everything worked. Now I don't know and it's really stressful." Familiar patterns create safety and security. However, when the pattern is broken, it can create a sense of unease and insecurity.

For their study, the researchers showed people a series of geometric shapes, like our row of triangles, then another with one triangle out of line. Researchers measured how much the disrupted pattern bothered the participants. What they found might surprise you. Those who scored high on discomfort for the broken patterns also had greater dislike of people who were different, including people of different races.[21] So if someone looks or behaves differently than the norm, a prejudice against that person begins to take root. The individual may not even be fully aware of his or her forming prejudice, nor might he or she hold blatantly racist beliefs.

This in no way lets people off the hook for racist actions, nor does it mitigate the harm done, but it provides insight as to why people behave as they do. Because the study is correlational—showing a relationship between the two factors of discomfort with broken patterns and prejudice toward people who are different—and not causal, we can't yet prove that dislike for broken patterns is at the root of prejudice, but it is a compelling step forward.

To change our automatic reactions to those who are different, we require exposure to stories and connections with individuals who are different. An extensive review of the research literature found that public perception of Black men creates barriers and causes many injustices. The authors write, "Among the most important mechanisms for maintaining (or changing) these perceptions are the mass media with their significant power to shape popular ideas and attitudes."[22]

Mass media, including film, television, and even comics, has the power to refashion our unconscious attitudes and automatic reactions to people who are different from us. When I asked Anton Gollwitzer, the lead researcher for the broken pattern study, about the potential impact of *Black Panther*, he said, "When you are watching the movie and you see so many Black actors, the pattern is Black actors, so they are no longer seen as the outliers. Now they are the pattern."

> *"Black Panther is a Hollywood movie, and Wakanda is a fictional nation. But . . . they must also function as a place for multiple generations of Black Americans to store some of our most deeply held aspirations."*
>
> —writer Carvell Wallace[23]

## WHY BLACK PANTHER MATTERS TO US

This is why *Black Panther* matters to us. It creates a new pattern, it upends the unconscious biases, and it makes the vision of heroic and ingenious Black men and women seem familiar and true. It succeeds beautifully at creating a new schema for us, one where we expect to see heroic Black men and brilliant Black women.

At first, breaking a pattern stirs discomfort, but often it is the necessary step to creating a better model. *Black Panther* is arguably the first international blockbuster to challenge the old pattern lodged in our brains. *Rolling Stone* writer Tre Johnson reflects on the title character: "He's not being played for laughs. He's not a sidekick or born out of dire circumstances. His story, one of an ingrained birthright, legacy and royalty is a stark difference for how we tend to treat most Black superheroes—and Black superhero movies."[24] *Black Panther* breaks the pattern and replaces it with something better, something more dignified and noble.

Though some segments of the public grumble and complain, the positive response to the film has far overshadowed the hatred. As one of the top-10 grossing films of all time, the movie is a powerful trailblazer that helps us experience Black men as courageous and not scary—and Black women as shrewd and not easily dismissed. The film has made its mark. A new pattern, one with a worldwide audience, has begun.

When I asked Daniel what he thought of the movie, he said, "It made me proud." During our 30-minute conversation, he used the word *proud* no less than a dozen times. That *Black Panther* makes a young Black man proud of himself and his heritage should make this film matter to us all.

I asked Daniel what stood out to him about the movie. "It was a movie about Africa," he said. He's right. This superhero film is, at its heart, a story of Africa. Even though Wakanda is fictional, the culture of Africa with its rich heritage—the dress, the rituals, the community, the beauty—was all there, he explained. "I'd never seen Africans who were superheroes in a big movie before," he said. And then it hit me: We've seen Black superheroes in film before—Blade, Storm, Nick Fury, Luke Cage, War Machine, Falcon, and others—but we hadn't seen an African superhero. *Black Panther* celebrates Africa itself. Writing for the *Washington Post*, Ishaan Tharoor goes further: "As an idealized homeland, Wakanda also represents the powerful promise of Black liberation dreamed by generations of African Americans."[25] In his *New York Times Magazine* essay, Carvell Wallace wrote, "Never mind that most of us had never been to Africa. The point was not verisimilitude or a precise accounting of Africa's reality. It was the envisioning of a free self."[26]

*Black Panther* gives my Black son a superhero who looks like him and reveals an aspirational vision of Africa that makes him proud. It matters to us all because our children have a new vision of Black men and women as heroes—courageous, sacrificial, tenacious heroes. Michelle Obama tweeted to the *Black Panther* team, "Because of you, young people will finally see superheroes that look like them on the big screen."[27]

As a psychologist, I've seen the profoundly negative impact prejudice and racism has had on young men and women of color. As the father of two children of Africa who are now citizens of the United States, I've seen it even more up close and personal. But *Black Panther* has made a difference. It has made my son—and many other Black sons—proud of who they are and where they have come from. The film gives us a reason for optimism and an opportunity for us all to celebrate our common humanity. It is a movie that matters to me and to my son, and also one that matters to us all.

Dave and Daniel during the writing of this chapter.

## NOTES

1. Johnson (2017).
2. *Black Panther* #40 (2008).
3. GoFundMe (2018).
4. Brewbaker (1960); Watson (2008).
5. Since *Fantastic Four* #52–53 (1966).
6. *Captain America: Civil War* (2016 motion picture); *Black Panther* (2018 motion picture).
7. Starting with *March: Book One* (2013).
8. Cavna (2016).
9. *Pray the Devil Back to Hell* (2008 documentary motion picture).
10. Personal communication (2009, April 18).
11. *Black Panther* (2018 motion picture).
12. Jones et al. (2018); Madani & Romero (2018).
13. Roberts (2018).
14. Beginning with *Black Panther* #1 (2016).
15. Coates (2015), p. 10.
16. Hagerman (2018).
17. Hagerman (2018).
18. Entman (2006).
19. Oshiro & Valera (2018).
20. Todd et al. (2016).
21. Gollwitzer et al. (2017).
22. Opportunity Agenda (2011), p. 13.
23. Wallace (2018).
24. Johnson (2017).
25. Tharoor (2018).
26. Wallace (2018).
27. Obama (2018).

# 19

# ILLUSTRATION, INSPIRATION & THE IMPORTANCE OF IDENTIFICATION

## INTERVIEW WITH ARTISTS ARVELL JONES AND KEN LASHLEY

### Travis Langley

*"I love it when a plan comes together."*
—T'Challa[1]

> *"It's not in the draftsmanship; it's in the man."*
> —Black Panther co-creator, artist Jack Kirby[2]

**B**lack Panther has emerged as an inspirational character in a way that not too many characters of any kind, not just comic book superheroes, ever rival. This is especially impressive considering how erratic the character's publication history has been and the fact that his live-action film debut came a full five decades after he first appeared in comics.[3] Black Panther has proven to be a strong, exciting character with an appeal that crosses boundaries of race, age, culture, and other demographics, and yet he also has a special place in the hearts of many who have rightly felt underrepresented.

When the US Supreme Court made its landmark ruling that declared school segregation to be unconstitutional in the *Brown v. Board of Education* case in 1954, the justices took into consideration evidence that the existing system had fostered antiBlack prejudices, even among African Americans themselves. Among other things, they learned that researchers had found that when given a choice between Black dolls and White dolls, most African-American children then preferred the White dolls.[4] In the subsequent decades, as desegregation became law and public discourse on racial issues expanded, African-American children became increasingly likely to prefer Black dolls and African-American adults came to view themselves more favorably with regard to characteristics such as intelligence, initiative, and reliability. And yet, in South Africa, where apartheid institutionalized segregation by law until the 1990s, researchers who showed photos to schoolchildren in a multiracial school in South Africa found that Black children said they would prefer the White children in the photos—and that was in the 21st century.[5]

Some people want to see positive examples of *in-group* members, people in the same groups as themselves, and others need to see positive examples of *out-group* members to help them overcome their own biases. As author Christopher Priest mentioned to us (chapter 8), he strove to show the progression of the outsider Everett K. Ross's views as Ross came to understand both T'Challa and Wakanda better through ongoing exposure and experience with them. We also spoke with artists who worked on Black Panther stories over the years, for their insight on what Black Panther meant to them in younger days and today.

## DREAMING AND DRAWING

Detroit-born artist Arvell Jones first broke into the comic book industry as an uncredited assistant drawing backgrounds for artist Rich Buckler on writer Don McGregor's earliest "Panther's Rage" stories in *Jungle Action*.[6] Jones went on to work as the lead illustrator on titles for both Marvel (e.g., *Iron Man, Daredevil, The Avengers*) and DC Comics (e.g., *All-Star Squadron, The Superman Family, Superboy and the Legion of Super-Heroes*). While penciling *Marvel Premiere*, starring Iron Fist, he and writer Tony Isabella turned one of Jones's creations into Misty Knight, the bionic-armed detective featured prominently in *The Defenders, Luke Cage*, and *Iron Fist* television series.[7] More recently, he worked on production art for the *Black Panther* motion picture, providing hundreds of sketches that became the foundation for movie posters and actor Chadwick Boseman's own poses.

Hailing from farther north in Toronto, artist Ken Lashley worked on such DC Comics titles as *Action Comics, Superman*, and *The Secret Six* before he got to fulfill a lifelong dream illustrating *Black Panther* and *X-Men: Gold* for Marvel Comics. Each of these men worked with Black Panther at critical times in the character's history—the earliest stories with T'Challa as the lead, the storyline in which Shuri becomes a Black Panther, and the motion picture that unleashed him into the wider array of our world's popular culture. During conventions where we've appeared together, both men spoke with me about their personal experiences as Black Panther fans and artists, and here they share some thoughts on why the character really matters.[8]

**Arvell Jones:** I was Richard Buckler's assistant back in the day when he was doing *Jungle Action* with the Black Panther. So I was sitting there doing backgrounds, listening to Don McGregor and Rich discuss the character and when they created Killmonger. I watched

Don come over to Richard's house and stand up on his table, do the poses. He was very much involved in every aspect of building that book as best he could.

Rich and I were both from Detroit, along with Jim Starlin, Allen Milgrom, Terry Austin, Keith Pollard, Tom Orzechowski—I can go on. There's about 15 of us. Detroit was one of the first cities to host a comic con. There were stores that sold old comic books, where I kept running into these guys, and we all became friends. We all started off together, and we sort of formed a little informal club, a workshop for ourselves to develop our art and learn how to get into the business. We made a pact that if one of us got into the industry, we were all going to get in. Rich was first.

Under Rich, the very first comic he called me up to do was *Jungle Action* with the Black Panther. For the part, I didn't get paid. He housed me and took me out to the movies and fed me. He was a little more advanced than me, so I was a student. I was learning and helping him out.

**Travis Langley:** Ken, how did you wind up working on *Black Panther?*

**Ken Lashley:** I was working at DC on a *Cyborg* mini-series,[9] when I got a call from Max Alonso where he said to me, "I hear you would love to draw Black Panther at some point in your life."

I go, "Dude, don't play with me. Don't play with me, right?"

"No, we have a thing, [writer] Reggie Hudlin is writing it, [artist] Larry Stroman's in it, and we wanted you to be part of it. Would you want to do it?"

"Yes it was my favorite thing growing up 100 percent, but I am still under contract at DC."

So I kind of was working at DC and the day my

contract was over—literally, Tuesday it was over, then Wednesday morning I put the DC stuff on the side table and started working. I think it was an annual and the first thing I did was to draw a female Black Panther in that one. So I think the *Cyborg* mini-series I was pretty unprofessional because I didn't finish *Cyborg*. I was doing my dream, what I really loved. I should've just said, "I can't do it anymore," but I didn't, so they cut the *Cyborg* mini-series by an issue. That's how I got my first *Black Panther* gig and then after that I got "The Deadliest of the Species."[10]

**Travis:** The one where Shuri first becomes a Black Panther.

**Ken:** Yes, Yes issue number 5 where she actually dons the suit for the first time. I got to design it with the fur. That's my design. There's not a lot you can do with that look. Give her some fur to maybe feminize it a bit, but that was kind of it. It was fun to do.

   It's one of the most over-the-top things I've ever done in my career—being able to draw a book that I loved as a kid. My mom bought me my first book. She bought me a lot of different books, but the Black Panther was one of the first that I remember her buying. I don't think she read a lot of the issues she gave me because one of the issues I really loved was Black Panther fighting the KKK.[11]

**Travis:** McGregor's second storyline.

**Ken:** It was crazy! But on the cover, he was fighting what looked like the KKK. That's how I got hooked on the Black Panther, so drawing it was amazing.

**Travis:** Arvell, how did you wind up doing your recent work on the *Black Panther* movie?

**Arvell:** The creative director assigned to *Black Panther* went to high school with me, and he remembered me. He called me up and said, "Hey, man, you did draw the Black Panther, didn't you?"

I said, "Yeah, why?"

"You know how to draw him?"

"Yes, I know how to draw him!"

"Send me a drawing."

So I did the drawing real quick and I sent it to him. He says, "You're perfect! You're working with me on the *Black Panther* movie posters."

**Travis:** When you're working on a movie poster, input comes from a zillion different people. How much freedom do you have on that as an artist?

**Arvell:** My job was very specific, and that was to pose the Black Panther. My job was to sketch what poses Chadwick Boseman was supposed to take. They said, "We don't know what a Black Panther does. What does a Black Panther do?" He'd have me do a number of thumbnails, then take some of those and finalize them, make them look a little better. He'd say, "Send more, send me more, because tomorrow we're shooting him, and we need these poses." So I did about 200 drawings. The next day, he was sending me 200 pictures of Chadwick Boseman in all the poses that I drew. Later on, they were being retouched. I'd say, "That leg doesn't look right. He doesn't look panther-like enough." "So how do we make it more panther-like?" I'd find myself on Photoshop sketching over some of the work.

**Travis:** Why do you think this character is so important? Why was he important to you?

**Arvell:** He stopped me from getting beat up by bullies.

**Travis:** That's important.

**Arvell:** I was walking around with the first issue with Black Panther, where he beats the Fantastic Four.[12] I'm reading about him being the king, being one of the richest men in the world in a country that no one knew about, which I thought was perfect. The guys were like,

"Here's the nerd coming again with his bag of comic books," and they would take my stuff. One of them asked me one day, luckily for me, "Why you like comic books so much?" And I said, "Look at this particular one right here." I explained who the character was, and the bullies stopped pounding on me and started wanting to borrow my books, like I was a library or something. Instead of demanding quarters from me, they'd say, "You got that latest *Captain America* or that latest *Fantastic Four* with the Black Panther in it?" I'd go, "Yeah." "Well, you should give that up." I'd say, "You need to give the other one back first." So it went from me taking shots to me being the shot-caller.

**Ken:** That's pretty cool. I never had that experience. I was on the bigger side, so I didn't have to worry about that too much. So kids didn't mess with me, I played football and all that jazz. But when I said I wanted to be a comic book artist, it was very interesting how people perceive that. The perception of a Black guy from Canada who wants to draw comic books? How's that going to work? I just had to believe in my ability to do it, and I'm very fortunate to have been able to do my career having worked for Marvel and DC and Lucasfilm. I've been fortunate. But I definitely believed I could do it from the time I was young.

**Arvell:** For me, it was that I needed to see some people, some characters, that were doing more than just robbing things, getting shot at, or being clowns. What made the Black Panther important to me personally was that he was regal, that he was his own individual. He wasn't showing a little girl how to tap up a flight of stairs and come back down.[13] He had more meaning in his life than saying, "Yassah," and "Yes, ma'am," to anybody. He had an important job to do, to clean up a country. I'm sure that still resonates. I went through the sixties and the seventies, looking at movies and television, and I didn't recognize the Black people that I saw on-screen. The characters were very cartoony. I didn't see people that looked like me. They just didn't remind me of anybody. I was raised by a strong mother who was a night nurse that carried a .38 in her purse, then she would be home in time to make the breakfast and take me to kindergarten in the morning. Before the *Black Panther* movie, can you think of another multimillion-dollar movie where the cast was primarily African Americans or Africans? There wasn't one.

Forget the Afrofuturism aspect. Forget the pomp and circumstance. As a person who got familiar with the Black Panther as a kid growing up and then being able to work on anything related to Black Panther, to any superhero, the important thing for me is that I needed some heroes. I needed some people to look up to. I think that today, despite all the other deep meaning that you might be able to glean from it, why are superheroes important anyway? They're somebody to look up to. They're the modern mythos. They could fulfill a sense of pride, at least in terms of having somebody that looked like me in my mind.

**Ken:** Many reasons. Representation. People talk about that as one of the things that is very important—being identified, being able to identify yourself. I saw myself in this character. Sure, there are some traits of the X-Men that I really liked. I liked Colossus, the big guy that draws. But when you see your face in a comic book, it's different. I don't think a lot of people who are not minority really understand what power that is when you open a comic book and see it. "That's me! That's us!"

And now I see kids dressing up like Black Panther,

kids of any race. Ten years ago, I would not have expected that. It's a great thing to see.

## A GREAT THING TO SEE

As we're growing up, we're particularly prone to the influence of *identification*, connecting our own self-concepts to the identities of others.[14] By emulating adults, children learn not only actions but also aspects of their own identities as well. Identification helps them figure out who they are. Though adults feel this influence less because their personalities have more fully formed, we feel its tug as well. We still want positive role models in the world, and not just for the kids.

Black Panther can be a hero to anyone.

## NOTES

1. *Black Panther* #41 (2008).
2. Kirby (1970).
3. *Black Panther* (2016 motion picture), 50 years after *Fantastic Four* #52 (1966).
4. Clark & Clark (1947).
5. Shutts et al. (2011).
6. *Jungle Action* #6–8 (1973–1974).
7. Comics: First mentioned in *Marvel Premiere* #20, Knight debuted in *Marvel Premiere* #21. Television: Played by actress Simone Missick, the character made her live-action debut in Marvel's *Luke Cage* episode 1–01, "Moment of Truth" (September 30, 2016).
8. Langley & Jones (2019); Lashley (2019).
9. *Cyborg* #1–2 (2008).
10. *Black Panther* #1–6 (2009).
11. *Jungle Action* #19–21 (1976).
12. *Fantastic Four* #52 (1966).
13. Shirley Temple danced on a staircase with Bill "Bojangles" Robinson in *The Little Colonel* (1935 motion picture), the first interracial pair to dance together on-screen.
14. George & Hoppe (1979); Quintana et al. (2010); Tarrant et al. (2006).

# FINAL WORD

## FOREVER

### Travis Langley

*"Whether by adopting the aesthetic or its principles, all people can find inspiration or practical use for Afrofuturism to both transform their world and break free of their own set of limitations."*

—*Afrofuturism* author Ytasha L. Womack[1]

*"Wakanda forever!"*
—Wakandan rallying cry[2]

We need heroes who look like us. We also need to recognize and value heroes who do not. The Black Panther is both to different people.

Not only does the character exemplify heroism, but also diversity between individuals and complexity within.[3] His stories celebrate culture, possibilities, and hope. The Oscar-winning film elevated Black Panther to greater recognition and influence through its "vivid re-imagination of something black Americans have cherished for centuries—Africa as a dream of our wholeness, greatness, and self-realization."[4]

His nation of Wakanda is the modern equivalent of classic magical kingdom fantasies but told as science fiction instead of fantasy, as potential instead of impossible. It's a counterfactual dream of what could have been, and a hope for how things could become for the individual, for the people, for the world. The Black Panther and Wakanda represent many things, including the hope that people previously overlooked might improve the future of the world for everyone.

Forever.

> *"Sense of identity, sense of culture, sense of who you are and your heritage. I'm not just talking about Africans or African Americans. I'm talking about everybody."*
> —actor Michael B. Jordan on *Black Panther's* importance[5]

*"This is not our destination. This is where our journey begins."*
—T'Challa[6]

## NOTES

1. *Black Panther* (2018 motion picture).
2. Womack (2013), p. 192.
3. Mohammed (2018); Johnson (2018); Smith (n.d.).
4. Wallace (2018).
5. Mohammed (2018).
6. *Fantastic Four* #607 (2012).

# ABOUT THE EDITOR

**Travis Langley, PhD,** editor, is a psychology professor who teaches courses on crime, media, and social behavior at Henderson State University. He received his bachelor's from Hendrix College and his graduate degrees from Tulane University in New Orleans. Dr. Langley is the series editor and lead writer for his Popular Culture Psychology books on *The Walking Dead, Game of Thrones, Doctor Who, Star Wars, Star Trek, Supernatural, Westworld,* many superheroes, and the Joker. He authored the acclaimed book *Batman and Psychology: A Dark and Stormy Knight. Psychology Today* carries his blog, "Beyond Heroes and Villains." Travis regularly speaks on media and heroism at universities, conferences, and conventions throughout the world. The documentary *Legends of the Knight* spotlighted how he uses fiction to teach real psychology, and he has appeared as an expert interviewee in programs such as *Superheroes Decoded, Necessary Evil: Super-Villains of DC Comics, Batman & Bill, Robert Kirkman's Secret History of Comics,* and Neil deGrasse Tyson's *StarTalk.* During graduate school, he was an undefeated champion on the *Wheel of Fortune* game show even though none of the puzzles were about psychology or superheroes.

Follow him as **@Superherologist** on Twitter, where he ranks among the 10 most popular psychologists. Also keep up with him and this book series through **Facebook.com/ThePsychGeeks**.

# ABOUT THE CO-EDITOR

**Alex Simmons** is an award-winning freelance writer, comic book creator, playwright, teaching artist, and educational consultant. He has written for Disney Books, Penguin Press, Simon & Schuster, DC Comics, and Archie Comics. Simmons is the creator of the acclaimed adventure comic book series *Blackjack*. He has helped develop concepts and scripts for an animation studio in England. As a teaching artist, Simmons has created and taught creative arts workshops for students and educators in the US, West Indies, Africa, and five countries in Europe. Simmons has served on panels and delivered lectures on children's entertainment media, as well as empowering young people through the arts. Simmons founded the annual family event Kids Comic Con, as well as three comic arts exhibits that have traveled abroad. He is currently developing a comics and creative arts program for children in the U.S., Europe, and Africa. Visit his website: **SimmonsHereAndNow.com.**

# ABOUT THE SPECIAL CONTRIBUTOR

**Don McGregor** has become one of the foremost writers in comic books today. With almost thirty years of experience in the field, Don incorporates a deep understanding of human nature into his stories, blending humanity with humility and pain with glory. He creates without compromise, making his characters' heroics poignantly real. Don has an intense desire to know, to dare, and to care about what he writes, and these attributes come through in his passionate style.

After working as a proofreader and eventually editor on several of Marvel Comics B&W line of comic magazines, he was assigned to write the Black Panther Feature in Marvel's *Jungle Action* comics. The "Panther's Rage" series that began in 1973 was the first mainstream comic to feature an essentially all-Black cast of comics, and would later feature prominently in the *Black Panther* motion picture story. Don created Killmonger together with artist Rich Buckler for "Panther's Rage" and later Queen Ramonda with artist Gene Colan in "Panther's Quest."

:

# ABOUT THE CONTRIBUTORS

 **Travis Adams, MSW,** received his MSW from the University of Southern California and is currently a peer support specialist working with United States military veterans. He is a Marine Corps veteran who specializes in serving veterans who have been diagnosed with PTSD, anxiety, depression, substance use disorder, and other diagnoses. He utilizes various types of therapy to aid veterans in their recovery, and he has incorporated the use of popular culture in conjunction with standardized treatment models. He has previously authored chapters in *Supernatural Psychology, Daredevil Psychology,* and *Westworld Psychology.* You can find Travis Adams on Twitter @ themarine_peer.

 **Apryl A. Alexander, PsyD,** is a clinical assistant professor at the Graduate School of Professional Psychology at the University of Denver. Dr. Alexander primarily teaches in the master's in forensic psychology program and serves as director of the Forensic Institute of Research, Service, and Training (Denver FIRST) Outpatient Competency Restoration Program and co-director of the University of Denver Prison Arts Initiative (DU PAI). Her research broadly focuses on violence and victimization, forensic assessment, and trauma- and culturally informed practice.

**Brea M. Banks, PhD, LPC,** is an assistant professor of psychology at Illinois State University. Her research interests include the cognitive consequences of microaggression and student of color experiences in higher education. She has published material surrounding autism spectrum disorder, literacy in refugee children, and behavioral treatment integrity. Her teaching interests surround cognitive assessment, multicultural counseling, and diversity in psychology. In her spare time, she and her spouse enjoy introducing sports and strategy games to their infant daughter and exploring the outdoors with their pup.

**Jenna Busch** is the founder of Legion of Leia, a website to promote and support women in fandom, now part of Vital Thrills. She co-hosted *Cocktails with Stan* with Black Panther co-creator and comic legend Stan Lee and hosted the weekly entertainment show *Most Craved*. In addition to appearing in the documentary *She Makes Comics,* Jenna has been a guest on ABC's *Nightline, Attack of the Show,* NPR, Al Jazeera America, and multiple episodes of *Tabletop with Wil Wheaton.* Busch has co-authored chapters and features in every book in this Popular Culture Psychology series from *Star Wars Psychology: Dark Side of the Mind* onward. Her work has appeared all over the web. She can be reached on Twitter @JennaBusch.

Writer. Publisher. Graphic Designer. Educator. **Victor Dandridge, Jr.,** is a leading new voice for innovation and production within the self-publishing market. He's found acclaim with his own imprint, Vantage: Inhouse Productions; the weekly internet review series Black, White & Read All Over; and the pop culture podcast Hall of Justice. Wanting not only to entertain but also to educate, Victor launched his U Cre-8 Comics line, a unique bridge between comics and classroom fundamentals.

 **Larisa A. Garski, MA, LMFT,** is a psycho-therapist and supervisor at Empowered Therapy in Chicago, IL. She specializes in working with women, families, and young adults who identify as outside the mainstream—such as those in the geek and LGBTQIA communities. She regularly appears at pop culture conventions, speaking on panels related to mental health and geek wellness. Her work as a clinical writer and researcher whose work has appears in a variety of books including but not limited to *Supernatural Psychology: Roads Less Traveled, Daredevil Psychology: The Devil You Know,* and *Westworld Psychology: Violent Delights.*

 **Amber Hewitt, PhD,** is a counseling psychologist with expertise in gendered-racial identity development and socialization of African American children and adolescents. She currently works at the intersection of health science and public policy serving as a manager of policy and advocacy at Nemours Children's Health System in Washington, DC. In this role, she and oversees a portfolio of issues including social determinants of health, nutrition, and children's health care coverage.

 **Vanessa Hicks, PsyD,** is a licensed clinical psychologist in Wisconsin. She earned her doctorate in psychology from The Chicago School of Professional Psychology in 2016. She has served on several convention panels focused on critical discussions of the manifestations of psychological concepts in various aspects of American popular culture. She is an active proponent of multicultural counseling and theory, and works dynamically with clients in therapy to understand how each individual makes meaning of the world within their various cultural contexts. In addition, when clinically beneficial, Dr. Hicks incorporates elements of popular culture into treatment ("geek therapy").

 **Asher Johnson, MA,** is completing his PhD in clinical psychology, emphasizing in forensics and crime. He has spoken on various geek psychology panels at San Diego Comic-Con International and LA Comic Con to discuss his application of superhero redemption therapy to inmates and parolees. He spent two years providing mental health services to state prisoners and three years working with federal and county probationers. Currently he provides specialized treatment to registered sexual offenders who are on parole.

 **J. Scott Jordan, PhD,** is a cognitive psychologist who studies the roots of cooperative behavior. He often uses popular culture in his classes to illustrate the relevance of social-cognitive psychology to daily life. He has contributed chapters to *Captain American vs. Iron Man: Freedom, Security, Psychology*; *Wonder Woman Psychology: Lassoing the Truth*; *Star Trek Psychology: The Mental Frontier*; *Supernatural Psychology: Roads Less Traveled*; and *Daredevil Psychology: The Devil You Know*. He is extremely proud of his international comic book collection.

 **Daniel Jun Kim** is a writer, editor, and founder of PopMythology.com. His mission is to find creative ways to fuse geek and popular culture with practical philosophy, psychology, religion, and activism. His collaborative with J. Scott Jordan in *Black Panther Psychology* is his first contribution to Travis Langley's Popular Culture Psychology series. When not reading, writing, or marching in the streets, he enjoys cosplaying (sometimes all at the same time) but refuses to cosplay any character whose outfit isn't black.

 **Alex Langley, MS,** is the author of five books (including *Make a Nerdy Living* from Sterling Publishing and *The Geek Handbook* series), a graphic novel, and chapters and features in the Popular Culture Psychology series. He teaches psychology, writes about gaming for ArcadeSushi.com, oversees NerdSpan.com's gaming section, co-created the webseries Geeks and Gamers Anonymous, appears on panels at comic con panels, and shares both sense and nonsense on Twitter as @RocketLlama.

 **Justin F. Martin, PhD,** is a professor of psychology at Whitworth University. He teaches development psychology, moral development, and courses related to statistics and research methods. His research interests are in socio-moral development and the socio-moral understanding of superheroes. When he is not consuming superhero media for "research," he enjoys playing basketball and watching Scandinavian crime dramas. He lives in Nine Mile Falls, Washington, with his wife Nicole and three-month-old son Zion.

 **Justine Mastin, MA, LMFT,** is the owner of Blue Box Counseling in Minneapolis. She specializes in working with clients who self-identify as being outside the mainstream, such as those in the geek, secular, and LGBTQIA communities. Justine is also the fearless leader of YogaQuest, a yoga organization that blends geek narratives with yoga. She appears at pop culture conventions, teaching yoga and speaking on geek wellness topics. Justine previously contributed chapters to *Supernatural Psychology: Roads Less Traveled, Daredevil Psychology: The Devil You Know,* and *Westworld Psychology: Violent Delights.* Find more information about Justine's work www.bluebox-counseling.com or follow her on Twitter @mindbodyfandom.

 **Brittani Oliver** obtained her master's degree in family therapy at the University of Houston–Clear Lake. Oliver is currently completing her PsyD in Couples and Family Therapy at Alliant International University. Oliver has presented in the United States and internationally on topics including grief and loss, and sexual and cultural influences on bereavement research. Oliver is currently a contributing writer for grief and loss in the black and LatinX community. She has also taught at Mesa College.

 **Leandra Parris, PhD,** is an assistant professor of school psychology at Illinois State University. A school psychologist by training, Leandra specializes in peer relationships, trauma-informed care, social justice, and school climate. A devotee of popular culture, Leandra often uses narrative therapy and media in her work as a researcher and educator. Outside of work, Leandra strives to pass on her love of science fiction/fantasy, Pink Floyd, and storytelling to her children.

 **Craig Pohlman, PhD,** is a neurodevelopmental psychologist who helps struggling learners find success. He has written several books, including *CinemAnalysis* and *How Can My Kid Succeed in School?* which helps parents and educators understand and help students with learning challenges. Craig is the CEO of Southeast Psych, a private practice and media company in Charlotte, North Carolina and Nashville, Tennessee. He wrote chapters for *Star Wars Psychology: Dark Side of the Mind*, *Star Trek Psychology: The Mental Frontier*, and *Daredevil Psychology: The Devil You Know*. He regularly contributes to Shrink Tank and Psych Bytes. Follow him on Twitter @DrCraigPohlman.

 **Sarah Rizkallah, GDip, MPsych (Clin),** is a graduate psychologist completing her clinical registrar program with Queensland Health in Brisbane, Australia. She did her undergraduate studies at Macquarie University, then earned her graduate diploma at Bond University and her Master's at the Australian Catholic University. She first picked up a comic book in her second last year of high school and it was love at first read.

 **Billy San Juan, PsyD,** earned his psychology doctorate from Alliant International University. He is a contributor to several of the Popular Culture Psychology series of books, as well as a fiction writer. Dr. Billy is a professor at Argosy University and an outreach coordinator for the American Addiction Centers. He has spoken on panels at various conventions, including San Diego Comic-Con, WonderCon, and LA Comic Con.

 **Janina Scarlet, PhD,** is a licensed clinical psychologist, author, and full-time geek. She uses Superhero Therapy to help patients with anxiety, depression, and PTSD at the Center for Stress and Anxiety Management. Dr. Scarlet authored the books *Superhero Therapy*, *Therapy Quest*, *Dark Agents*, and *Harry Potter Therapy*. She has regularly authored chapters in multiple books in this Popular Culture Psychology series. Reach Janina via her website at superhero-therapy.com or on Twitter: @shadowquill.

**Dave Verhaagen** is a licensed and board-certified psychologist, the author or co-author of eight books and nine book chapters, an internationally known speaker, and the father of four adopted young adult children, including two born southwest of Wakanda.

 **Tracy Vozar, PhD,** is a clinical assistant professor and director of the Infant and Early Childhood Mental Health Specialty at the Graduate School of Professional Psychology at the University of Denver. Dr. Vozar teaches courses on perinatal and infant and early childhood mental health. Her research and clinical interests include promoting healthy parent-child relationships, parenting self-efficacy, culturally informed practice, and perinatal mood and anxiety disorders.

 **Eric D. Wesselmann, PhD,** is an associate professor of psychology at Illinois State University. He publishes research on various topics, such as social exclusion, stigma, and religion/spirituality. He has been a comic fan since grade school and loves that he now gets to read comics and consider it "work." When not at the university, he and his spouse train their four little superheroes at home to be the best heroes they can be. Eric has contributed to the majority of volumes in the Popular Culture Psychology series.

# REFERENCES

## COMIC BOOK REFERENCES

*A + X* #3 (2012). "Black Panther + Storm." Script: J. Aaron. Art: P. Ferry.

*Action Comics* #1 (1938). "Superman, Champion of the Oppressed." Script: J. Siegel. Art: J. Shuster. New York, NY: National Comics.

*All-Star Comics* #8 (1941). Publisher: All-Star Publications.

*Amazing Fantasy* #15 (1962). "Spider-Man!" Script: S. Lee. Art: S. Ditko.

*Amazing Spider-Man* #35 (2001). "Coming Out." Script: J. M. Straczynski. Art: J. Romita, Jr., & S. Hanna.

*Avengers* #52 (1968). "Death Calls for the Arch-Heroes." Script: R. Thomas. Art: J. Buscema & V. Colletta.

*Avengers* #62 (1969). "The Monarch and the Man-Ape!" Script: F. Thomas. Art: J. Buscema & G. Klein.

*Avengers* #73 (1970). "The Sting of the Serpent." Script: R. Thomas. Art: F. Giacoia & H. Trimpe.

*Avengers* #77 (1970). "Heroes for Hire!" Writer: R. Thomas Art: J. Buscema & T. Palmer.

*Avengers* #21 (2014). "The Bomb." Script: J. Hickman. Art: V. Schiti & S. Larrocca.

*Avengers* #8 (2018). "Inside Avengers Mountain." Script: J. Aaron. Art: D. Marquez.

*Avengers vs. X-Men* #9 (2012). "Part Nine." Script: J. Aaron. Art: A. Kubert & J. Dell.

*Black Panther* #1 (1998). "The Client." Script: C. Priest. Art: M. Texeira.

*Black Panther* #2 (1998). "Invasion." Script: C. Priest. Art: S. Velluto.

*Black Panther* #3 (1998). "Original Sin." Script: C. Priest. Art: M. Texeira.

*Black Panther* #5 (1998). "Lord of the Damned." Script: C. Priest. Art: V. Evans.

*Black Panther* #11 (1998). "Enemy of the State: Book Three." Script: C. Priest. Art: M. Bright.

*Black Panther* #15 (1998). "Hulk Smash." Script: C. Priest. Art: S. Velluto.

*Black Panther* #24 (1998). "Her Name Is Malice." Script: C. Priest & M. D. Bright. Art: W. Wong.

*Black Panther* #34 (1998). "Gorilla Warfare, Part 1." Script: C. Priest. Art: J. Calafiore.

*Black Panther* #35 (1998). "Gorilla Warfare, Part 2." Script: C. Priest. Art: M. McKone.

*Black Panther* #6 (1999). "Hunted." Script: C. Priest. Art: J. Jusko.

*Black Panther* #8 (1999). "That Business with the Avengers." Script: C. Priest. Art: J. Jusko & J. Palmiotti.

*Black Panther* #9 (1999). "Enemy of the State, Book 1." Script: C. Priest. Art: M. Manley.

*Black Panther* #13 (1999). "Call of the Cat." Script: C. Priest. Art: S. Velluto & B. Almond.

*Black Panther* #19 (2000). "Freefall." Script: C. Priest. Art: S. Velluto & B. Almond.

*Black Panther* #20 (2000). "Retribution." Script: C. Priest. Art: S. Velluto & B. Almond.

*Black Panther* #21 (2000). "Victory." Script: C. Priest. Art: S. Velluto & B. Almond.

*Black Panther* #3 (2001). "A Story of Love and War, Book 3: The Trade of Kings." Script: C. Priest. Art: S. Velluto.

*Black Panther* #29 (2001). "Sturm und Drang—A Story of Love & War, Conclusion: The Continuation of Politics by Other Means." Script: C. Priest. Art: S. Velluto, M. McKenna, & W. Martineck.

*Black Panther* #34 (2001). "Gorilla Warfare, Part 1 of 2: Hell(o), I Must Be Going." Script: C. Priest. Art: J. Calafiore & J. Livesay.

*Black Panther* #45 (2002). "Enemy of the State II, Book Four: 60 Minutes." Script: C. Priest. Art: S. Velluto & S. Geiger.

*Black Panther* #48–49 (2002). "The Death of the Black Panther" Script: C. Priest. Art: S. Velluto & B. Almond.

*Black Panther* #60 (2003). "Ascension, Part 2." Script: C. Priest. Art: P. Zircher & N. Rapmund.

*Black Panther* #61 (2003). "Ascension, Part 3." Script: C. Priest, Art: J. Calafiore & N. Rapmund.

*Black Panther* #1–6 (2005). "Who Is the Black Panther? " Script: R. Hudlin. Art: J. Romita, Jr. & K. Janson.

*Black Panther* #14 (2006). "Bride of the Panther, Part One." Script: R. Hudlin. Art: S. Eaton & K. Janson.

*Black Panther* #23–25 (2007). "War Crimes." Script: R. Hudlin. Art: M. To, D. Ho., & J. De Los Santos.

*Black Panther* #26 (2007). "Two Plus Two, Part One, Home Invasion." Script: R. Hudlin. Art: F. Portela, & V. Olazaba.

*Black Panther* #2 (2008). "The Deadliest of the Species, Part 2." Script: R. Hudlin Art: K. Lashley.

*Black Panther* #3 (2008). "The Deadliest of the Species, Part 3." Script: R. Hudlin. Art: K. Lashley.

*Black Panther* #4 (2008). "The Deadliest of the Species, Part 4." Script: R. Hudlin. Art: K. Lashley.

*Black Panther* #40 (2008). "See Wakanda and Die, Part 2." Script: J. Aaron. Art: J. Palo.

*Black Panther* #41 (2008). "See Wakanda and Die, Part 3." Script: J. Aaron. Art: J. Palo.

*Black Panther* #1–6 (2009). "The Deadliest of the Species." Script: R. Hudlin. Art: K. Lashley & P. Neary.

*Black Panther* #1 (2016). "A Nation Under Our Feet, Part 1." Script: T. Coates. Art: B. Stelfreeze.

*Black Panther* #2 (2016). "A Nation under Our Feet, Part 2." Script: T. Coates. Art: B. Stelfreeze.

*Black Panther* #3 (2016). "A Nation Under Our Feet, Part 3." Script: T. Coates. Art: B. Stelfreeze.

*Black Panther* #4 (2016). "A Nation under Our Feet, Part 4." Script: T. Coates. Art: B. Stelfreeze.

*Black Panther* #5 (2016). "A Nation Under Our Feet, Part 5." Script: T. Coates. Art: C. Sprouse & K. Story.

*Black Panther* #6. (2016). "A Nation under Our Feet, Part 6." Script: T. Coates. Art: C. Sprouse & K. Story.

*Black Panther* #7 (2016). "A Nation Under Our Feet, Part 7." Script: T. Coates. Art: C. Sprouse & K. Story.

*Black Panther* #8 (2016). "A Nation Under Our Feet, Part 8." Script: T. Coates. Art: C. Sprouse, K. Story, & W. Wong.

*Black Panther* #10 (2016). "A Nation Under Our Feet, Part 10" Script: T. Coates. Art: C. Sprouse & K. Story.

*Black Panther* #12 (2016). "A Nation Under Our Feet: Epilogue." Script: T. Coates. Art: B. Stelfreeze, C. Sprouse, K. Story, & S. Hanna.

*Black Panther* #14 (2016). "Avengers of the New World, Part 2." Script: T. Coates. Art: W. Torres & J. Burrows.

*Black Panther* #2 (2017). "World of Wakanda: Dawn of the Midnight Angels, Part 2." Script: R. Gay. Art: A. Richardson.

*Black Panther* #10 (2017). "A Nation Under Our Feet, Part 10." Script: T. Coates. Art: C. Sprouse & K. Story.

*Black Panther* #12 (2017). "A Nation Under Our Feet, Part 12." Script: T. Coates. Art: B. Stelfreeze, C. Sprouse, K. Story, & S. Hanna.

*Black Panther* #167 (2017). "Avengers of the New World, Part 8." Script: T. Coates. Art: L. Kirk, M. Deering, & L. Martin.

*Black Panther* #168 (2017). "Avengers of the New World, Part 9." Script: T. Coates. Art: C. Sprouse, K. Story, & W. Wong.

*Black Panther Annual* #1 (2008). "Black to the Future." Script: R. Hudlin. Art: L. Stroman, K. Lashley, R. Paris, C. Cuevas, & J. Sibal.

*Black Panther Annual* #1 (2018). "Panther's Heart." Script: D. McGregor. Art: D. Acuña.

*Black Panther: Panther's Prey* #1 (1990). "Homes." Script: D. McGregor. Art: D. Turner.

*Black Panther: The Man without Fear!* #513 (2010). "Urban Jungle." Script: D. Liss. Art: F. Francevilla.

*Black Panther: The Man without Fear!* #519 (2011). "Storm Hunter, Part One." Script: D. Liss. Art: F. Francavilla & J. Palo.

*Black Panther: World of Wakanda* #1 (2016). "Dawn of the Midnight Angels, Part 1." Script: R. Gay. Art: A. E. Martinez.

*Black Panther: World of Wakanda* #3 (2016). "Dawn of the Midnight Angels, Part 3." Script: R. Gay. Art: A. E. Martinez.

*Black Panther: World of Wakanda* (2017). "Dawn of the Midnight Angels, Part 2." Script: R. Gay. Art: A. Richardson.

*Captain America Comics* #1 (1941). "Meet Captain America." Script: J. Simon. Art: J. Kirby & A. Liederman.

*Civil War Battle Damage Report* #1 (2007). "Battle Damage Report." Script: A. Flamini & R. Byrd. Art: S. Kolins.

*Cyborg* #1 (2008). "Rage Against the Machine." Script: M Sable. Art: K. Lashley & J. Giapion.

*Cyborg* #2 (2008). "Rage Against the Machine, Part Two." Script: M Sable. Art: K. Lashley & J. Giapion.

*Dazzler* #9 (1981). "The Sound and the Fury!" Script: D. Fingeroth. Art: F. Springer & V. Colletta.

*Detective Comics* #33 (1939). "The Legend of the Batman—Who He Is and How He Came to Be." Script: B. Finger. Art: B. Kane. New York, NY: Detective Comics.

*Exiles* #2 (2009). "Deja Vu." Writer: J. Parker, Art: D. Bullock, M. Irwin, & T. Washington.

*Fantastic Four* #1 (1966). "The Fantastic Four." Script: S. Lee. Art: J. Kirby, G. Klein, & C. Rule.

*Fantastic Four* #52 (1966). "The Black Panther!" Script: S. Lee. Art: J. Kirby & J. Sinnott.

*Fantastic Four* #53 (1966). "The Way It Began..!" Script: S. Lee. Art: J. Kirby & J. Sinnott.

*Fantastic Four* #52 (1966). "The Black Panther!" Script: S. Lee. Art: J. Kirby & J. Sinnott.

*Fantastic Four* #53 (1966). "The Way It Began!" Script: S. Lee. Art: J. Kirby & J. Sinnott.

*Fantastic Four* #311 (1988). "I Want to Die!" Script: S. Englehart. Art: K. Pollard & J. Sinnott.

*Fantastic Four* #312 (1988). "The Turning Point!" Script: S. Englehart. Art: K. Pollard & J. Sinnott.

*Fantastic Four* #607 (2012). "Inert." Script: J. Hickman. Art: G. Camuncoli & K. Kesel.

*Jungle Action* #6 (1973). "Panther's Rage!" Script: D. McGregor. Art: R. Buckler & K. Janson.

*Jungle Action* #7 (1973). "Death Regiments beneath Wakanda!" Script: D. McGregor. Art: R. Buckler & K. Janson.

*Jungle Action* #8 (1974). "Malice by Crimson Moonlight." Script: D. McGregor. Art: R. Buckler & K. Janson, and T. Orzechowski.

*Jungle Action* #9 (1974). "But Now the Spears are Broken." Script: D. McGregor. Art: G. Kane, K. Janson, & T. Orzechowski.

*Jungle Action* #10 (1974). "King Cadaver Is Dead and Living in Wakanda." Script: D. McGregor. Art: B. Graham & K. Janson.

*Jungle Action* #11 (1974). "Once You Slay the Dragon." Script: D. McGregor. Art: B. Graham & K. Janson.

*Jungle Action* #13 (1974). "The God Killer." Script: D. McGregor. Art: B. Graham & C. Russell.

*Jungle Action* #15 (1975). "Thorns in the Flesh in the Mind." Script: D. McGregor. Art: B. Graham & D. Green.

*Jungle Action* #16 (1975). "And All Our Past Decades Have Seen Revolutions." Script: D. McGregor. Art: B. Graham.

*Jungle Action* #17 (1975). "Of Shadows and Rages." Script: D. McGregor. Art: B. Graham & V. Redondo.

*Jungle Action* #18 (1975). "Epilogue!" Script: D. McGregor. Art: B. Graham & B. McLeod.

*Jungle Action* #19 (1976). "Blood and Sacrifices!" Script: D. McGregor. Art: B. Graham & B. McLeod.

*Jungle Action* #21 (1976). "A Cross Burning Darkly Blackening the Night!" Script: D. McGregor. Art: B. Graham & B. McLeod.

*Ka-Zar* #17 (1998). "Misery." Script: C. Priest. Art: K. Martinez & A. Rodriguez.

*March: Book One* (2013). Script: J. Lewis & A. Aydin. Art: N. Powell.

*Marvel Comics Presents* #14 (1989). "Panther's Quest, Part 2: Forgotten Corpses." Script: D. McGregor. Art: G. Colan & T. Palmer.

*Marvel Comics Presents* #14 (1989). "God's Country, Part 5: The Secret is There's No Secret." Script: A. Nocenti. Art: R. Leonardi & P. C. Russell.

*Marvel Comics Presents* #27 (1989). "Panther's Quest, Part 15: Last Night I Wept for Freedom." Script: D. McGregor. Art: G. Colan & T. Palmer.

*Marvel Graphic Novel* #27 (1987). "Emperor Doom." Story: D. Michelinie, M. Gruenwald, & J. Shooter. Art: B. Hall & K. Williams.

*Marvel Premiere* #20 (1975). "Batroc and Other Assassins." Script: T. Isabella. Art: A. Jones & D. Green.

*Marvel Premiere* #21 (1975). "Daughters of the Death–Goddess." Script: T. Isabella. Art: A. Jones & V. Colletta.

*New Avengers* #7 (2013). "Thrones." Script: J. Hickman. Art: M. Deodato.

*New Avengers* #8 (2013). "What Maximus Made." Script: J. Hickman. Art: M. Deodato & F. Martin.

*New Avengers* #12 (2013). "Infinity: Epilogue." Script: J. Hickman. Art: M. Deodato.

*New Avengers* #18 (2014). "Into the Breach." Script: J. Hickman. Art: V. Schiti & S. Larroca.

*New Avengers* #21 (2014). "The Bomb." Script: J. Hickman. Art: V. Schiti & S. Larroca.

*New Avengers* #24 (2014). "The Cabal." Script: J. Hickman. Art: V. Schiti.

*Rise of the Black Panther* #1 (2018). "The King at the End of Everything." Script: E. Narcisse. Art: P. Renaud & S. Paitreau.

*Rise of the Black Panther* #4 (2018). "Stalemate." Script: E. Narcisse. Art: J. Pine.

*Secret Wars* #2 (2015). "Doom Messiah." Script: J. Hickman. Art: E. Ribic.

*Sensation Comics* #1 (1941). ["Wonder Woman Comes to America."] Script: W. M. Marston (as C. Moulton). Art: H. G. Peter. New York, NY: All-American Publications.

*Sgt. Fury and His Howling Commandos* #1 (1963). "Seven Against the Nazis!" Script: S. Lee. Art: J. Kirby & D. Ayers.

*Shuri* #1 (2018). "Gone." Script: N. Okorafor. Art: L. Romero.

*Super-Villain Team-Up* #14 (1977). "A World for the Winning!" Script: B. Mantlo. Art: B. Hal, D. Perlin, & D. Vohland.

*Ultimates* #1 (2016). "Start with the Impossible." Script: A. Ewing. Art: K. Rocofort.

## OTHER REFERENCES

Abrams, D., & Hogg, M. A. (2006*). Social identifications: A social psychology of intergroup relations and group processes.* New York, NY: Routledge.

Advisory Board to the President's Initiative on Race. (1998). *One America in the 21st century: Forging a new future.* Washington, DC: U.S. Government Printing Office.

Ainsworth, M. D. S., Blehar, M. C., Waters, E., & Wall, S. (1978). *Patterns of attachment: A psychological study of the strange situation.* Oxford, UK: Lawrence Erlbaum.

Allen, M. D. (2018). If you can see it, you can be it: *Black Panther*'s Black Woman Magic. Africology: *Journal of Pan African Studies, 11*(9), 20–22.

Allen, Q. (2016). "Tell your own story": Manhood masculinity and racial socialization among black fathers and sons. *Ethnic & Racial Studies, 39*(10), 1831–1848.

Allison, S. T., & Goethals, G. R. (2011). *Heroes: What they do and why we need them.* New York, NY: Oxford University Press.

Allison, S. T., & Goethals, G.R. (2013). *Heroic leadership: An influence taxonomy of 100 exceptional individuals.* New York, NY: Routledge.

Allport, G. W. (1954). *The nature of prejudice.* Oxford, England: Addison-Wesley.

American Psychiatric Association (2000). *Diagnostic and statistical manual of mental disorders* (DSM-IV-TR) (4th ed., revised). Washington, DC: American Psychiatric Association.

American Psychiatric Association (2013). *Diagnostic and statistical manual of mental disorders* (5th ed.). Arlington, VA: American Psychiatric Association.

American Psychological Association (2010/2013). *Publication manual of the American Psychological Association* (6th ed., 7th printing). Washington, DC: American Psychological Association.

American Psychological Association. (2017). *Ethical principles of psychologists and code of conduct.* Washington, DC: American Psychological Association.

Analayo, B. (2018). *Rebirth in early Buddhism and current research.* Somerville, MA: Wisdom.

Anderson, L. M. (1997). *Mammies no more: The changing image of Black women on stage and screen.* Lanham, MD: Rowman & Littlefield.

Anyiwo, N., Ward, L. M., Fletcher, K. D., & Rowley, S. (2018). Black adolescents' television usage and endorsement of mainstream gender roles and the Strong Black Woman Schema. *Journal of Black Psychology, 44*(4), 371–397.

Arnett, J. J., & Tanner, J. L. (Eds.). (2006). *Emerging adults in America: Coming of age in the 21st century.* Washington, DC: American Psychological Association.

Arsenio, W. F., & Willems, C. (2017). Adolescents' conceptions of national wealth distribution: Connections with perceived societal fairness and academic plans. *Developmental Psychology, 53*(3), 463–474.

Arvedon, J. (2018, January 24). *Black Panther's sister Shuri is the "smartest person in the world."* CBR: https://www.cbr.com/black-panther-shuri-smartest-person.

Asch, S. E. (1952). *Social psychology.* Englewood Cliffs, NJ: Prentice-Hall.

Atkinson, D. R. (2004). *Counseling American minorities* (6th ed.). New York, NY: McGraw-Hill.

Bailey, M., & Trudy (2018). On misogynoir: Citation, erasure, and plagiarism. *Feminist Media Studies, 18*(4), 762–768.

Bainbridge, J. (2007). "This is the Authority. This planet is under our protection"—An exegesis of superheroes' interrogations of law. *Law, Culture & the Humanities, 3*(3), 455–476.

Bainbridge, J. (2015). "The call to do justice": Superheroes, sovereigns and the State during wartime. *International Journal for the Semiotics of Law—Revue Internationale de Sémiotique Juridique, 28*(2), 745–763.

Bandura, A., Underwood, B., & Fromson, M. E. (1975). Disinhibition of aggression through diffusion of responsibility and dehumanization of victims. *Journal of Research in Personality, 9*(4), 253–269.

Banks, L. M. (2006). The History of Special Operations Psychological Selection. In A. D. Mangelsdorff (Ed.), *Psychology in the service of national security* (pp. 83–95). Washington, DC: American Psychological Association.

Bargh, J. A., & Chartrand, T. L. (1999). The unbearable automaticity of being. *American Psychologist, 54*(7), 462.

Barlé, N., Wortman, C., & Latack, J. A. (2015). Traumatic bereavement: Basic research and clinical implications. *Journal of Psychotherapy Integration, 27*(2), 127–139.

Barry, H. (1969). Parental deaths: An investigative challenge. *Contemporary Psychology, 14*(2), 102–104.

Batson, C. D., Chang, J., & Rowland, J. (2002). Empathy, attitudes, and action: Can feeling for a member of a stigmatized group motivate one to help the group? *Personality & Social Psychology Bulletin, 28*(12), 1656–1666.

Baumeister, R. (1999). *Evil inside human violence and cruelty.* New York, NY: Holt.

Beauboeuf-Lafontant, T. (2007). You have to show strength: An exploration of gender, race, and depression. *Gender & Society, 21*(1), 28–51.

Becker, E. (1972). *The denial of death.* New York, NY: Basic.

Becker, S. W., & Eagly, A. H. (2004). The heroism of women and men. *American Psychologist, 59*(3), 163–178.

Berggraf, L., Ulvenes, P. G., Hoffart, A., McCullough, L, & Warmpold, B. E. (2014). Growth in sense of self and sense of others predicts reduction in interpersonal problems in short-term dynamic but not in cognitive therapy. *Psychotherapy Research, 24*(4), 456–469.

Behm-Morawitz, E., & Ortiz, M. (2013). Race, ethnicity, and the media. In K. E. Dill (Ed.), *The Oxford handbook of media psychology* (pp. 252–266). New York, NY: Oxford University Press.

Benore, E. R., & Park, C. L. (2004). Death-specific religious beliefs and bereavement: Belief in an afterlife and continued attachment. *International Journal for the Psychology of Religion, 14*(1), 1–22.

Blackhart, G. C., Knowles, M. L., Nelson, B. C., & Baumeister, R. F. (2009). Rejection elicits emotional reactions but neither causes immediate distress nor lowers self-esteem: A meta-analytic review of 192 studies on social exclusion. *Personality & Social Psychology Review, 13*(4), 269–309.

Boyd-Franklin, N. (2003). *Black families in therapy* (2nd ed.). New York, NY: Guilford.

Boulware, D. L., & Bui, N. H. (2016). Bereaved African American adults: The role of social support, religious coping, and continuing bonds. *Journal of Loss & Trauma, 21*(3), 192–202.

Bowlby, J. (1969). *Attachment and loss.* New York, NY: Basic.

Bowlby, J. & Fry, M. (1953). *Child care and the growth of love.* Melbourne, Victoria, Australia: Penguin.

Bowman, P. J. (2013). A strength-based social psychological approach to resiliency: Cultural diversity, ecological, and life span issues. In S. Prince-Embury & D. Saklofske (Eds.), *Resilience in children, adolescents, and adults* (pp. 299–324). New York, NY: Springer.

Box Office Mojo (n.d.). *Genres: Superhero—origin.* Box Office Mojo: https://www.boxofficemojo.com/genres/chart/?id=superheroorigin.htm.

Bracha, H. S., Ralston, T. C., Matsukawa, J. M., Williams, A. E., & Bracha, A. S. (2004). Does "fight or flight" need updating? *Psychosomatics: Journal of Consultation & Liaison Psychiatry, 45*(5), 448–449.

Bradshaw, G. A. (2017). *Carnivore minds: Who these fearsome animals really are.* New Haven, CT: Yale University Press.

Brameld, T. (1946). *Minority problems in public schools.* New York, NY: Harper.

Brewbaker, J. J. (1960). *Desegration in the Norfolk public schools.* Norfolk, VA: Southern Regional Council.

Brewer, M. B., & Chen, Y. R. (2007). Where (who) are collectives in collectivism? Toward conceptual clarification of individualism and collectivism. *Psychological Review, 114*(1), 133.

Bromwich, J. E. (2018, February 27). *Disney to donate $1 million of "Black Panther" proceeds to Youth STEM Programs.* New York Times: https://www.nytimes.com/2018/02/27/movies/disney-black-panther-stem.html.

Brown, B. (2015). *Daring greatly: How the courage to be vulnerable transforms the way we live, love, parent, and lead.* New York, NY: Penguin.

Brown, J. A. (2000). *Black superheroes, Milestone comics, and their fans.* Jackson, MS: University Press of Mississippi.

Browne Graves, S. (1999). Television and prejudice reduction: When does television as a vicarious experience make a difference? *Journal of Social Issues, 55*(4), 707–727.

Bulkeley, K. (1998). Penelope as dreamer: A reading of book 19 of The Odyssey. *Dreaming, 8*(4), 229–242.

Burpo, C., & Vincent, L. (2010). *Heaven is real: A little boy's astounding story of his trip to Heaven.* Edinburgh, Scotland: Mockingbird.

Calhoun, L. G., & Tedeschi, R. G. (2006). The foundations of posttraumatic growth: An expanded framework. In L. G. Calhoun & R. G. Tedeschi (Eds.), *Handbook of posttraumatic growth: Research and practice* (pp. 3–23). Mahwah, NJ: Erlbaum.

Campbell, J. (1949). *The hero with a thousand faces.* Princeton, NJ: Princeton University Press.

Capuzzi, D., & Stauffer, M. D. (Eds.). (2015). *Foundations of couples, marriage, and family counseling.* Hoboken, NJ: Wiley.

Carter, C. (2010). *Science and the near-death experience: How consciousness survives death*. Rochester, VT: Inner Traditions.

Cavna, M. (2016, November 17). Rep. *John Lewis's National Book Award is a milestone moment for graphic novels*. Washington Post: https://www.washingtonpost.com/news/comic-riffs/wp/2016/11/17/rep-john-lewiss-national-book-award-win-is-a-milestone-moment-for-graphic-novels/?utm_term=.89307e430c7d.

Chang, L. C., Rajagopalan, S., & Mathew, S. J. (2016). The history of ketamine use and its clinical indications. In S. J. Mathew & C. A. Zarate, Jr. (Eds.), *Ketamine for treatment-resistant depression: The first decade of progress* (pp. 1–12). Cham, Switzerland: Springer.

Chapman, T. (2018). *Black Panther's 16-year-old sister is smarter than Tony Stark*. ScreenRant: https://screenrant.com/black-panther-sister-shuri-smarter-tony-stark/.

Charon, J. M., & Cahill, S. (2004). *Symbolic interactionism: An introduction, an interpretation, an integration* (8th ed.). Upper Saddle River, NJ: Pearson Prentice Hall.

Chetty, R., Hendren, N, Jones, M. R., & Porter, S. R. (2018). Race and economic opportunity in the United States: An intergenerational perspective. *National Journal of Economic Research*. (Working Paper 24441). Harvard University: https://scholar.harvard.edu/hendren/publications/race-and-economic-opportunity-united-states-intergenerational-perspective.

Chowns, G. (2008). "No, you don't know how we feel": Groupwork with children facing parental loss. *Groupwork: An Interdisciplinary Journal for Working with Groups, 18*(1), 14–37.

Christenfeld, N., Phillips, D. P., & Glynn, L. M. (1999). What's in a name: Mortality and the power of symbols. *Journal of Psychosomatic Research, 47*(3), 241–254.

Christopher, J. C., & Hickinbottom, S. (2008). Positive psychology, ethnocentrism, and the disguised ideology of individualism. *Theory & Psychology, 18*(5): 563–589.

Clark, K., & Clark, M. (1947). Racial identification and preference in Negro children. In T. M. Newcomb & E. L. Hartley (Eds.). *Readings in social psychology*. New York, NY: Holt.

Coates, T. (2015). *Between the world and me*. New York, NY: Spiegel & Grau.

Cochran, D. L. (1997). African American fathers: A decade review of the literature. *Families in Society, 78*(4), 340–351.

Cohen, E., Mundry, R., & Kirschner, S. (2014). Religion, synchrony, and cooperation. *Religion, Brain & Behavior, 4*(1), 20–30.

Coke, J. S., Batson, C. D., & McDavis, K. (1978). Empathic mediation of helping: A two-stage model. *Journal of Personality & Social Psychology, 36*(7), 752–766.

Coleman, A. L. (2018, February 22). *There's a true story behind Black Panther's strong women. Here's why that matters.* Time: http://time.com/5171219/black-panther-women-true-history.

Collier, C. D. A. (2003). Tradition, modernity, and postmodernity in symbolism of death. *Sociological Quarterly, 44*(4), 727–749.

Collins, P. H. (2012). It's all in the family: Intersections of gender, race, and nation. In K. E. Rosenblum & T. C. Travis (2012). *The meaning of difference: American constructions of race, sex and gender, social class, sexual orientation, and disability* (pp. 245–254). New York, NY: McGraw Hill.

Coman, A., Momennejad, I., Drach, R. D., & Geana, A. (2016). Mnemonic convergence in social networks: The emergent properties of cognition at a collective level. *Proceedings of the National Academy of Sciences, 113*(29), 8171–8176.

Coogan, P. (2006). *Superhero: The secret origin of a genre.* Austin, TX: MonkeyBrain.

Cooley, S., & Killen, M. (2015). Children's evaluations of resource allocation in the context of group norms. *Developmental Psychology, 51*(4), 554–563.

Cook, B. A. (Ed.). (2006). *Women and war: A historical encyclopedia from antiquity to the present* (Vol. 2). Santa Barbara, CA: ABC-Clio.

Cornum, R., Matthews, M. D., & Seligman, M. E. P. (2011). Comprehensive soldier fitness: Building resilience in a challenging institutional context. *American Psychologist, 66*(1), 4–9.

Crenshaw, K. (1992). Whose story is it, anyway? Feminist and antiracist appropriations of Anita Hill. In T. Morrison (Ed.). *Race-ing justice, en-gendering power: Essays on Anita Hill, Clarence Thomas, and the construction of social reality* (pp. 436). New York, NY: Random House.

Crimston, D., Bain, P. G., Hornsey, M. J., & Bastian, B. (2016). Moral expansiveness: Examining variability in the extension of the moral world. *Journal of Personality & Social Psychology, 111*(4), 636–653.

Crimston, D., Hornsey, M. J., Bain, P. G., & Bastian, B. (2018). Toward a psychology of moral expansiveness. *Current Directions in Psychological Science, 27*(1), 14–19.

Culver, D. (2018). *Marvel Black Panther the illustrated history of a king: The complete comics chronology.* San Rafael, CA: Insight Editions.

Curtis, N. (2013). Superheroes and the contradiction of sovereignty. *Journal of Graphic Novels & Comics, 4*(2), 209–222.

CyberSpacers (2004). *How to be a real super hero!* CyberSpacers: http://www.cyberspacers.com/exclusive/08020302.html.

Daily Mail Reporter (2012, November 21). Rest in peace: Patients lie in coffins to "die" as part of bizarre treatment for stress in China. The Daily Mail: https://www.dailymail.co.uk/news/article-2236294/Patients-lie-coffins-die-bizarre-treatment-stress-China.html.

Deci, E. L. & Ryan, R. M. (2000). The "what" and "why" of goal pursuits:

Human needs and the self-determination of behavior. *Psychological Inquiry*, *11*(4), 227–268.

DeGroot, G. J. (2001). A few good women: Gender stereotypes, the military and peacekeeping. *International Peacekeeping*, *8*(2), 23–38.

De las Cuevas, C., Peñate, W., & Sanz, E. J. (2014). The relationships of psychological reactance, health locus of control, and sense of self-efficacy with adherence to treatment in psychiatrist outpatients with depression. *BMC Psychiatry, 14,* ArtID 324.

Dohner, J. V. (2017). *The encyclopedia of animal predators*. North Adams, MA: Storey.

DeLoache, J. S. (1995). Early understanding and use of symbols: The model model. *Current Directions in Psychological Science*, *4*(4), 109–113.

Deme, M. K. (2009). Heroism and the supernatural in the African epic: Toward a critical analysis. *Journal of Black Studies*, *39*(3), 402–419.

Dennett, D. C., & LaScola, L. (2015). *Caught in the pulpit: Leaving belief behind*. Durham, NC: Pitchstone.

Derrick, J. E., Gabriel, S., & Hugenberg, K. (2009). Social surrogacy: How favored television programs provide the experience of belonging. *Journal of Experimental Social Psychology 45,* 352–362.

D'Exelle, B., & Riedl, A. (2013). Resource allocations and disapproval voting in unequal groups. *Journal of Conflict Resolution*, *57*(4), 627–652.

Dovidio, J. F. (2001). On the nature of contemporary prejudice: The third wave. *Journal of Social Issues, 57*(4), 829–849.

Doyle, M. E., & Peterson, K. A. (2005). Re-entry and reintegration: Returning home after combat. *Psychiatric Quarterly*, *76*(4), 361–370.

Drolet, J. (1990). Transcending death during early adulthood: Symbolic immortality, death anxiety, and purpose in life. *Journal of Clinical Psychology*, *46*(2), 148–160.

Druckman, J. N., Trawalter, S., Montes, I., Fredendall, A., Kanter, N., & Rubenstein, A. P. (2017). Racial bias in sport medical staff's perceptions of others' pain. *The Journal of Social Psychology*, *158*(6), 721–729.

Duchardt, K. (2012, December 4). *Coffin therapy: Relaxing of depressing?* Reuters: https://www.reuters.com/video/2012/12/04/coffin-therapy-relaxing-or-depressing?videoId=239642188&videoChannel=4.

Duffy, D., & Jennings, J. (2010). *Black comix: African American independent comics, art and culture*. New York, NY: Mark Batty.

Duffy, J. T. (2010). A heroic journey: Re-conceptualizing adjustment disorder through the lens of the hero's quest. *Journal of Systemic Therapies*, *29*(4), 1–16.

Dunne, S., Gallagher, P., & Matthews, A. (2015). Existential threat or dissociative response? Examining defensive avoidance of point-of-care testing devices through a terror management theory framework. *Death Studies, 39*(1), 30–38.

Easterbrook, G. (2001, March 5). I'm OK, you're OK. *The New Republic*, 20–23.

Edwards, M. B. (2006). The relationship between the internal working model of attachment and patterns of grief experienced by college students after the death of a parent. *Dissertation Abstracts International Section A*, *66*, 4197.

Efthimiou, O., & Allison, S.T. (2017). Heroism science: Frameworks for an emerging field. *Journal of Humanistic Psychology*, *58*(5), 556–570.

Elbert, T., Schauer, M., & Neuner, F. (2015). Narrative exposure therapy (NET): Reorganizing memories of traumatic stress, fear, and violence. In U. Schnyder & M. Cloitre (Eds.), *Evidence based treatments for trauma-related psychological disorders: A practical guide for clinicians* (pp. 229–253). Basel, Switzerland: Springer.

Elenbaas, L., & Killen, M. (2016). Children rectify inequalities for disadvantaged groups. *Developmental Psychology*, 52(8), 1318–1329.

Elenbaas, L., & Killen, M. (2017). Children's perceptions of social resource inequality. *Journal of Applied Developmental Psychology*, *48*, 49–58.

Eliot, G. (1871). *Middlemarch*. https://www.planetebook.com/free-ebooks/middlemarch.pdf.

Ellithorpe, M. E., & Bleakley, A. (2016). Wanting to see people like me? Racial and gender diversity in popular adolescent television. *Journal of Youth & Adolescence*, *45*(7), 1426–1437.

Elnitsky, C. A., Chapman, P. L., Thurman, R. M., Pitts, B. L., Figley, C., & Unwin, B. (2013). Gender differences in combat medic mental health services utilization, barriers, and stigma. *Military Medicine*, *178*(7), 775–784.

Endler, N. S., & Shedletsky, R. (1973). Trait versus state anxiety, authoritarianism, and ego threat versus physical threat. *Canadian Journal of Behavioural Science*, *5*(4), 347–361.

Engel, G.L. (1979). The biopsychosocial model and the education of health professionals. *General Hospital Psychiatry*, *1*(2), pp. 156–165.

Entman, R. M. (2006). *Young men of color in the media: Images and impacts*. Washington, DC: Joint Center for Political and Economic Studies.

Faithful, G. (2018). Dark of the world, shine on us: The redemption of Blackness in Ryan Coogler's Black Panther. *Religions*, *9*, 1–15.

Fallahi, C. R., & Lesik, S. A. (2009). The effects of vicarious exposure to the recent massacre at Virginia Tech. *Psychological trauma: Theory, Research, Practice, & Policy*, *1*(3), 220–230.

Fiske, S. T. (2002). What we know now about bias and intergroup conflict, the problem of the century. *Current Directions in Psychological Science*, *11*(4), 123–128.

Florian, V., & Mikulincer, M. (1998). Symbolic immortality and the management of the terror of death: The moderating role of attachment style. *Journal of Personality & Social Psychology*, *74*(3), 725–734.

Foster III, W. H. (2005). *Looking for a face like mine: The history of African Americans in comics.* Waterbury, CT: Fine Tooth Press.

Foster III, W. H. (2010). *Dreaming of a face like ours: Collected essays, articles and scholarly presentations on the changing image of Blacks in comics.* Waterbury, CT: Fine Tooth Press.

Fouad, N. A., & Arredondo, P. (2007). *Becoming culturally oriented: Practical advice for psychologists and educators.* Washington, DC: American Psychological Association.

Fraley, R. C., & Shaver, P. R. (2016). Attachment, loss, and grief: Bowlby's views, new developments, and current controversies (Chapter 3). In J. Cassidy & P. R. Shaver (Eds.), *Handbook of attachment: Theory, research, and clinical applications.* New York, NY: Guilford.

Francisco, B., & Gorman, L. (2010). Living in the new normal: Helping children thrive through good and challenging times. In *Military Child Education Coalition Conference.* https://www.militarychild.org/programs/living-in-the-new-normal-linn.

Franco, Z. E., Allison, S. T., Kinsella, E. L., Kohen, A., Langdon, M., & Zimbardo, P. G. (2018). Heroism research: A review of theories, methods, challenges, and trends. *Journal of Humanistic Psychology, 58*(4), 382–396.

Franco, Z. E., Blau, K., & Zimbardo, P. G. (2011). Heroism: A conceptual analysis and differentiation between heroic action and altruism. *Review of General Psychology, 15*(2), 99–113.

Franco, Z., & Zimbardo, P. G. (2006). The banality of heroism. *Greater Good, 3*(2), 30–35.

Frankl, V. E. (1946). . . . *trotzdem Ja zum Leben sagen: Ein Psycholog erlebt das Konzentrationslager* [. . . Nevertheless say "yes" to life: A psychologist experiences the concentration camp]. Vienna, Austria: Verlag.

Frankl, V. (1984). *Man's search for meaning: An introduction to Logotherapy.* New York, NY: Simon & Schuster.

Freud, A. (1936). *The ego and the mechanisms of defense.* London, UK: Imago.

Friston, K. (2010). The free-energy principle: a unified brain theory? *Nature Reviews Neuroscience, 11*(2), 127.

Furuya, H., Ikezoe, K., Shigeto, H., Ohyagi, Y., Arahata, H., Araki, E., & Fujii, N. (2009). Sleep- and non-sleep-related hallucinations—relationship to ghost tales and their classifications. *Dreaming, 19*(4), 232–238.

Gabriel, S., Read, J. P., Young, A. F., Bachrach, R. L., & Troisi, J. D. (2017). Social surrogate use in those exposed to trauma: I get by with a little help from my (fictional) friends. *Journal of Social & Clinical Psychology, 36*(1), 41–63.

Gabriel, S., & Young, A. F. (2011). Becoming a vampire without being bitten: The narrative collective-assimilation hypothesis. *Psychological Science, 22*(8), 990–994.

Gallagher, S. & Tollefsen, D. (2017). Advancing the 'We' through narrative. *Topoi,* 1–9. https://link.springer.com/article/10.1007/s11245-017-9452-1.

Garbarino, J. (1987). Children's response to a sexual abuse prevention program: A study of the Spiderman comic. *Child Abuse & Neglect, 11*(1), 143–148.

Garve, R., Garve, M., Türp, J. C., Fobil, J. N., & Meyer, C. G. (2017). Scarification in sub-Saharan Africa: Social skin, remedy and medical import. *Tropical Medicine & International Health, 22*(6), 708–715.

George, D. M., & Hoppe, R. A. (1979). Racial identification, preference, and self-concept: Canadian Indian and White schoolchildren. *Journal of Cross-Cultural Psychology, 10*(1), 85–100.

Gewirtz, A. H., Erbes, C. R., Polusny, M. A., Forgatch, M. S., & Degarmo, D. S. (2011). Helping military families through the deployment process: Strategies to support parenting. *Professional Psychology: Research & Practice, 42*(1), 56–62.

Ghee, K. (2013). "Will the 'real' Black superheroes please stand up?!" A critical analysis of the mythological and cultural significance of black superheroes. In S. C. Howard & R. L. Jackson II (Eds.), *Black comics: Politics of race and representation* (pp. 223–237). London, UK: Bloomsbury.

Glazer, M. P., & Glazer, P. M. (1999). On the trail of courageous behavior. *Sociological Inquiry, 69*(2), 276–295.

GoFundMe (2018). *Black Panther challenge*. GoFundMe: https://www.gofundme.com/cause/black-panther-challenge.

Goldberg, A. P., & Michaels, G. Y. (1985). *Empathy: Development, training, and consequences*. Hillsdale, NJ: Lawrence Erlbaum.

Gollwitzer, A., Marshall, J., Wang, Y., & Bargh, J. A. (2017). Relating pattern deviancy aversion to stigma and prejudice. *Nature Human Behaviour, 1*(12), 920–927.

Gonsalkorale, K., & Williams, K. D. (2007). The KKK won't let me play: Ostracism even by a despised outgroup hurts. *European Journal of Social Psychology, 37*(6), 1176–1186.

Grand, S., & Salberg, J. (2017). Introduction. In S. Grand & J. Salberg (Eds.), *Trans-generational trauma and the Other: Dialogues across history and difference* (p. 1). New York, NY: Routledge.

Grant, P. R. (1991). Ethnocentrism between groups of unequal power under threat in intergroup competition. *Journal of Social Psychology, 131*(1), 21–28.

Gray, J. W. (2016, April 4). *A conflicted man: An interview with Ta-Nehisi Coates About Black Panther*. The New Republic: https://newrepublic.com/article/132355/conflicted-man-interview-ta-nehisi-coates-black-panther.

Greene, D. (2018, February 15). *Director Ryan Coogler says "Black Panther" brought him closer to his roots*. NPR: https://www.npr.org/2018/02/15/585702642/director-ryan-coogler-says-black-panther-brought-him-closer-to-his-roots.

Greyson, B. (2000). Dissociation in people who have near-death experiences: Out of their bodies or out of their minds? *Lancet, 355*(9202), 460–463.

Grof, S. (1980). *LSD psychotherapy*. Pomona, CA: Hunter House.

Hagan, J. C., III (2017). *The science of near-death experiences.* Columbia, MO: University of Missouri Press.

Hagerman, M. (2018). *White kids: growing up with the privilege in a racially divided America.* New York, NY: NYU Press.

Haidt, J., & Joseph, C. (2004). Intuitive ethics: How innately prepared intuitions generate culturally variable virtues. *Daedalus, 133*(4), 55–66.

Halstead, R. W. (2000). From triumph to tragedy: Counselor as companion on the hero's journey. *Counseling & Values, 44*(2), 100–106.

Hare, R. D. (1996). Psychopathy: A clinical construct whose time has come. *Criminal Justice & Behavior, 23*(1), 25–54.

Harris, J. E. (1982/1993). Introduction. In J. E. Harris (Ed.), *Global dimensions of the African diaspora* (pp. 8–9). Washington, DC: Howard University Press.

Hartmann, D., & Zimberoff, D. (2009). The hero's journey of self-transformation: Models of higher development from mythology. *Journal of Heart-Centered Therapies, 12*(2), 3–93.

Hastie, R., & Dawes, R. M. (2010). *Rational choice in an uncertain world: The psychology of judgment and decision making.* Thousand Oaks, CA: SAGE.

Hayes, J., & Schimel, J. (2018). Unintended effects of measuring implicit processes: The case of death-thought accessibility in mortality salience studies. *Journal of Experimental Social Psychology, 74*, 257–269.

Hays, P. A. (2008). *Addressing cultural complexities in practice: Assessment, diagnosis, and therapy* (2nd ed.). Washington, DC: American Psychological Association.

Hayslip, B. J., Pruett, J. H., & Caballero, D. M., (2015). The "how" and "when" of parental loss in adulthood: Effects on grief and adjustment. *OMEGA—Journal of Death and Dying, 71*(1), 3–18.

Heflick, N. A., Goldenberg, J. L., & Kamp, S. (2015). Death awareness and body–self dualism: A why and how of afterlife belief. *European Journal of Social Psychology, 45*(2), 267–275.

Helwig, C. C. (1995). Adolescents' and young adults' conceptions of civil liberties: Freedom of speech and religion. *Child Development, 66*(1), 152–166.

Helwig, C. C. (1997). The role of agent and social context in judgments of freedom of speech and religion. *Child Development, 68*(3), 484–495.

Helwig, C. C. (1998). Children's conceptions of fair government and freedom of speech. *Child Development, 69*(2), 518–531.

Helwig, C. C., Hildebrandt, C., & Turiel, E. (1995). Children's judgments about psychological harm in social context. *Child Development, 66*(6), 1680–1693.

Helwig, C. C., Ruck, M. D., & Peterson-Badali, M. (2013). Rights, civil liberties, and democracy. In M. Killen & J. G. Smetana (Eds.), *Handbook of moral development* (2nd ed., pp. 46–69). New York, NY: Psychology Press.

Hewitt, A. A. (2018, February 25). *"Black Panther" and the importance of racial socialization.* Psychology Today: https://www.psychologytoday.com/us/

blog/you-empowered/201802/black-panther-and-the-importance-racial-socialization.

Hinduja, S. & Patchin, J. (2007). Offline consequences of online victimization: School violence and delinquency. *Journal of School Violence, 6*(3), 89–112.

Hirschberger, G., Florian, V., & Mikulincer, M. (2002). The anxiety buffering function of close relationships: Mortality salience effects on the readiness to compromise mate selection standards. *European Journal of Social Psychology, 32*(5), 609–625.

Hoffman, M. L. (2000). *Empathy and moral development: Implications for caring and justice.* New York, NY: Cambridge University Press.

Hoffman, K. M., & Trawalter, S. (2016). Assumptions about life hardship and pain perception. *Group Processes & Intergroup Relations, 19*(4), 493–508.

Hofstede, G. (1980). *Culture's consequences.* Beverly Hills, CA: SAGE.

Hofstede, G. (2001). *Culture's consequences: Comparing values, behaviors, institutions, and organizations across nations* (2nd ed.). Thousand Oaks, CA: SAGE.

Holmbeck, G. N., O'Mahar, K., Abad, M., Colder, C., & Updegrove, A. (2006). Cognitive-behavioral therapy with adolescents: Guides from developmental psychology. In P. C. Kendall (Ed.) *Child & Adolescent Therapy: Cognitive Behavioral Procedures* (3rd ed., pp. 419–464). New York, NY: Guilford.

Holoien, D. S., & Shelton, J. N. (2012). You deplete me: The cognitive costs of colorblindness on ethnic minorities. *Journal of Experimental Social Psychology, 48*(2), 562–565.

House, R. J., Hanges, P. J., Javidan, M., Dorfman, P. W., & Gupta, V. (Eds.). (2004). *Culture, leadership, and organizations: The GLOBE study of 62 societies.* Thousand Oaks, CA: SAGE.

Howard, S., & Borgella, A. (2018). "Sinking" or sinking?: Identity salience and shifts in Black women's athletic performance. *Psychology of Sport & Exercise, 39*, 179–183.

Hughes, D., Rodriguez, J., Smith, E. P., Johnson, D. J., Stevenson, H. C., & Spicer, P. (2006). Parents' ethnic-racial socialization practices: A review of research and directions for future study. *Developmental Psychology, 42*(5), 747–770.

Hughes, K. (2018). *How World War I helped give US women the right to vote.* Army: https://www.army.mil/article/192727/how_world_war_i_helped_give_us_women_the_right_to_vote.

Hui, V. K., & Coleman, P. G. (2012). Do reincarnation beliefs protect older adult Chinese Buddhists against personal death anxiety? *Death Studies, 36*(10), 949–958.

Hui, V. K., & Coleman, P. G. (2013). Afterlife beliefs and ego integrity as two mediators of the relationship between intrinsic religiosity and personal death anxiety among older adult British Christians. *Research on Aging, 35*(2), 144–162.

Hynes, J. (2010). Changing lives through sport: The story of the positive mental attitude sports foundation trust. *Advances in Dual Diagnosis, 3*(1), 26–31.

Ickes, W., Park, A., & Johnson, A. (2012). Linking identity status to strength of sense of self: Theory and validation. *Self & Identity, 11*(4) 531–544.

Ijiyemi, S. (2012). *Don't die sitting: Nothing is worse than doing nothing.* Baltimore, MD: Mastars.

Inamori International Center for Ethics and Excellence (n.d.). *About the Center.* Case Western Reserve University: https://case.edu/inamori/about-the-center.

Jackman, M. R., & Senter, M. S. (1981). Beliefs about race, gender, and social class different, therefore unequal: Beliefs about trait differences between groups of unequal status. In D. J. Treiman & R. V. Robinson (Eds.), *Research in stratification and mobility* (Vol. 2). Greenwich, CT: JAI Press.

Jambon, M., & Smetana, J. G. (2014). Moral complexity in middle childhood: Children's evaluations of necessary harm. *Developmental Psychology, 50*(1), 22–33.

Janet, P. (1889). *L'automatisme psychologique [The psychological automatism].* Paris, France: Fëlix Alcan.

Janet, P. (1894). *L'Etat mental des hysterigues: Les accidents mentaux [The mental state of the hysterics: Mental accidents].* Paris, France: Rueff & Cie.

Janet, P. (1898). *Nevroses et iddes fixes* (Vol. I). Paris, France: Fëlix Alcan.

Jayson, J. (2017, June 10). *Black Panther: Forest Whitaker is like Obi-Wan Kenobi to T'Challa.* ComicBook: https://comicbook.com/marvel/2017/06/10/black-panther-forest-whitaker-zuri/.

JinxxyWinxxy (2012, July 15). *Gerard Way from My Chemical Romance.* Teen Ink: http://www.teenink.com/nonfiction/celebrity_interviews/article/479227/Gerard-Way-from-My-Chemical-Romance/.

Johnson, T. (2017, October 17). *Black superheroes matter: Why a 'Black Panther' movie is revolutionary.* Rolling Stone: https://www.rollingstone.com/movies/movie-news/black-superheroes-matter-why-a-black-panther-movie-is-revolutionary-198678/.

Johnson, T. (2018, February 23). *Black Panther is a gorgeous, groundbreaking celebration of black culture.* Vox: https://www.vox.com/culture/2018/2/23/17028826/black-panther-wakanda-culture-marvel.

Jones, M. G., Howe, A., & Rua, M. J. (2000). Gender differences in students' experiences, interests, and attitudes towards science and scientists. *Science Education, 84*(2), 180–192.

Jones, S., Watts, A., & Almasy, S. (2018, April 14). *Teen says he was asking for directions, but homeowner shot at him.* CNN: https://www.cnn.com/2018/04/14/us/michigan-man-shoots-at-teen-asking-for-directions/index.html.

Jordan, J. S. (2013). The wild ways of conscious will: What we do, how we do it, and why it has meaning. *Frontiers in Psychology, 4.* https://www.frontiersin.org/articles/10.3389/fpsyg.2013.00574/full.

Jordan, J. S. (2018). *Wild narratives: The science of consciousness and the stories we tell.* Paper presented at The Science of Consciousness conference, Tucson, AZ.

Jordan, J. S., Bai, Jiuyang, Cialdella, V., & Schloesser, D. (2015). Foregrounding the background: Cognitive science as the study of embodied context. In E. Dzhafarov & J. S. Jordan (Eds.), *Contextuality from physics to psychology* (pp. 209–228). Berlin, Germany: Springer.

Jordan, J. S., Cialdella, V. T., Dayer, A., Langley, M. D., & Stillman, Z. (2017). Wild bodies don't need to perceive, detect, capture, or create meaning: They ARE meaning. *Frontiers in Psychology, 4.* https://www.frontiersin.org/articles/10.3389/fpsyg.2017.01149/full.

Jordan, J. S., & Wesselmann, E. D. (2015). The contextually grounded nature of prosocial behavior: A multi-scale, embodied approach to morality. In W. G. Graziano & D. Schroeder (Eds.), *Oxford handbook of prosocial behavior* (pp. 153–165). New York, NY: Oxford University Press.

Jung, C. G. (1942/1961). *Alchemical studies.* CW13. Princeton, NJ: Princeton University Press.

Jung, C. G. (1948/1969). *The archetypes and the collective unconscious.* CW9. Princeton, NJ: Princeton University Press.

Jung, C. G. (1953/1999). *The collected works of C. G. Jung (Vol.12): Psychology and alchemy.* Princeton, NJ: Princeton University Press.

Jung, C. G. (1963). *Memories, dreams, reflections.* (C. Winston & R. Winston, Trans.). New York, NY: Random House.

Kahan, J. P., & Rapoport, A. (1975). Decisions of timing in conflict situations of unequal power between opponents. *Journal of Conflict Resolution, 19*(2), 250–270.

Karney, B. R., & Crown, J. S. (U.S.), & United States Office of the Secretary of Defense. (2007). *Families under stress: An assessment of data, theory, and research on marriage and divorce in the military* (1st ed.). Santa Monica, CA: RAND Corporation.

Kaul, H., & Ventikos, Y. (2014). On the genealogy of tissue engineering and regenerative medicine. *Tissue Engineering Part B: Reviews, 21*(2), 203–217.

Keller, H. (2013). Attachment and culture. *Journal of Cross-Cultural Psychology, 44*(2), 175–194.

Kelley, M. L. (2006). Single military parents in the new millennium. In C. A. Castro, A. B. Adler, and T. W. Britt (Eds.), *Military life: The psychology of serving in peace and combat* (pp. 93–103). Westport, CT: Praeger Security International.

Killen, M., Richardson, C., & Kelly, M. C. (2010). Developmental perspectives. In J. F. Dovidio, M. Hewstone, P. Glick & V. M. Eesses (Eds.), *Handbook of prejudice and discrimination* (pp. 97–114). Thousand Oaks, CA: SAGE.

Killen, M., & Smetana, J. G. (1999). Social interactions in preschool classrooms and the development of young children's conceptions of the personal. *Child Development, 70*(2), 486–501.

Kinsella, E. L., Ritchie, T. D., & Igou, E. R. (2015). Zeroing in on heroes: A prototype analysis of hero features. *Journal of Personality & Social Psychology, 108*(1), 114–127.

Kirby, J. (1970, August). *Jack "King" Kirby.* Presentation at San Diego's Golden State Comic-Con, San Diego, CA.

Klasen, F., Daniels, J., Oettingen, G., Post, M., & Hoyer, C. (2010). Posttraumatic resilience in Ugandan child soldiers. *Child Development, 81*(4), 1096–1113.

Kohli, R., & Solórzano, D. G. (2012). Teachers, please learn our names!: Racial microaggressions and the K-12 classroom. *Race, Ethnicity & Education, 15*(4), 441–462.

Kolp, K., Young, M. S., Friedman, H., Krupitsky, Jansen, K., O'Connor, K. (2007). Ketamine-enhanced psychotherapy: Preliminary clinical observations on its effects in treating death anxiety. *International Journal of Transpersonal Studies, 26*(1), 1–17.

Komolova, M., Pasupathi, M., Wainryb, C., & Lucas, S. (2017). Children's and adolescents' conceptions of personhood: A narrative approach. *International Journal of Behavioral Development, 41*(3), 350–359.

Koziol, L. F., Budding, D. E., & Chidekel, D. (2012). From movement to thought: executive function, embodied cognition, and the cerebellum. *The Cerebellum, 11*(2), 505–525.

Kramer, H. (2017, May 17). *Seven most religious superheroes of the Marvel Universe.* The Complete Pilgrim: http://thecompletepilgrim.com/seven-religious-superheroes-marvel-universe.

Krysinska, K., & Lester, D. (2006). Comment on the Werther effect. *Crisis: The Journal of Crisis Intervention & Suicide Prevention, 27*(2), 100.

Kungurtsev, I. (1991). "Death-rebirth" psychotherapy with ketamine. *Albert Hoffman Foundation Bulletin, 2*(4), 2–6.

Kuniak, S., & Blink, M. (2015). Hillbilly to hero: The transformation of Daryl Dixon. In T. Langley (Ed.), *The Walking Dead psychology: Psych of the living dead* (pp. 234–245). New York, NY: Sterling.

Labek, K., Berger, S., Buchheim, A., Bosch, J., Spohrs, J., Dommes, L., Beschoner, P., Stingl, J., Viviani, R. (2017). The iconography of mourning and its neural correlates: A functional neuroimaging study. *Social Cognitive & Affective Neuroscience, 12*(8), 1303–1313.

Lakin, J. L., Jefferis, V. E., Cheng, C. M., & Chartrand, T. L. (2003). The chameleon effect as social glue: Evidence for the evolutionary significance of nonconscious mimicry. *Journal of Nonverbal Behavior, 27*(3), 145–162.

Lambert, R. D. (2003). Constructing symbolic ancestry: Befriending time, confronting death. *OMEGA: Journal of Death & Dying, 46*(4), 303–321.

Langley, A. (2015). These archetypes you're looking for. In T. Langley (Ed.), *Star Wars psychology: Dark side of the mind* (pp. 111–122). New York, NY: Sterling.

Langley, T. (2012). *Batman and psychology: A dark and stormy knight.* Hoboken, NJ: Wiley.

Langley, T. (Ed.) (2016). *Captain America vs. Iron Man: Freedom, security, psychology.* New York, NY: Sterling.

Langley, T. (2017). Virtue file I: Justice. In T. Langley & M. Wood (Eds.), *Wonder Woman psychology: Lassoing the truth.* New York, NY: Sterling.

Langley, T. (Ed.) (2018). *Daredevil psychology: The devil you know.* New York, NY: Sterling.

Langley, T., & Jones, A. (2019, January). *Welcome to Wakanda: Black Panther forever!* Panel presented at Wizard World New Orleans Comic Con, New Orleans, LA.

Lashley, K. (2019, January 6). Personal communication. New Orleans, LA.

Lauderdale, P. (1976). Deviance and moral boundaries. *American Sociological Review, 41*(4), 660–676.

Lawrence, E, Jeglic, E. L., Matthews. L. T., & Carolyn, M. P. (2005). Gender differences in grief reactions following the death of a parent. *OMEGA, 52* (4), 323–337.

Lawson, G. (2005). The hero's journey as a developmental metaphor in counseling. *Journal of Humanistic Counseling, Education, & Development, 44,* 134–144.

LeBel, E. P., Berger, D., Campbell, L., & Loving, T. J. (2017). Falsifiability is not optional. *Journal of Personality & Social Psychology, 113*(2), 254–261.

Lee, S. A. (2016). Religion and pet loss: Afterlife beliefs, religious coping, prayer, and their associations with sorrow. *British Journal of Guidance & Counseling, 44*(1), 123–129.

Lemstra, M., Nielsen, G., Rogers, M., Thompson, A., & Moraros, J. (2012). Risk indicators and outcomes associated with bullying in youth aged 9–15 years. *Canadian Journal of Public Health, 103*(1), 9–13.

Lester, P., Peterson, K., Reeves, J., Knauss, L., Glover, D., Mogil, C., Duan, N., Saltzman, W., Pynoos R., Wilt, K, & Beardslee, W. (2010). The long war and parental combat deployment: Effects on military children and at-home spouses. *Journal of the American Academy of Child & Adolescent Psychiatry, 49*(4), 310–320.

Lewis, A. M. (2014). Terror management theory applied clinically: Implications for existential-integrative psychotherapy. *Death Studies, 38*(6), 412–417.

Lewis, J. A., Mendenhall, R., Harwood, S. A., & Huntt, M. B. (2013). Coping with gendered racial microaggressions among Black women college students. *Journal of African American Studies, 17*(1), 51–73.

Lim, T. S., Kim, S. Y., & Kim, J. (2011). Holism: A missing link in Individualism-Collectivism research. *Journal of Intercultural Communication Research, 40*(1), 21–38.

Li-Vollmer, M. (2002). Race representation in child-targeted television commercials. *Mass Communication & Society, 5*(?), 207–228.

Lilienfeld, S. O. (2017). Microaggressions: Strong claims, inadequate evidence. *Perspectives on Psychological Science, 12*(1), 138–169.

Long, J., & Perry, P. (2016). *God and the afterlife: The groundbreaking new evidence for God and near-death experience.* San Francisco, CA: HarperOne.

Lord Tennyson, A. (1842). *Ulysses.* Available online: https://www.poetryfoundation.org/poems/45392/ulysses.

Lovallo, W. R. (2015). *Stress and health: Biological and psychological interactions* (3rd ed.). Thousand Oaks, CA: SAGE.

Love, M. (2007). Security in an insecure world: An examination of individualism-collectivism and psychological sense of community at work. *Career Development International, 12*(3), 304–320.

Lu, F. G. (2005). Personal transformation through an encounter with death: A study of Akira Kurosawa's Ikiru on its fiftieth anniversary. *Journal of Transpersonal Psychology, 37*(1), 34–42.

Ludvico, L. R., & Kurland, J. A. (1995). Symbolic or not-so-symbolic wounds: The behavioral ecology of human scarification. *Ethology & Sociobiology, 16*(2), 155–172.

Lynch, R., Palestis, B. G., & Trivers, R. (2017). Religious devotion and extrinsic religiosity affect in-group altruism and out-group hostility oppositely in rural Jamaica. *Evolutionary Psychological Science, 3*(4), 335–344.

Madani, D., & Romero, D. (2018, October 12). *Retired firefighter found guilty for shooting at lost black teen on doorstep.* NBC News: https://www.nbcnews.com/news/us-news/retired-firefighter-found-guilty-shooting-lost-black-teen-doorstep-n919656.

Maguen, S., Ren, L., Bosch, J. O., Marmar, C. R., & Seal, K. H. (2010). Gender differences in mental health diagnoses among Iraq and Afghanistan veterans enrolled in veterans affairs health care. *American Journal of Public Health, 100*(12), 2450–2456.

Main, M., & Hesse, E. (1990). Parents' unresolved traumatic experiences are related to infant disorganized attachment status: Is frightened and/or frightening parental behavior the linking mechanism? In M. T. Greenberg, D. Cicchetti, & E. M. Cummings (Eds.), *Attachment in the preschool years: Theory, research, and intervention* (pp. 161–182). Chicago, IL: University of Chicago Press.

Main, M., Kaplan, N., & Cassidy, J. (1985). Security in infancy, childhood and adulthood: A move to the level of representation. *Monographs of the Society for Research in Child Development, 50*(1–2, Serial. No. 209), 66–104.

Main, M., & Solomon, J. (1990). Procedures for identifying infants as disorganized/disoriented during the Ainsworth Strange Situation. In M. T. Greenberg, D. Cicchetti, & E. M. Cummings (Eds.), *Attachment in the preschool years: Theory, research, and intervention* (pp. 121–160). Chicago, IL: University of Chicago Press.

Major, R. J., Whelton, W. J., & Duff, C. T. (2016). Secure your buffers or stare at the sun? Terror management theory and psychotherapy integration. *Journal of Psychotherapy Integration, 26*(1), 22–35.

Mar, R. A., Oatley, K., Hirsh, J., de la Paz, J., & Peterson, J. B. (2006). Bookworms versus nerds: Exposure to fiction versus non-fiction, divergent associations with social ability, and the simulation of fictional social worlds. *Journal of Research in Personality, 40*(5), 694–712.

March, J. G. (1994). *Primer on decision making: How decisions happen.* New York, NY: Simon & Schuster.

Markell, K. A., & Markell, M. A. (2013). *The children who lived: Using Harry Potter and other fictional characters to help grieving children and adolescents.* New York, NY: Routledge.

Markus, C. (2018, February 9). *The Black Panther royal family tree.* Marvel: https://www.marvel.com/articles/comics/the-black-panther-royal-family-tree.

Markus, H. R., & Kitayama, S. (1991). Culture and the self: Implications for cognition, emotion, and motivation. *Psychological Review, 98*(2), 224–253.

Marsh, H. W., Nagengast, B., Morin, A. J., Parada, R. H., Craven, R. G., & Hamilton, L. R. (2011). Construct validity of the multidimensional structure of bullying and victimization: An application of exploratory structural equation modeling. *Journal of Educational Psychology, 103*(3), 701–732.

Marston, W. M. (1928). *Emotions of normal people.* London, UK: Kegan, Paul, Trench, Trubner.

Martens, J. W. (2005). Definitions and omissions of heroism. *American Psychologist, 60*(4), 342–343.

Martin, J. (2018, July 27). *From Wakanda to America: Agreement, disagreement, and the complexity of social judgments.* Modern Treatise: http://www.moderntreatise.com/culture/2018/7/27/from-wakanda-to-america-agreement-disagreement-and-the-complexity-of-social-judgments.

Mastro, D. E., & Greenberg, B. S. (2000). The portrayal of racial minorities on prime time television. *Journal of Broadcasting & Electronic Media, 44*(4), 690–703.

Maslow, A. (1967). Self-actualization and beyond. In J. F. T. Bugental (Ed.), *Challenges of humanistic psychology* (pp. 279-286). New York, NY: McGraw-Hill.

Maslow, A. (1971). *The farther reaches of human nature.* New York, NY: Viking.

Masten, A. S. (2013). Afterword: What we can learn from military children and families. *The Future of Children, 23*(2), 199–212.

Mastin, J., & Garski, L. (2017). The hero's road trip. In T. Langley & L. S. Zubernis (Eds.), *Supernatural psychology: Roads less traveled* (pp. 243–253). New York, NY: Sterling.

McGregor, D. (2018). Foreword. In S. Wiacek (Author), *Black Panther: The ultimate guide* (p. 7). London, UK: Dorling, Kindersley.

McNeil, J., & Helwig, C. C. (2015). Balancing social responsibility and personal autonomy: adolescents' reasoning about community service programs. *Journal of Genetic Psychology, 176*(6), 349–368.

McNulty, S. S. (2012). Myth busted: Women are serving in ground combat positions. *Air Force Law Review, 68*, 119–165.

Mead, M., & Métraux, R. B. (1979). *Margaret Mead, some personal views.* Sydney, Australia Angus & Robertson.

Midgette, A., Noh, J. Y., Lee, I. J., & Nucci, L. (2016). The development of Korean children's and adolescents' concepts of social convention. *Journal of Cross-Cultural Psychology, 47*(7), 918–928.

Mikulincer, M., & Shaver, P. (2016). *Attachment in adulthood* (2nd ed.). New York, NY: Guilford.

Miller, N. S., & Brewer, M. B. (Eds.). (2013). *Groups in contact: The psychology of desegregation.* Orlando, FL: Academic Press.

Miller, W. R., & Rollnick, S. (2009). Ten things that motivational interviewing is not. *Behavioural & Cognitive Psychotherapy, 37*(2), 129–140.

Mohammed, S. (2018, February 13). *Michael B. Jordan on the importance of Black Panther and black representation in movies.* Glamour: https://www.glamourmagazine.co.uk/gallery/why-marvel-black-panther-is-important.

Monique (2018, March 28). *5 princes of color you can't help but celebrate.* Just Add Color: http://colorwebmag.com/2018/03/28/5-princes-of-color-you-cant-help-but-celebrate/.

Monk-Turner, E., Heiserman, M., Johnson, C., Cotton, V., & Jackson, M. (2010). The portrayal of racial minorities on prime time television: A replication of the Mastro and Greenberg study a decade later. *Studies in Popular Culture, 32*(2), 101–114.

Moody, R. (1975). *Life after life: The investigation of a phenomenon—survival of bodily death.* Fairhope, AL: Mockingbird.

Morris, S. M. (2010). Predicting the grief of midlife adults following the death of a parent: The role of meaning reconstruction. *Dissertation Abstracts International, 71,* 3363.

Morris, S. M. (2012). Black girls are from the future: Afrofuturist feminism in Octavia E. Butler's Fledgling. *Women's Studies Quarterly, 40*(3–4), 146–166.

Moskowitz, A., & Corstens, D. (2007). Auditory hallucinations: Psychotic symptoms or dissociative experience? *Journal of Psychological Trauma, 6*(2–3), 35–63.

Mulvey, K. L., & Killen, M. (2016). Keeping quiet just wouldn't be right: Children's and adolescents' evaluations of challenges to peer relational and physical aggression. *Journal of Youth & Adolescence, 45*(9), 1824–1835.

Mumper, M. L., & Gerrig, R. J. (2017). Leisure reading and social cognition: A meta-analysis. *Psychology of Aesthetics, Creativity, & the Arts, 1*(1), 109.

Murdoch, M., Bradley, A., Mather, S. H., Klein, R. E., Turner, C. L., & Yano, E. M. (2006). Women and war: What physicians should know. *Journal of General Internal Medicine, 21*(S3), S5–S10.

Murray, J., Farrington, D. P., & Sekol, I. (2012). Children's antisocial behavior, mental health, drug use, and educational performance after parental incarceration: A systematic review and meta-analysis. *Psychological Bulletin, 138*(2), 175–210.

Nadal, K. L., Whitman, C. N., Davis, L. S., Erazo, T., & Davidoff, K. C. (2016). Microaggressions toward lesbian, gay, bisexual, transgender, queer, and genderqueer people: A review of the literature. *Journal of Sex Research, 53*(4–5), 488–508.

Nama, A. (2009). Brave black worlds: Black superheroes as science fiction ciphers. *African Identities, 7*(2), 133–144.

Nama, A. (2011). *Super black: American pop culture and black superheroes.* Austin, TX: University of Texas Press.

Nansel, T., Overpeck, M., Pilla, R., Ruan, W., Simons-Morton, B., & Scheidt, P. (2001). Bullying behaviors among US youth: Prevalence and association with psychosocial adjustment. *Journal of American Medical Association, 285*(16), 2095–2100.

Neuner, F., Schauer, M., Klaschik, C., Karunakara, U., & Elbert, T. (2004). A comparison of narrative exposure therapy, supportive counseling, and psychoeducation for treating posttraumatic stress disorder in an African refugee settlement. *Journal of Consulting & Clinical Psychology, 72*(4), 579.

Nezlek, J. B., Wesselmann, E. D., Wheeler, L., & Williams, K. D. (2012). Ostracism in everyday life. *Group Dynamics: Theory, Research, and Practice, 16*(2), 91–104.

Nicholson, A. A., Rabellino, D., Densmore, M., Frewen, P. A., Paret, C., Kluetsch, R., Schmahl, C., Theberge, J., Ros, T. Neufeld, R. W. J., McKinnon, M. C., Reiss, J. P., Jetly, R., & Lanius, R. A. (2018). Intrinsic connectivity network dynamics in PTSD during amygdala downregulation using real-time fMRI neurofeedback: A preliminary analysis. *Human Brain Mapping, 39*(11), 4258–4275.

Nisbett, R. E., Peng, K., Choi, I., & Norenzayan, A. (2001). Culture and systems of thought: Holistic versus analytic cognition. *Psychological Review, 108*(2), 291.

Niu, R., Lei, D., Chen, F., Chen, Y., Suo, X., Li, L., Lui, S., Huang, X., Sweeney, J.A., & Gong, Q. (2018). Reduced local segregation of single-subject gray matter networks in adult PTSD. *Human Brain Mapping, 39*(12), 4884–4892.

Nucci, L. (1981). Conceptions of personal issues: A domain distinct from moral or societal concepts. *Child Development, 52*(1), 114–121.

Nucci, L., & Turiel, E. (2009). Capturing the complexity of moral development and education. *Mind, Brain, & Education, 3*(3), 151–159.

Obama, M. (2018, February 19). [Untitled tweet]. Twitter: https://twitter.com/MichelleObama/status/965641575584935936.

Okpewho, I. (1979). *The epic in Africa: Toward a poetics of the oral performance.* New York, NY: Columbia University Press.

Olweus, D. (1994). Bullying at school: Long term outcomes for the victims and an effective school-based intervention program. In L. R. Huesmann (Ed), *Aggressive behavior: Current perspectives* (pp. 97–130). New York, NY: Plenum.

Ong, A. D., Edwards, L. M., & Bergeman, C. S. (2006). Hope as a resource of resilience in later adulthood. *Personality & Individual Differences, 41*(7), 1263–1273.

Opotow, S. (1990). Moral exclusion and injustice: An introduction. *Journal of Social Issues, 46*(1), 1–20.

Opotow, S., Gerson, J., & Woodside, S. (2005). From moral exclusion to moral inclusion: Theory for teaching peace. *Theory into Practice, 44*(4), 303–318.

Opportunity Agenda, The (2011). *Media representations and impact on the lives of Black men and boys.* New York, NY: The Opportunity Agenda.

Osborne, J., Simon, S., & Collins, S. (2003). Attitudes towards science: A review of the literature and its implications. *International Journal of Science Education, 25*(9), 1049–1079.

Oshiro, M., & Valera, P. (2018). Framing physicality and public safety: A study of Michael Brown and Darren Wilson. In M. A. Bruce, & D. F. Hawkins (Eds.), *Research in Race & Ethnic Relations* (Vol. 20, pp. 207–228). Bingley, UK: Emerald.

Ostrom, T. M., & Sedikides, C. (1992). Out-group homogeneity effects in natural and minimal groups. *Psychological Bulletin, 112*(3), 536–552.

Oyserman, D., Coon, H. M., & Kemmelmeier, M. (2002). Rethinking individualism and collectivism: Evaluation of theoretical assumptions and meta-analyses. *Psychological Bulletin, 128*(1), 3–72.

Oyserman, D., & Lee, S. W. S. (2008). Does culture influence what and how we think? effects of priming individualism and collectivism. *Psychological Bulletin, 134*(2), 311–342.

Paganini-Hill, A., Kawas, C. H., & Corrada, M. M. (2018). Positive mental attitude associated with lower 35-year mortality: The leisure world cohort study. *Journal of Aging Research, 2018*(Article 2126368), 1–10.

Palmer, C. (2008, March 28). *Vicar offers tress relief in grave.* Reuters: https://www.reuters.com/article/us-germany-burials-odd/vicar-offers-stress-relief-in-grave-idUSREE85432520080328.

Palombo, J. (2017). The self as a complex adaptive system, part IV: Making sense of the sense of self. *Psychoanalytic Social Work, 41*(1), 37–53.

Passini, S. (2010). Moral reasoning in a multicultural society: Moral inclusion and moral exclusion. *Journal for the Theory of Social Behaviour, 40*(4), 435–451.

Patrick, C. J., Fowles, D. C., & Krueger, R. F. (2009). Triarchic conceptualization of psychopathy: Developmental origins of disinhibition, boldness, and meanness. *Development & Psychopathology, 21*(3), 913–38.

Pemment, J. (2013). Psychopathy versus sociopathy: Why the distinction has become crucial. *Aggression & Violent Behavior, 18*(5), 458–461.

Perfecting Your Craft (2018, September 3). *14 popular fantasy tropes—and how to make them feel new again*. Reedsy: https://blog.reedsy.com/fantasy-tropes.

Perry, A., & Lewis, S. (2016). Leaving legacies: African American men discuss the impact of their fathers on the development of their own paternal attitudes and behavior. *Journal of Family Social Work, 19*(1), 3–21.

Peterson, C., & Seligman, M. E. P. (2004). *Character strengths and virtues*. Washington, DC: American Psychological Association & Oxford University Press.

Pettigrew, T. F., & Tropp, L. R. (2006). A meta-analytic test of intergroup contact theory. *Journal of Personality & Social Psychology, 90*(5), 751–783.

Pew Research Center. (2018, March). *The generation gap in American politics*. Pew Research Center: http://www.people-press.org/2018/03/01/the-generation-gap-in-american-politics/.

Piaget, J. (1953). *The origin of intelligence in the child*. New York, NY: Routledge & Kegan Paul.

Pieracci, M. (1990). The mythopoesis of psychotherapy. *The Humanistic Psychologist, 18*(2), 208–224.

Pietrzak, R. H., Johnson, D. C., Goldstein, M. B., Malley, J. C., Rivers, A. J., Morgan, C. A., & Southwick, S. M. (2010). Psychosocial buffers of traumatic stress, depressive symptoms, and psychosocial difficulties in veterans of Operations Enduring Freedom and Iraqi Freedom: the role of resilience, unit support, and postdeployment social support. *Journal of Affective Disorders, 120*(1), 188–192.

Pietrzak, R. H., Johnson, D. C., Goldstein, M. B., Malley, J. C., & Southwick, S. M. (2009). Psychological resilience and postdeployment social support protect against traumatic stress and depressive symptoms in soldiers returning from Operations Enduring Freedom and Iraqi Freedom. *Depression & Anxiety, 26*(8), 745–751.

Piper, D., & Murphey, C. (2004). *90 minutes in heaven*. Grand Rapids, MI: Revell.

Prediger, S., Vollan, B., & Herrmann, B. (2014). Resource scarcity and antisocial behavior. *Journal of Public Economics, 119*, 1–9.

Predmore, R. (1977). Young Goodman Brown: Night journey into the forest. *Journal of Analytical Psychology, 22*(3), 250–257.

Prencipe, A., & Helwig, C. C. (2002). The development of reasoning about the teaching of values in school and family contexts. *Child Development, 73*(3), 841–856.

Putnam, F. W. (1989). Pierre Janet and modern views of dissociation. *Journal of Traumatic Stress, 2*(4), 413–429.

Pyszczynski, T., Wicklund, R. A., Floresku, S., Koch, H., Gauch, G., Solomon, S., & Greenberg, J. (1996). Whistling in the dark: Exaggerated consensus estimates in response to incidental reminders of mortality. *Psychological Science, 7*(6), 332–336.

Quintana, S. M., Herrera, T. A., & Nelson, M. L. (2010). Mexican American high school students' ethnic self-concepts and identity. *Journal of Social Issues, 66*(1), 11–28.

Rakoff, V., Sigal J. J., & Epstein, N. B. (1966). Children and families of concentration camp survivors. *Canada's Mental Health, 14,* 24–26.

Rapoport, A., Bornstein, G., & Erev, I. (1989). Intergroup competition for public goods: Effects of unequal resources and relative group size. *Journal of Personality & Social Psychology, 56*(5), 748–756.

Recchia, H. E., Brehl, B. A., & Wainryb, C. (2012). Children's and adolescents' reasons for socially excluding others. *Cognitive Development, 27*(2), 195–203.

Recchia, H. E., Wainryb, C., Bourne, S., & Pasupathi, M. (2015). Children's and adolescents' accounts of helping and hurting others: Lessons about the development of moral agency. *Child Development, 86*(3), 864–876.

Reddish, P., Fischer, R., & Bulbulia, J. (2013). Let's dance together: synchrony, shared intentionality and cooperation. *PloS One, 8*(8), e71182.

Reed, A., & Aquino, K. F. (2003). Moral identity and the expanding circle of moral regard toward out-groups. *Journal of Personality & Social Psychology, 84*(6), 1270–1286.

Reilly, K. (2017, January 6). *Read what Michelle Obama said in her final remarks as first lady.* Time: http://time.com/4626283/michelle-obama-final-remarks-transcript/.

Reijntjes, A., Stegge, H., & Terwogt, M. (2010). Children's coping with peer rejection: The role of depressive symptoms, social competence, and gender. *Infant & Child Development, 15*(1), 89–107.

Reiter-Scheidl, K., Papousek, I., Lackner, H. K., Paechter, M., Weiss, E. M., & Aydin, N. (2018). Aggressive behavior after social exclusion is linked with the spontaneous initiation of more action-oriented coping immediately following the exclusion episode. *Physiology & Behavior, 195*(15), 142–150.

Rivadeneyra, R., Ward, L. M., & Gordon, M. (2007). Distorted reflections: Media exposure and Latino adolescents' conceptions of self. *Media Psychology, 9*(2), 261–290.

Relentless. (2018, March 5). *Keith David implores you—don't forget to see the Black Panther.* YouTube: https://www.youtube.com/watch?v=1SxyvAgYtfc.

Resick, P. A., & Schnicke, M. K. (1992). Cognitive processing therapy for sexual assault victims. *Journal of Consulting & Clinical Psychology, 60*(5), 748–756.

Riekki, T., Linderman, M., & Lipsanen, J. (2013). Conceptions about the mind-body problem and their relations to afterlife beliefs, paranormal beliefs, religiosity, and ontological confusions. *Advances in Cognitive Psychology, 9*(3), 112–120.

Ring, K. (1980). *Life at death: A scientific investigation of the near-death experience.* New York, NY: Coward, McCann, & Geoghegan.

Rizzo, M. T., Elenbaas, L., Cooley, S., & Killen, M. (2016). Children's recognition of fairness and others' welfare in a resource allocation task: Age related changes. *Developmental Psychology, 52*(8), 1307–1317.

Roberts, N. (2018, November 13). *Protestors ready to raise hell outside Midlothian police department that refuses to name cop who killed Jemel Roberson.* Chicago Defender: https://chicagodefender.com/2018/11/13/protesters-ready-to-raise-hell-outside-midlothian-police-department-that-refuses-to-name-cop-who-killed-jemel-roberson/.

Robertson, D. L., & Lawrence, C. (2015). Heroes and mentors: A consideration of relational-cultural theory and "The Hero's Journey." *Journal of Creativity in Mental Health, 10*(3), 264–277.

Rollnick, S., Butler, C. C., Kinnersley, P., Gregory, J., & Mash, B. (2010). Motivational interviewing. *BMJ, 340*(7758), c1900.

Romero, R. E. (2000). The icon of the strong Black woman: The paradox of strength. In L. C. Jackson & B. Greene (Eds.), *Psychotherapy with African American women: Innovations in psychodynamic perspectives and practice* (pp. 225–238). New York, NY: Guilford.

Rose, P. I. (1999). Toward a more perfect union: The career and contributions of Robin M. Williams. *American Sociologist, 30*(2), 78.

Rosenberg, M., & Phillips, D. (2015). *All combat roles now open to women, Defense Secretary says.* New York Times: https://www.nytimes.com/2015/12/04/us/politics/combat-military-women-ash-carter.html.

Rosenblatt, P. C. (2017). Researching grief: Cultural, relational, and individual possibilities. *Journal of Loss & Trauma, 22*(8), 617–630.

Rothbaum, F., Rosen, K., Ujiie, T., & Uchida, N. (2002). Family systems theory, attachment theory, and culture. *Family Process, 41*(3), 328–350.

Rubin, L. C. (2009). Our heroic adventure: Creating a personal mythology. *Journal of Creativity in Mental Health, 4*(3), 262–271.

Rubin, L. *Using superheroes and villains in counseling and play therapy: A guide for mental health professionals.* New York, NY: Routledge.

Rubin, L., & Livesay, H. (2006). Look, up in the sky! Using superheroes in play therapy. *International Journal of Play Therapy, 15*(1), 117.

Ruff, S. R., & Keim, M. A. (2014). Revolving doors: The impact of multiple school transitions on military children. *The Professional Counselor, 4*(2), 103–114.

Rush, J. A. (2005). *Spiritual tattoo: A cultural history of tattooing, piercing, scarification, branding, and implants.* Berkeley, CA: Frog.

Ryan, D. P. J. (2001). *Bronfenbrenner's ecological systems theory.* Florida Health: http://www.floridahealth.gov/AlternateSites/CMS-Kids/providers/early_steps/training/documents/bronfenbrenners_ecological.pdf.

Salberg, J. (2015). The texture of traumatic attachment: Presence and ghostly absence in transgenerational transmission. *Psychoanalytic Quarterly, 84*(1), 21–46.

Salmon, K., & Reese, E. (2016). The benefits of reminiscing with young children. *Current Directions in Psychological Science, 25*(4), 233–238.

Savage, S. (2015). Covert cognition: My so-called near-death experience. *Skeptical Inquirer, 39*(4). Online archive: https://www.csicop.org/si/show/cove3rt_cognition_my_so-called_near-death_experience.

Sayer, N. A., Noorbaloochi, S., Frazier, P., Carlson, K., Gravely, A., & Murdoch, M. (2010). Reintegration problems and treatment interests among Iraq and Afghanistan combat veterans receiving VA medical care. *Psychiatric Services, 61*(6), 589–597.

Scarlet, J. (2016). *Superhero therapy: A hero's journey through acceptance and commitment therapy.* London, UK: Little, Brown.

Scarlet, J. (in press). Using Spidey senses during the storm of anxiety. In L. Rubin (Ed.), *Using superheroes and villains in counseling and play therapy: A guide for mental health professionals.* New York, NY: Routledge.

Schwarzbaum, S. E., & Thomas, A. J. (2008). *Dimensions of multicultural counseling: A life story approach.* Los Angeles, CA: SAGE.

Seaburn, P. (2018, September 27). *Psychologist buries patients alive for therapeutic purposes.* Mysterious Universe: https://mysteriousuniverse.org/2018/09/psychologist-buries-patients-alive-for-therapeutic-purposes/.

Seidel, E. M., Silani, G., Metzler, H., Thaler, H., Lamm, C., Gur, R. C., Kryspin-Exner, I., Habel, U., & Derntl, B. (2013). The impact of social exclusion vs. inclusion on subjective and hormonal reactions in females and males. *Psychoneuroendocrinology, 38*(12), 2925–2932.

Seligman, M. E. P. (1998). Building human strength: Psychology's forgotten mission. *APA Monitor, 29*(1), 1.

Sharon, T. (2005). Made to symbolize: Intentionality and children's early understanding of symbols. *Journal of Cognition & Development, 6*(2), 163–178.

Shaver, P. R., Mikulincer, M., Gross, J. T., Stern, J. A., & Cassidy, J. (2016). A lifespan perspective on attachment and care for others: Empathy, altruism and prosocial behavior. In J. Cassidy & P. R. Shaver (Eds.) *Handbook of attachment: Theory, research, and clinical applications* (pp. 878–916). New York, NY: Guilford.

Shaw, L. A., & Wainryb, C. (1999). The outsider's perspective: Young adults' judgments of social practices of other cultures. *British Journal of Developmental Psychology, 17*(3), 451–471.

Sheaves, B., Bebbington, P. E., Goodwin, G. M., Harrison, P. J., Espie, C. A., Foster, R. G., & Freeman, D. (2016). Insomnia and hallucinations in the general population: Findings from the 2000 and 2007 British psychiatric morbidity surveys. *Psychiatry Research, 241*, 141–146.

Sheppard, S. C., Malatras, J. W., & Israel, A. C. (2010). The impact of deployment on US military families. *American Psychologist, 65*(6), 599.

Sherif, M. (1966). *In common predicament: Social psychology of intergroup conflict and cooperation.* Boston, MA: Houghton-Mifflin.

Shpancer, N. (2010, August 21). *What doesn't kill you makes you weaker.*

Psychology Today: https://www.psychologytoday.com/us/blog/insight-therapy/201008/what-doesnt-kill-you-makes-you-weaker.

Shutts, K., Kinzler, K. D., Katz, R. C., Tredoux, C., & Spelke, R. S. (2011). Race preferences in children: Insights from South Africa. *Developmental Science, 14*(6), 1283–1291.

Silverman, P. R., Nickman, S., Worden J. W. (1992). Detachment revisited: The child's reconstruction of a dead parent. *American Journal of Orthopsychiatric Association, 62*(4).

Sinigaglia, C., & Rizzolatti, G. (2011). Through the looking glass: Self and others. *Consciousness & Cognition, 20*(1), 64–74.

Skeem, J., Schubert, C., Stowman, S., Beeson, S., Mulvey, E., Gardner, W., & Lidz, C. (2005). Gender and risk assessment accuracy: Underestimating women's violence potential.

Skinner, N. (2012). *Bronfenbrenner's ecological systems theory and applications for management ecological systems theory.* Academia: http://www.academia.edu/1779093/Bronfenbrenner_s_Ecological_Systems_Theory_and_Applications_for_Management.

Skowron, E. A. (2004). Differentiation of self, personal adjustment, problem solving, and ethnic group belonging among persons of color. *Journal of Counseling & Development, 82*(4), 447–456.

Skowron, E. A. & Dendy, A. K. (2004). Differentiation of self and attachment in adulthood: Relational correlates of effortful control. *Contemporary Family Therapy, 26*(3), 337–357.

Sleutjes, A., Moreira-Almedia, A., & Greyson, B. (2014). Almost 40 years investigating near-death experiences: An overview of mainstream scientific journals. *Journal of Nervous & Mental Disease, 202*(11), 833–836.

Smedley, J. W., & Bayton, J. A. (1978). Evaluative race-class stereotypes by race and perceived class of subjects. *Journal of Personality & Social Psychology, 36*(5), 530–535.

Smetana, J. G. (1981). Preschool children's conceptions of moral and social rules. *Child Development, 52*(4), 1333–1336.

Smetana, J. G., & Bitz, B. (1996). Adolescents' conceptions of teachers' authority and their relations to rule violations in school. *Child Development, 67*(3), 1153–1172.

Smetana, J. G., Rote, W. M., Jambon, M., Tasopoulos-Chan, M., Villalobos, M., & Comer, J. (2012). Developmental changes and individual differences in young children's moral judgments. *Child Development, 83*(2), 683–696.

Smith, B. N., Vaughn, R. A., Vogt, D., King, D. W., King, L. A., & Shipherd, J. C. (2013). Main and interactive effects of social support in predicting mental health symptoms in men and women following military stressor exposure. *Anxiety, Stress & Coping, 26*(1), 52–69.

Smith, J. (n.d.). *The revolutionary power of Black Panther.* Time: http://time.com/black-panther.

Snyder, J., Gewirtz, A., Schrepferman, L., Gird, S. R., Quattlebaum, J., Pauldine, M. R., Elish, K., Zamir, O., Hayes, C. (2016). Parent-child relationship quality and family transmission of parent posttraumatic stress disorder symptoms and child externalizing and internalizing symptoms following fathers' exposure to combat trauma. *Development & Psychopathology, 28*(4), 947–969.

Solomon, S., Greenberg, J., & Pyszczynski, T. (1991). A terror management theory of social behavior: The psychological functions of self-esteem and cultural worldviews. *Advances in Experimental Social Psychology, 24*, 93–159.

Solórzano, D., Ceja, M., & Yosso, T. (2000). Critical race theory, racial microaggressions, and campus racial climate: The experiences of African American college students. *Journal of Negro Education, 69*(1–2), 60–73.

Southwell, K. H., & MacDermid Wadsworth, S. M. (2016). The many faces of military families: Unique features of the lives of female service members. *Military Medicine, 181*(suppl_1), 70–79.

Sperry, L., & Sperry, J. J. (2012). *Case conceptualization: Mastering this competency with ease and confidence.* New York, NY: Routledge.

Steinberg, L. (2005). Cognitive and affective development in adolescence. *Trends in Cognitive Sciences, 9*(2), 69–74.

Stroebe, W. & Schut, H. (2001). Risk factors in bereavement outcome: A methodological and empirical review. In M. S. Stroebe, R. O. Handdon, W. Stroebe, & H. Schut (Eds.), *Handbook of bereavement research: Consequences, coping, and care* (pp. 349–371). Washington, D.C.: American Psychological Association.

Sue, D. W., Bucceri, J., Lin, A. I., Nadal, K. L., & Torino, G. C. (2007a). Racial microaggressions and the Asian American experience. *Cultural Diversity and Ethnic Minority Psychology, 13*(1), 72–81.

Sue, D. W., Capodilupo, C. M., Torino, G. C., Bucceri, J. M., Holder, A. M. B., Nadal, K. L., & Esquilin, M. (2007b). Racial microaggressions in everyday life: Implications for clinical practice. *American Psychologist, 62*(4), 271–286.

Summerfield, D. (2000). War and mental health: A brief overview. *BMJ Clinical Research, 321*(7255), 232–235.

Sun, H., Tan, Q., Fan, G., & Tsui, Q. (2014). Different effects of rumination on depression: Key role of hope. *International Journal of Mental Health Systems, 8*, article 53.

Tajfel, H. (1970). Experiments in intergroup discrimination. *Scientific American, 223*(5), 96–102.

Takahaski, Y., & Berger, D. (1996). Cultural dynamics and suicide in Japan. In A. A. Leenaars & De. Lester (Eds.), *Suicide and the unconscious* (pp. 248–258). Northvale, NJ: Jason Aronson.

Tarrant, M., MacKenzi, L., & Hewitt, L. A., (2006). Friendship group identification, multidimensional self-concept, and experience of developmental tasks in adolescence. *Journal of Adolescence, 29*(4), 627–640.

Tate, F. B. (1989). Impoverishment of death symbolism: The negative consequences. *Death Studies*, *13*(3), 305–317.

Taubman-Ben-Ari, O., Eherenfreund-Hager, A., & Findler, L. (2011). Mortality salience and positive affect influence adolescents' attitudes toward peers with physical disabilities: Terror management and broaden and build theories. *Death Studies*, *35*(1), 1–21.

Tavris, C. (2015). The scientist-practitioner gap. In S. O. Lilienfeld, S. J. Lynn, & J. M. Lohr (Eds.), *Science and pseudoscience in clinical psychology* (pp. ix–xx). New York, NY: Guilford.

Taylor, C. (1989). *Sources of the self: The making of the modern identity*. Cambridge, MA: Harvard University Press.

Tharoor, I. (2018, February 20). *"Black Panther": Why Wakanda matters*. Washington Post: https://www.washingtonpost.com/news/worldviews/wp/2018/02/20/why-wakanda-matters.

Thomas, D., Mitchell, T., & Arseneau, C. (2015). Re-evaluating resilience: From individual vulnerabilities to the strength of cultures and collectives among indigenous communities. *Resilience: International Policies, Practices & Discourses*, *4(2)*, 116–129.

Thompson, K. (2013). Rites of passage. *Culturescope*, *101*, 22.

Thorndike, E. L. (1920). Intelligence and its use. *Harper's Magazine*, *140*, 227–235.

Todd, A.R., Thiem, K.C., & Neel, R. (2016). Does seeing faces of young black boys facilitate the identification of threatening stimuli? *Psychological Science*, *27*(3), 384–393.

Trahan, D. P., Jr., & Lemberger, M. E. (2014). Critical race theory as a decisional framework for the ethical counseling of African American clients. *Counseling & Values*, *59(1)*, 112–124.

Trawalter, S., & Hoffman, K. M. (2015). Got pain? Racial bias in perceptions of pain. *Social and Personality Psychology Compass*, *9*(3), 146–157.

Tsai, J., Harpaz-Rotem, I., Pietrzak, R. H., & Southwick, S. M. (2012). The role of coping, resilience, and social support in mediating the relation between PTSD and social functioning in veterans returning from Iraq and Afghanistan. *Psychiatry: Interpersonal & Biological Processes*, *75*(2), 135–149.

Turiel, E. (1983). *The development of social knowledge: Morality and convention*. Cambridge, UK: Cambridge University Press.

Turiel, E. (2002). *The culture of morality: Social development, context, and conflict*. Cambridge, UK: Cambridge University Press.

Turiel, E. (2008). Thought about actions in social domains: Morality, social conventions, and social interactions. *Cognitive Development*, *23*(1), 136–154.

Turiel, E., Hildebrandt, C., Wainryb, C., & Saltzstein, H. D. (1991). Judging social issues: Difficulties, inconsistencies, and consistencies. *Monographs of the Society for Research in Child Development*, *56*(2), i–116.

TV Tropes (n.d.). *The Cavalry*. TV Tropes: https://tvtropes.org/pmwiki/pmwiki.php/Main/TheCavalry.

Ukpokolo, I. E. (2012). Memories in photography and rebirth: Toward a psychosocial therapy of the metaphysics of reincarnation among traditional Esan people of Southern Nigeria. *Journal of Black Studies, 43*(3), 289–302.

Urquhart, W. (2012, December 2). *"Coffin therapy" to prepare for death.* BBC News: https://www.bbc.com/news/av/world-europe-20571517/coffin-therapy-to-prepare-for-death.

Uslan, M. E. (2011). *The boy who loved Batman.* San Francisco, CA: Chronicle.

Vale, M. G., & Lenhers, Y. (2018). *Saint Joan of Arc.* Encyclopædia Britannica: https://www.britannica.com/biography/Saint-Joan-of-Arc.

Van Gennep, A. (1960/2013). *The rites of passage.* (M. B. Vizedom & G. L. Caffee, Trans.) London, UK: Routledge & Kegan Paul.

Van Hoorn, A. (2015). Individualist-collectivist culture and trust radius: A multilevel approach. *Journal of Cross-Cultural Psychology, 46*(2), 269–276.

Van IJzendoorn, M. H. (1995). Adult attachment representations, parental responsiveness, and infant attachment: a meta-analysis on the predictive validity of the Adult Attachment Interview. *Psychological Bulletin, 117*(3), 387–403.

Van Lommel, P. (2010). *Consciousness beyond life: The science of near-death experience.* San Francisco, CA: HarperOne.

Van Slyke, J. (2013). *Post-traumatic growth.* Naval Center for Combat and Operational Stress Control: https://pdfs.semanticscholar.org/b2aa/8aed76f97e16d36c1450f50fc66784f4f010.pdf.

Vasquez, M. (2013). Women of color leaders: Benefits for all. In L. Comas-Diaz, B. Greene, & M. Vasquez (Eds.), *Psychological health of women of color: Intersections, challenges, and opportunities* (pp. 355–372). Santa Barbara, CA: ABC-CLIO.

Vedat, S., Koyuncu, A., Ozturk, E., Yargic, L. I., Kundakci, T., Yazici, A., Kuskonmax, E., & Aksüt, D. (2007). Dissociative disorders in the psychiatric emergency ward. *General Hospital Psychiatry, 29*(1), 45–50.

Vélez-Agosto, N. M., Soto-Crespo, J. G., Vizcarrondo-Oppenheimer, M., Vega-Molina, S., & García Coll, C. (2017). Bronfenbrenner's bioecological theory revision: Moving culture from the macro into the micro. *Perspectives on Psychological Science, 12*(5), 900.

Volini, J. A. (2017). An introduction to global family therapy: Examining the empirical evidence of terror management theory within the family and social system. *American Journal of Family Therapy, 45*(2), 79–94.

Volkan, V. D. (2001). Transgenerational transmissions and chosen traumas: An aspect of large-group identity. *Group Analysis, 34*(1), 79–97.

Von Robertson, R., & Chaney, C. (2017). "I know it (racism) still exists here:" African American males at a Predominantly White Institution (PWI). *Humboldt Journal of Social Relations, 1*(39), 260–282.

Vos, J., Craig, M., & Cooper, M. (2015). Existential therapies: A meta-analysis of their effects on psychological outcomes. *Journal of Consulting & Clinical Psychology, 83*(1), 115–128.

Wagner, E. E., Rathus, J. H., & Miller, A. L. (2015). Mindfulness in Dialectical Behavioral Therapy (DBT) for Adolescents. In R. A. Baer (Eds.), *Mindfulness-based treatment approaches: Clinician's guide to evidence base and applications.* Burlington, MA: Elsevier.

Wainryb, C. (1991). Understanding differences in moral judgments: The role of informational assumptions. *Child Development, 62*(4), 840–851.

Wainryb, C., & Brehl, B. A. (2006). I thought she knew that would hurt my feelings: Developing psychological knowledge and moral thinking. In R. Vail (Ed.), *Advances in child development and behavior* (Vol. 34, pp. 131–171). San Diego, CA: Elsevier.

Wainryb, C., Brehl, B. A., & Matwin, S., Sokol, B. W., & Hammond, S. (2005). Being hurt and hurting others: Children's narrative accounts and moral judgments of their own interpersonal conflicts. *Monographs of the Society for Research in Child Development, 70*(3), i–122.

Wallace, C. (2018, February 12). *Why 'Black Panther' is a defining moment for Black America.* New York Times: https://www.nytimes.com/2018/02/12/magazine/why-black-panther-is-a-defining-moment-for-black-america.html.

Ward, L. M. (2004). Wading through the stereotypes: positive and negative associations between media use and black adolescents' conceptions of self. *Developmental Psychology, 40*(2), 284–294.

Wardlaw, C. (2018, February 19). *"Black Panther": How T'Challa avoids toxic masculinity.* Hollywood Reporter: https://www.hollywoodreporter.com/heat-vision/black-panther-how-tchalla-avoids-toxic-masculinity-1085741.

Warner, W. L. (1949). *Democracy in Jonesville, a study in quality and inequality.* Oxford, UK: Harper.

Waterman, A. S. (1984). *The psychology of individualism.* New York, NY: Praeger.

Watson, D. N. (2008, October 3). *The Norfolk 17 face a hostile reception as schools reopen—when the walls came tumbling down, part 6.* The Virginian-Pilot: https://pilotonline.com/news/local/projects/massive-resistance/article_05745bcd-a24e-5d1d-9c5c-ce22313d963d.html.

Watson, N. N., & Hunter, C. D. (2016). "I had to be strong": Tensions in the Strong Black Woman schema. *Journal of Black Psychology, 42*(5), 424–452.

Watson-Singleton, N. N. (2017). Strong Black Woman schema and psychological distress: The mediating role of perceived emotional support. *Journal of Black Psychology, 43*(8), 778–788.

Waytz, A., Hoffman, K. M., & Trawalter, S. (2015). A superhumanization bias in Whites' perceptions of Blacks. *Social Psychological & Personality Science, 6*(3), 352–359.

Webster, V., Brought, P., & Daly, K. (2016). Fight, flight, or freeze: Common responses for follower coping with toxic leadership. *Journal of the International Society for the Investigation of Stress, 32*(4), 346–354.

Wein, S. (2012). Heroism and the fear of death. *Journal of Palliative Medicine, 15*(7), 731–732.

Weinhold B. (2006). Epigenetics: the science of change. *Environmental Health Perspectives, 114*(3), A160–7.

Wesselmann, E. D., Grzybowski, M. R., Steakley-Freeman, D. M., DeSouza, E. R., Nezlek. J. B., & Williams. K. D. (2016). Social exclusion in everyday life. In P. Riva & J. Eck (Eds.), *Social exclusion: Psychological approaches to understanding and reducing its impact* (pp. 3–23). Basel, Switzerland: Springer.

Wesselmann, E. D., & Parris, L. (in press). Inclusion, exclusion, and group psychotherapy: The importance of a trauma-informed approach. In C. D. Parks & G. A. Tasca (Eds.), *Group psychology and group psychotherapy: An interdisciplinary handbook.* Washington, DC: American Psychological Association.

Wesselmann, E. D., Schneider, K. T., Ford, T. E., & DeSouza, E. R. (2018, April). *Disparaging humor as a form of social exclusion.* Presentation at the meeting of the Society for Industrial and Organizational Psychology, Chicago, IL.

Weston, G. (2013). Superheroes and comic-book vigilantes versus real-life vigilantes: An anthropological answer to the Kick-Ass paradox. *Journal of Graphic Novels & Comics, 4*(2), 223–234.

Whetten, K., Ostermann, J., Whetten, R., O'Donnell, K., Thielman, N., & Positive Outcomes for Orphans Research Team (2011). More than the loss of a parent: Potentially traumatic events among orphaned and abandoned children. *Journal of Traumatic Stress, 24*(2), 174–82.

Wiacek, S. (2018). *Black Panther: The ultimate guide.* London, UK: Dorling Kindersley.

Wiese, B. (2006). *23 minutes in hell: One man's story about what he saw, heard, and felt in that place of torment.* Lake Mary, FL: Charisma House.

Williams, D., Martins, N., Consalvo, M., & Ivory, J. D. (2009). The virtual census: Representations of gender, race and age in video games. *New Media & Society, 11*(5), 815–834.

Williams, G. W. (1963). Highway hypnosis: An hypothesis. *International Journal of Clinical & Experimental Hypnosis, 11*(3), 143–151.

Williams, K. D. (2009). Ostracism: Effects of being excluded and ignored. In M. P. Zanna (Ed.), *Advances in experimental social psychology* (Vol. 41, pp. 275–314). New York, NY: Academic Press.

Williams, K. D., Freedman, G., & Beer, J. S. (2016). Softening the blow of social exclusion: The responsive theory of social exclusion. *Frontiers in Psychology, 7*, 1570.

Williams, R. M., Jr. (1947). The reduction of intergroup tensions: A survey of research on problems of ethnic, racial, and religious group relations. *Social Forces, 26*(4), 484–485.

Wilson, J. (2016, January 12). *The meaning of #BlackGirlMagic, and how you can get some of it.* Huffington Post: https://www.huffpost.com/entry/what-is-black-girl-magic-video_n_5694dad4e4b086bc1cd517f4.

Wilson, J. P., Droždek, B., & Turkovic, S. (2006). Posttraumatic shame and guilt. *Trauma, Violence, & Abuse, 7*(2), 122–141.

Wiltermuth, S. S., & Heath, C. (2009). Synchrony and cooperation. *Psychological science, 20*(1), 1–5.

Wisman, A., & Goldenberg, J. L. (2005). From the grave to the cradle: Evidence that mortality salience engenders a desire for offspring. *Journal of Personality & Social Psychology, 89*(1), 46–61.

Wisman, A., & Heflick, N. A. (2016). Hopelessly mortal: The role of mortality salience, immortality, and trait self-esteem in personal hope. *Cognition & Emotion, 30*(5), 868–889.

Wohn, D. Y. (2011). Gender and race representation in casual games. *Sex Roles, 65*(3–4), 198–207.

Wolson, P. (2005). The existential dimension of psychoanalysis (EDP): Psychic survival and the fear of psychic death (nonbeing). *Psychoanalytic Review, 92*(5), 675–699.

Womack, Y. L. (2013). *Afrofuturism: The world of Black sci-fi and fantasy culture.* Chicago, IL: Lawrence, IL.

Wu, H. (2011). The protective effects of resilience and hope on quality of life of the families coping with the criminal traumatization of one of its members. *Journal of Clinical Nursing, 20*(13–14), 1906–1915.

Xu, W., Fu, Z., He, L., Schoebi, D., & Wang, J. (2015). Growing in times of grief: Attachment modulates bereaved adults' posttraumatic growth. *Psychiatry Research, 230* (1), 108–115.

Yan, G. W., McAndrew, L., D'Andrea, E. A., Lange, G., Santos, S. L., Engel, C. C., & Quigley, K. S. (2013). Self-reported stressors of national guard women veterans before and after deployment: The relevance of interpersonal relationships. *Journal of General Internal Medicine, 28*(S2), 549–555.

Yaszek, L. (2006). Afrofuturism, science fiction, and the history of the future. *Socialism & Democracy, 20*(3), 41–60.

Yoon, H. (2016, January 19). *Seoul's "bizarre" death experience.* Timeout: https://www.timeout.com/seoul/things-to-do/seouls-bizarre-death-experience.

Zeanah, C. H. & Smyke, A. T. (2009). Attachment disorders. In C. H. Zeanah, Jr. (Ed.), *Handbook of infant mental health* (pp. 421–434). New York, NY: Guilford.

Zimbardo, P. (2008). *The Lucifer effect: Understanding how good people turn evil.* New York, NY: Random House.

Zimbardo, P. & Ebbeson, E. (1970). *Influencing attitudes and changing behavior. A basic introduction to relevant methodology, theory, and applications.* Menlo Park, CA: Addison-Wesley.

Zimbardo, P. G., Breckenridge, J. N., & Moghaddam, F. M. (2013). "Exclusive" and "inclusive" visions of heroism and democracy. *Current Psychology, 32*(3), 221–233.

# INDEX

Black women
Afrofuturist feminism and, 122–123,
   126, 129, 130
in *Black Panther*, 122
defying tropes and, 122–125
group therapy with, 125
heroic, vision of, 236
image and stereotype of, 18
as leaders, 121–130
media representation of, 121, 123,
   124
misogynoir and, 125–127
narrative, 129
negative stereotypes of, 124
racism and sexism and, 126
representation of, 129–130
stereotypes, 124–125
strong Black woman (SBW) trope
   and, 124, 125
"wives-in-training" and, 125, 127
Bowen, Murray, 184
Bradford, E.J., 232
*Brown v. Board of Education*, 226, 241
Buckler, Rich, 242, 243
"Building bridges," 44
Bullying
cyberbullying, 168
defined, 167
physical, 168
relational, 167–168
verbal, 167

Call to adventure, 63
Campbell, Joseph, 61
Carter, Ruth E., 138–139
*Character Strengths and Virtues: A
   Handbook and Classification* (CSV),
   205
Children
attitudes towards race and racism,
   233
caregivers, 73, 185

of color, adopting, 226–227
communal caregiving, 76–77
development of moral treatment of
   others, 23
disorganized attachment style, 73
family genes influence, 183
family system influence, 183
learning by emulating adults, 248
legacy and, 77
parents reminiscing with, 91
racial socialization and, 46–47
resolving situations of indirect
   harm, 28
rules and authority and, 23–24
secure attachment style, 74
of service members, 133–135
socio-conventional and moral
   considerations and, 29
trust of caregiver, 74
understanding of moral domain
   and, 23
Chinese culture, 84
Choices, moral, 22
Chronosystem, 134
Coates, Ta-nehisi, 71, 126–127, 232
Cognitive behavior therapy, 100
Cognitive restructuring, 176
Collective
definition of, 98
sacrifice for betterment of, 102
trust in, 102
Collective memories, 91
Collective mindset, 98
Collective narratives, 95
Collectivism
defined, 87
group-based, 87, 88, 89
relational, 87, 88, 89
Collectivistic culture, 101–102
Compassion, 86, 174, 176
Conflict resolution, 26
Conformity, 40